DOOM!

For my dear Fred,
Käthe and
Martyn

for Ted x

BOOM!

a baby boomer memoir, 1947-2022

Ted Polhemus

*how the baby boomers did and didn't
change the world*

Copyright © 2011 Ted Polhemus

All rights reserved. No part of this publication may be reproduced, stored in a retrieval system or transmitted in any form or by any means, electronic, mechanical, photocopying, recording or otherwise, without the permission of the author.

Orbiting Neptune -a baby boomer memoir is an illustrated companion volume to *BOOM!*.
For more information see www.tedpolhemus.com
> What's Up?

This book was typeset and produced using Open Source software. LyX was used for typesetting and layout. My sincere thanks to all who work in Open Source. Special thanks also to Alan L Tyree whose *Self-publishing with LyX* got even me from a to b. Also huge thanks to all who contribute to Wikipedia (from someone old enough to remember when checking a date meant getting up, finding the right book, changing your glasses and then finding the right page - then repeating the process in reverse).

ISBN 978-1-4709-9995-7

for my parents,
Charles and Peggy Polhemus

With thanks to Lynn Procter, Emilia Telese,
Belén Asad, Philippa Morrow, Steve Dawson,
Alistair Gentry, Phil White, John the Cobbler,
Kaustav SenGupta, David Marshall, Nancy Savoth,
Joe Polhemus, Amber & Nisha at Broken Hearts
and Andrew White.

Front Cover: The first photo of the author,
Ted Polhemus, with his father Charles Polhemus,
Oak Terrace, Neptune City, New Jersey, 1947.
Back Cover: The author in 1969 and 'Tillie' once
the iconic face of Palace Amusements, Asbury Park,
New Jersey.

Contents

1	1947	1
2	Coming Home	31
3	Suburban Life	49
4	Modern Times	75
5	Sex	97
6	Drugs	125
7	Rock 'n' Roll	155
8	Protest	179
9	Swinging London	211
10	No Future	247
11	2022	285
I	Sources & Inspirations	317
II	Timeline	353

Chapter 1

1947

The aliens and their fire-farting machines from hell invaded on the 4th of July 1947. A town of about 4,000 souls, Hollister California was on that fateful day hosting a motorcycle rally. But as well as the clean cut, all-American sportsmen who turned up to compete in the races, there arrived thousands of barbarian hordes – scruffy, filthy, dirty denim and black leather clad, no good punks bent on spitting on the American Dream.

The tiny local police force couldn't control this alien and alienated mob and the good upstanding citizens of Hollister were virtually taken hostage for the next few days. Drink flowed. Fights broke out. Impromptu drag races ripped through the town – some crazed Bikers ending up in hospital, some in jail. Completely outnumbered, in desperation the cops sealed off a side street seething with these degenerates and ordered a band to play on late into the night in the hope that frenzied, demonic dancing would exhaust the subhuman hordes. Then, a few days later, they were gone as suddenly as they had arrived – hopefully back to whatever sordid, strange, sinister world from whence they had come.

And that might have been that – at least as far as the wider world was concerned – except that an LA journalist named Frank Rooney researched and wrote up the story of 'The Cyclists' Raid' and eventually, in 1953, it became the film *The Wild One* featuring Marlon Brando, who had recently found fame as the T-shirted, working-class, take-no-prisoners Stanley Kowalski in Tennessee William's *A Streetcar Named Desire*. Riding his own Triumph Thunderbird motorcycle, Brando personified a new breed of devil-may-care outsider who when asked what he was rebelling against famously shrugs 'Wha ya got?'

If we time travel along the road which Brando's 'Johnny' and his gang roar off down we soon spot the emergence of the Hells Angels (so tough they even thumb their noses at the punctuation police) and other formally organized, outlaw-style gangs. Further down the road, as well as the tribalism of Biker gangs, we see the independence of the *Easy Rider* who, as well as being deliberately estranged from 'normal society', the odd mate aside, has opted to go it alone. The important thing, as Johnny prescribes in *The Wild One*, is just to 'go'.

More broadly, even though in reality those Bikers who stormed into Hollister were, like Brando, twenty or even thirty something men rather than teenagers, the cyclists' raid on Hollister in 1947 and *The Wild One* flagged up the notion of a new generation of out of control 'juvenile delinquents' – deranged, dangerous kids just out for kicks; youthful 'punks' who flaunted their bad attitude as proudly as their greasy jeans and battered leather jackets. In 1947 this 'Wha ya got?' shrug and disdainful curl of the lip was exceptional and, confounding rational explanation, seemed extraterrestrial or perhaps communist in origin. Today, on the other hand, the shrug and disdainful curled lip of 'whatever' – the rejection of the world as it is but with no alternative agenda – seems sometimes to have become our age's default setting.

In an interview which took place shortly after the film's release, Brando classified *The Wild One* as a 'hipster' movie and the dialogue of the film is indeed replete with go-daddy-o jive talk, finger popping and give-me-five handshakes. Viewed in the 21st century this feels out of date and inauthentic, since we now appreciate that the line of evolutionary descent of the jazz-fueled Hipsters owed more to the bohemian, bongo-bashing Beats than the barbarian Bikers – a descent which, by the mid '60s, (to the consternation of many a truly hip cat) would see the straight-from-the-fridge Hipsters transformed into wear a flower in your hair Hippies. But, in common with the Bikers, this flight from all things square, normal, conventional and less than copacetic involved going *On the Road*. And, again, this is a road trip which sets off in 1947.

Jack Kerouac had heard a lot about this guy Neal Cassady: how he had been working on a ranch out West, how he had been in prison before that, how he'd criss-crossed America on Greyhounds or just with his thumb stuck out, how he'd been raised virtually on the street by an alcoholic bum of a father, how he'd been born when his parents were just passing through Salt Lake City on their way somewhere else. *Somewhere else* - that Beat Nirvana which was just beginning to take shape in Jack's fired-up imagination. And he'd heard that Cassady – like his parents before him - was the kind of cat who was perpetually on his way *somewhere else*. And now, with a new wife in tow and a passion for literature kick-started in the prison library, he'd rolled up in New York City.

Cassady had arrived at the end of 1946, but it was early in 1947 when Kerouac – from a middle-class family in respectable, solid Lowell, Massachusetts, a famed high school athlete who had served in the merchant navy during the war and now, in NYC, was determined to become a writer – went to meet him in a dingy, cold-water apartment in Spanish Harlem. Before long the pair would be crisscrossing the continent together, and the experiences generated by their friendship and their adventures would become *On the Road*, which would not get published until 1957 but which instantly became a classic when it did. And, more importantly, instantly became a template for an alternative way of life which offered a way out of the post-war, increasingly suburbanized, standardized and conformist America which, like Kool-Aid, was sweet but failed to quench one's thirst.

On the Road also starts out in 1947. Like *The Wild One*'s Johnny, Sal Paradise and Dean Moriarty (the fictional counterparts of Kerouac and Cassady) say 'go!' and they are gone – far gone, beat, worn out, wasted but inextinguishable ethnographers of American life. They are looking for what we all increasingly recognize as the most precious and rapidly disappearing of things: authenticity. The Real Thing. In their quest they tended towards the wrong side of the tracks (home turf for Cassady, bohemian adventure for Kerouac) and to dress in clothes like denim jeans, work shirts, chinos, sweat shirts and sneakers which had previously been worn only for work or sport – in the process, ironically, becoming the style leaders and trendsetters of the modern age. And where style goes so too goes lifestyle: Sal and Dean's laid-back, rootless, love the one you're with, try anything once, Just Do It approach to life setting out the timeless, enduring parameters for a life less square. (The difference between then and now being that, for a few dollars more, you can buy jeans which have been stained, stone washed, ripped and patched by some worker in China who, on a pittance an hour, must surely wonder at the mindset of Western people who want and will pay more for clothes which make you look like a tramp.)

While Kerouac and Cassady were meeting in that apartment in East Harlem, down on 55th Street, near 5th Avenue, in a one room basement flat behind a Chinese laundry, a young white jazz musician and arranger – Gil Evans – and his friends were sat all over the bed and on the floor listening to Jazz and classical records on Gil's phonograph. Friends like the trumpet player Miles Davis and the saxophonist Charlie Parker.

When they'd worn down the grooves on Gil's vinyl this creative coterie might amble round to Minton's Playhouse to hear Thelonious Monk lay down his sparse, startling, incomparable melodies – melodies like 'Round Midnight' and 'Straight No Chaser' which have now become part of The Great American Songbook but which, in 1947, sounded all wrong except to a tiny group of musical pioneers for whom they sounded more than all right. Bebop had already led the way but here was something else, something modern, something cool.

For the first time as band leader, Monk began recording his distinctive Modern Jazz, for Blue Note, in October of 1947 but *The Genius of Modern Music Volume 1* would not be released until 1951. Miles Davis, Gil Evans and a nonet which included Gerry Mulligan, Max Roach, John Lewis and Lee Konitz began recording their own take on this new, modern form of jazz in September 1948 but they would have to wait even longer than Monk before their efforts were available in the shops. But when *Birth of the Cool* did finally come out in 1957, as well as underlining the shift from bebop to modern jazz in its title as well as its restrained minimalist sound, it defined not only a musical genre but a lifestyle ideal which would go mainstream in decades to come: cool rather than hot, less rather than more.

While Swing and then Bebop had burst a blood vessel to stoke it up, this new Modern Jazz would take it easy, exercise restraint, opt for the subtle rather than the bombastic. Time travel up this road and we come to the sharp, single-breasted suits and Mondrian-thin ties of Don Draper in his less is more office or, after hours, having casual sex – for casual is cool – with his bohemian, hip-chick mistress. Or we find Hugh Hefner in the Playboy Mansion – the man so laid-back and casual he wears only pyjamas. Or there's Frank, Dean and Sammy in Vegas – a city so futuristic it is built completely of neon and unlikely dreams. Or, come to that, John Kennedy the first straight from the fridge President presiding over his short-lived Camelot.

The temperature is cool, the color blue – *Kind of Blue*, International Kline Blue. The style is modern: a popular American modernism which, unlike that founded in Europe, isn't afraid to break the rules of orthodox minimalism to wrap everything up in chrome and jutting, thrusting, functionless, fantastic fins. For the future has arrived and, God damn it, it works – a gas guzzling, on the go, on the way up, so hip it hurts future where technology has solved all the old problems, the economy is booming and the beat goes on and on. Of course now, in our postmodern world, the wide-eyed, bring it on optimism which fueled this era seems so naïve and childish. The *Mad Men*'s slick marketing manipulations seem utterly Machiavellian and sinister. The failure of this *Brave New World* to foresee the environmental and social costs of suburban sprawl and unchecked technology seem downright criminal. But we're not about to throw the baby out with the bathwater: the sharp suit stays, play it again Thelonious, Cool Rules.

While temperatures were plunging on 52nd Street in Manhattan, things were getting decidedly hot and steamy (in decades to come one would say 'funky') in the Club Granada, where ex-professional boxer turned singer-songwriter Roy Brown was belting out his latest composition 'Good Rockin' Tonight'. Injecting the call and response dynamics of Gospel (which Brown had learned as a boy, at his mother's side in church in his native New Orleans) into the devil's domain of the dancehall, Brown had hit upon the magic formula which, in time, would propel the emerging genre of 'Rhythm & Blues' on its trajectory to world domination. In Galveston in 1947, however, there was just one small problem: the owner of the Club Granada was wise to the fact that Brown had been rocking and rolling with his wife, and the only thing for it was for Brown to hightail it back to his native New Orleans where he soon unleashed 'Good Rockin' Tonight' on the crowds at the Dew Drop Inn.

Not satisfied with this, when the successful Blues 'shouter' Wynonie Harris came to New Orleans, Brown, using Harris' own band between sets, performed 'Good Rockin' Tonight' for his hero. But Harris wasn't interested. Undeterred, Brown went down the street to another club where a singer named Cecil Gant was appearing, and Gant phoned up the president of De Luxe Records in the middle of the night and had Brown sing 'Good Rockin' Tonight' for him over the phone. Roy Brown's recording of his song got to #13 in a 1947 Billboard Magazine 'Rhythm & Blues' chart.

The following year Wynonie Harris changed his mind and his version of 'Good Rockin' Tonight' (complete with Gospel-style hand clapping) got to #1. But this was just a #1 'Race Record' and so it was exceedingly unlikely that anything more would come of the new gospel feel, which Roy Brown's song had brought to Rhythm & Blues. Unlikely but not impossible. Strangely, whenever he played anywhere near Memphis, Brown was surprised and amused to see that some redneck, hillbilly white kid kept turning up and, on one occasion, even begged Brown to let him join him on stage. It was only when this kid chose to record 'Good Rockin' Tonight' as his second single that Brown learned that his name was Elvis Presley.

'Good Rockin' Tonight' wasn't a big hit for Presley. Roy Brown's career eventually stalled and, at least for a time, he made his living as a door to door encyclopedia salesman. Yet when Bruce Springsteen became 'the future of rock & roll', he chose to kick off the concerts of his 'Darkness Tour' with a down and dirty rendition of 'Good Rockin' Tonight', and a comeback concert of Roy Brown's in the '80s, shortly before his death, had a wide-eyed Paul Mc-

Cartney sitting in the front row. But the magic formula of mixing a bit of Gospel into the simmering pot of Rhythm & Blues, which Brown concocted in 1947, did even more than lay the foundations for Rock 'n' Roll, Rock and Soul: the fusion of the seemingly incompatible musical traditions of white Country & Western and black Rhythm & Blues would, in time, slowly but inevitably make the logic and desirability of racial segregation unsustainable. The multiracial DNA of Rhythm & Blue's bastard child Rock 'n' Roll was both undeniable and, roll up the carpet, something to be celebrated.

All these exciting new musical genres, visual styles and subcultures beginning to take shape way back in 1947. 1947! Yet, the odd bit of journalism like 'The Cyclists' Raid' aside, very little of these seminal events made any splash in the media at the time. Within less than a decade the media and its public — whether pro or con — couldn't get enough about Rock 'n' Roll, Teens, juvenile delinquents, Hells Angels, Beatniks and Hipsters, and Thelonious Monk was on the cover of *Time*. In 1947, however, what held the world transfixed and preoccupied the media didn't come from Hollister, Galveston, New York City or *On the Road* somewhere in between. It came from Paris, France and instead of celebrating that wrong side of the tracks popular culture which would in fact shape, define and distinguish the coming era, it celebrated the return of an elitist, Old World High Culture and aesthetic which looked down from a great height on anything plebeian — especially if it wasn't

European.

In 1942, in *Casablanca*, war still raging, Bogart comforts Bergman, 'We'll always have Paris'. But when Victory in Europe was finally achieved on May 8th 1945 the question on many minds was 'Will Paris always *be* Paris?' The city from which Rick and Ilsa escaped as the German victors rolled in had for centuries been the unchallenged capital not only of France but of global Culture – the wellspring of all that is avant-garde, chic, beautiful, fashionable, stylish, civilized and worth emulating. Now much of Europe was in ruins, on its knees economically, in debt both metaphorically and literally to the Americans. While Paris itself had been spared extensive physical damage, it was a city nervously divided into those who had heroically resisted and those who had feebly (or even energetically) collaborated.

America emerged from the war triumphant culturally as well as economically and militarily – its Jazz, Hollywood stars like Bogart and Bergman, sleek skyscrapers, jive-talking Hipsters, dance crazes and even its hamburgers now world renowned symbols of a New World culture – a popular culture (no capital 'C' required) – which increasingly challenged the presumption that things would simply carry on as before with Europe calling the shots, and with Culture (capital 'C' if you please) controlled by an aristocratic (even if sometimes nouveau riche) elite. Would Paris, against the odds, find some way of reigniting its old magic? The answer came (or seemed to) on

February 12th 1947, when the up and coming French designer Christian Dior launched his Spring collection and the world's fashion press, hardly able to contain their excitement, dubbed it the 'New Look'.

In the 17th and 18th centuries dolls called 'Pandoras' (because they were sealed inside wooden boxes) were dressed in the latest Parisian fashions and shipped to the four corners of the globe. It is said that at least one such doll went into the harbor at the Boston Tea Party. Full-sized copies of these doll's dresses might be made-up by local dress makers under license or, in a sort of early form of mail order, the wealthy, even as far afield as Australia, might order such garments direct from the dressmakers of France. The underlying presumption was that, as in art, music and ballet, Paris possessed some special, preordained power to decree what was beautiful, chic, avant-garde and worthy of imitation. When the doors were opened at Christian Dior's new salon at 30 Avenue Montaigne on February 12th 1947 and the international fashion press, buyers and well-heeled customers raced to grab a little gold chair, the old tradition of the Parisian Pandoras was being reestablished – only now, with the advantage of photography.

If we join the throng and push our way into Dior's 'private house' we find a scene remarkably different to a big name fashion show today. There is no blaring pop music – indeed, there is no music at all. Nor are there the latest pop stars nestled into reserved front row seats. No, nothing so vulgar my dear. Not even a raised 'catwalk'. This is a 'salon' and the models – 'mannequins' – will simply walk amongst us; lit only by the chandeliers hanging from the ornate ceiling.

Note also that these mannequins are not the scrawny size zero teens one might see at a fashion show today: they are fully adult women with fully adult curves and, always, an aristocratic air about them. They might not be as rich as Dior's customers, but you can be sure they all come from good families and have proper lady-like educations – not one an 'ordinary' girl spotted on the street, as would happen years later with international supermodels like Twiggy or Naomi Campbell. Speaking of which, although blatantly obvious it still needs to be mentioned: as we scan the faces of those seated as well as modeling at 30 Avenue Montaigne in 1947, we are not surprised to discover that all are white.

The clothes being modeled take the breath away. After so many years of wartime austerity, cloth rationing, no nonsense masculine lines and short skirts, here are huge, flouncy, ultra feminine skirts which swish and swirl copious amounts of gorgeous fabric at calf length – but tapering sharply up to a tiny 'wasp' waist. Even more than its aesthetic outlandishness, the broader implications of this 'New Look' are staggering. The war is over. This we knew (even if rationing is still very real for many of us) but Dior is also, at a stroke, rolling back the unprecedented socio-cultural changes which came about during the war years.

Far from working in a munitions factory or such like, the New Look woman symbolizes a return to traditional, pre-war notions of femininity. And the supremacy of the upper class – throughout the war challenged by the rise of a new meritocracy and by egalitarianism born of the need to pull together for the common good – was now elegantly, extravagantly yet so firmly reasserted. And all in the seemingly insignificant context of a fashion show.

Beyond this, Dior was reasserting the cultural supremacy of the Old World in general – and of Paris in particular. Once again Paris would decree what was 'in' and the rest of the world would race to keep up and fall into line. Women like my mother in suburban America would have seen photos of the New Look in the latest issue of *Life* magazine. Although she always liked to claim that she wasn't interested in fashion (and although she most certainly couldn't afford a Dior original), given time, like most women in America, my mother's wardrobe would slowly but surely shift within the style parameters which Dior had decreed.

Sometime in the early '50s the women members of the Hamilton Methodist Church choir – which included my mother – decided that they would adopt a sort of uniform: they would all wear pastel dresses, the skirt would be flouncy, full and long, and the waist would be pulled in tight (with, as was the custom at the time, the aid of a girdle worn beneath). In contrast to the world today, what was remarkable about this was not that a designer like

Dior should decree a new 'direction' but that millions of women around the world, like my mother and her friends in the Hamilton Methodist Church choir, should so readily and willingly do exactly as they were told. Today we would dismissively label someone so sheep-like and unoriginal a 'fashion victim'.

In 1947 the unparalleled international success of Dior's New Look seemed to suggest that the fashion system had returned to its natural and eternal order as a strict but benign dictatorship. Moreover, that the natural and eternal seat of this power would once again be Paris. Not only in fashion but in culture in the broadest sense, the Old World Order had been reestablished. It was almost as if the war had never happened. Gum chewing, hip swinging, finger snapping, jive-talking pop culture had been put in its place, shown the door. Elegance, style, good taste and beauty would once again be created and defined within the heady heights of the upper class before, magnanimously, being allowed slowly to 'trickle down' to the likes of my mother in Neptune, New Jersey, USA. As before the war (indeed, as throughout history) Culture would be for and by the wealthy, established elite – who, after all, knew about these things and had the taste, education, experience and refinement to avoid the vulgar, crass and tasteless.

Or so it seemed at the time. In fact, as we will see throughout this book, exactly the opposite happened: the second half of the 20th century was characterized by an unprecedented triumph of popular culture over Old World elitism. And, as we have seen, the roots of this revolution were already visible – if you knew where to look and looked hard enough – in 1947. Yet, the historical importance of even this extraordinary and seismic cultural shift – POP! - would in the end be overshadowed by something else which kicked off in 1947: the big bang of the baby boom. For despite everything which happened in fashion, style and music, 1947's most significant historical influence was ultimately one of simple demographics.

There were 3.9 million of us born in America in 1947. It had been 3.47 million in 1946. Compared to only 2.8 million in 1945. A similar 'baby boom' occurred throughout much of the world following in the wake of the end of WWII, and had a remarkable impact on world history – a reverberating impact which is still being felt in the 21st century; this simple demographic blip and its underlining of a generational model of history ('my generation') becoming the key storyline which shaped the narrative of the post-war world.

As well as an obvious spur to economic growth, the expansion of the education system, housing and so on, the emergence and the subsequent development of the 'Boomers' had a profound, unprecedented impact on the values, attitudes and beliefs not only of the Boomers themselves but of the entire culture which surrounded them – the life cycle of this particular generation, as it swept through each decade like a great tsunami, at each and every stage distorting and shape-shifting all of Western culture.

Accordingly, the late '40s and early '50s saw babies, children and the 2.5 kids family (waving from their new station wagon or barbecuing in the backyard of their new suburban home) become the focal point of advertising, cinema, popular music, the emerging television industry and design. But the really profound impact came in the early '60s when the Boomers began to enter their adolescent years. It was not only their sheer numbers but the fact that a great many of these 'teenagers' had spending power. This combination of demographics and economics was too tempting to resist, and those companies which wanted to sell anything from soft drinks to pop music, fashion to automobiles, cinema tickets to make-up, record players to magazines adjusted their product and its marketing and advertising to appeal to the tastes, desires and dreams of that huge new target market, the teenage Baby Boomers. (Although, as will be discussed in 'Rock 'N' Roll', it is curious and important to note that the first chapter in the inexorable rise of the 'teenager' occurred in the mid '50s before the Boomers had themselves entered their teen years. But what had begun as an eye-catching spark in the '50s ignited into an awesome explosion, when the adolescent Boomers joined in the teen fun/angst at the start of the '60s.)

Thus it came to pass not only that 'youth culture' became a recognized, established phenomenon but, more broadly, that all of Western culture underwent a process of what might be termed 'youthification'. In 1947 (as throughout its entire previous history) fashion such as that offered up by Dior in Paris took absolutely no interest in the dress style of adolescent girls (who, naturally, followed the lead of their mothers). By the early 1960s, however, in part a result of old, too-long-established Paris' inability to get down with the kids, the capital of world fashion shifted to Swinging London where a new breed of younger designers like Mary Quant used adolescently thin (rather than middle-aged curvaceous) models like Twiggy (born 1949) to show off clothes which looked good on teens but, as far too many mothers of teenage daughters discovered the hard way, looked ridiculous on women of an age more suited to the (now completely passé) New Look.

Similar examples of 'youthification' are unavoidable in late '50s and early '60s cinema, popular music, television, food, packaging, object design, typography, even architecture and art. And, above all else, in worldview: with, in less than a decade, Western culture throwing traditional notions of the value and wisdom of maturity out the window and embracing instead the bright, shiny spark of youthful exuberance. This was particularly appropriate in America, an adolescent country propelled center stage – shoving Old Europe aside – by recent history.

However, '50s America was a 'young' country with a much revered and cherished but – hardly in sync with the spirit of the times – old leader, President 'Ike' Eisenhower, the former five-star general. Then in 1960, after presiding over his young country like a kindly old uncle for his maximum eight-year term, out went Ike and in came JFK – in the very same year when all of us Boomers born in 1947 entered the first year of our teens. Many contend that Nixon lost because he looked bad on TV. And so he did. But, even more importantly and the reason why he looked bad on TV, he looked *old* at a time when - the adolescent zeitgeist on the verge of becoming the cornerstone of Western culture - age no longer carried positive connotations. In another parallel universe, one without the exaltation of all things teenage and youthful, Kennedy's age (only 44), his limited political experience and his boyish looks would have given Nixon a clear advantage.

While the Baby Boomers reconfigured the world around them (doing so not by any revolutionary act but simply by growing in mass into adolescence) they were of course themselves profoundly, forever, changed in the process. We – my generation – were defined by our youth. For the first time in human history the primary, critical defining feature of identity for a huge number of people wasn't what tribe you belonged to, your nationality, ethnicity, income, class, educational level, religion or race: what mattered most was simply how old you were.

The world became fundamentally, irrevocably divided into YOUTH and, on the other hand, those who were either too young or too old to belong to this blessed In-crowd. As the sharp-eyed British writer Colin MacInnes observed in his perceptively titled novel *Absolute Beginners*: even in 1958 the year in which the novel is set, 'This teenage thing is getting out of hand'. As our bright spark narrator laments, at the ripe old age of eighteen years he will 'very soon be out there among the oldies'. In Britain as in America and much of Europe, the fundamental line which divided humanity became that between the Teens - the *Absolute Beginners* - and the Oldies who, sadly, regrettably but inevitably, were no longer where *it* – that magic engine of all things happening, with it and cutting edge – was at.

Of course, when MacInnes and I are proposing age as the critical criteria of identity, we are speaking about that segment of society to which we ourselves belonged: the white middle class. But then, by the late '50s and early '60s, there were a hell of a lot of white, middle class teenagers and that is why this group's perception of age as the single most important criteria of identity is significant; why it shaped the broader culture around it. For a black kid growing up in Alabama (or, indeed, in New Jersey where I grew up) skin color would have been more important than age. Likewise, a working class kid growing up in South London or a Catholic kid in Belfast would have seen class and religion, respectively, as the key criteria of 'People Like Us'. But during this period, especially but not only in America, the demographic collision of, on the one hand, the swelling numbers of adolescent Boomers and, on the other hand, the swelling ranks of the middle class, demanded that the big story – that which most defined the zeitgeist of this era and most tellingly drew a line between 'Us' and 'Them' – was youth. Teens in the early '60s were not simply a new social phenomenon, they were a separate species.

Or so it seemed at the time and, most importantly, we teenagers *saw ourselves* in this way – as something separate from the rest of humanity. Year after year of being categorized and marketed to as 'youth' left a deep existential imprint on the character of an entire, huge generation. As Hippies in the late '60s we warned 'Never Trust Anyone Over 35' because we knew irrefutably that those who were middle aged and older were a different, less evolved species that lacked our capacity to see the world clearly.

The problem in the end was that, to our considerable surprise, incredulity and consternation, even we Boomers aged. We ceased being teenagers. We became young adults – entering our twenties towards the end of the '60s. But still we clung to the idea that we were – and would always be, damn it – youth. Yet by the end of the '70s (as if it wasn't enough that the Age of Aquarius had failed to materialize) we were ourselves suddenly teetering on the edge of the ageist abyss: in our thirties and (the horror of it) looking at turning 35, middle aged and, ipso facto, not to be trusted. How could this be? Surely we the blessed generation – the generation for whom (as we saw it) 'youth culture' had been created and who had from the start been defined and categorized as 'youth' – surely we were immune to this sort of thing?

So throughout the '70s we struggled to convince ourselves – and, naturally, everyone else – that youthfulness was such an intrinsic part of our being that, a whole, ginormous generation of Dorian Grays, middle age would never catch us as it had our parents – who, after all, lacked our magical powers because they, sad things, came from the prehistoric, antediluvian time before the invention of teenagers. (Jon Savage in his book *Teenage* provides indisputable proof that, in fact, the term and the significance of 'teenagers' long predated the adolescent flowering of the Boomers but, as with sex, drugs and Rock 'n' Roll, we Boomers would prefer to cling to the belief that – the evidence aside – the 'teenager' was yet another thing which we invented in the '60s.)

And for a long time, well into the '70s, we more or less got away with it. What helped in this deception was that, having long ago chucked out the old, grey, squares who had previously been running the worlds of pop music, TV, journalism, fashion, cinema and even politics (on the grounds that we were young, bright, hip and uniquely plugged into the pulsing supernova of 'youth culture'), we the Boomers were now running the show and, crucially, controlling the institutions which shaped perception and ideology. Only problem (aside from that of physical degeneracy but there was always jogging, aerobics and/or, if all else failed, plastic surgery) was that, after all these years of our promoting and fetishizing the merits of 'youth', irony of ironies, a new generation was snapping at our heels and – the audacity of it! – heckling us Baby Boomers as a bunch of 'Boring Old Farts'.

Naturally we ignored these naive, upstart, acned kids and carried on with the business of saving the world by making Rock (the 'Roll' having been dispensed with) 'serious' and 'Progressive'. But by 1976 the pent-up, frustrated, crazed power of youth once again burst forth like a particularly virulent eruption of spots on the face of a particularly unfortunate sixteen-year-old. This youth revolution came courtesy of the Punk generation who, like kids rebelling against their parents, deliberately and precisely positioned themselves in opposition to the previous generation of omnipotent, omnipresent Hippies: instead of love & peace, kick-ass 'bother boots', instead of flowers in the hair, a safety-pin jabbed through the cheek, instead of the hopeful promise of The Age of Aquarius, No Future. At long last youth – real youth, not its worn, faded facade – had triumphed and youth culture was once again giving the world a good kicking. It didn't last of course. These things never do. But that isn't to say it will never happen again.

There are those who believe that my generation, the Baby Boomers, liberated the world from countless centuries of repression and tedium. On the other hand there are those (including some self-deprecating Boomers) who blame the Boomers – and their golden decade, the '60s – for destroying civilization and all that decent, right-thinking people everywhere hold dear.

Strictly speaking, however, neither of these assertions is true. Rock 'n' Roll, Modern Jazz, Surfing, Recreational Drugs, Let It All Hang Out Do It In the Road Sex, The Electric Guitar, Same Sex Sex, Experimental Cinema, Streetstyle, Subcultures, Gender Bending, The Counter Culture and so forth and so on, were all rolled out of the factory in the '50s (or long before that) by lone, courageous/mad pioneers who were themselves born long before WWII had even started let alone finished. Even all the great 'youth' or 'counter culture' figures of the '60s were, in fact, pre-Boomers: John Lennon (born 1940), Frank Zappa (born 1940), Bob Dylan (born 1941), Jimi Hendrix (born 1942), Brian Wilson (born 1942), Mick Jagger (born 1943), Pete Townshend (born 1945). Or, again, even earlier: Timothy Leary (born 1920), Andy Warhol (born 1928), Ken Kesey (born 1935), Elvis Presley (born 1935). They led and we Boomers followed rather passively, all the time perversely bending history persistently to recategorize them – these pioneering pre-Boomer heroes – as 'Us'. Not to mention the fact that the whole Teenage thing – youth culture, call it what you will - was already Rocking 'n' Rolling in the mid-50s when we Boomers were working on our merit badges in the Boy Scouts and Girl Scouts.

Nevertheless we did change the world. Not by pioneering, revolutionary action, clever creativity or ingenious invention but, as always with Boomers, simply by virtue of our numbers. We were only the audience – but a huge and generally accommodating one, and where would any performer, artist, visionary or ideological movement be without an audience? We were that great Baby Boomer multitude which sat on our butts at Woodstock and thereby changed the world (or something like that). Thanks (?) to us what had begun in the '50s as alternative, idiosyncratic and unusual became, by the late '60s and into the '70s, commonplace, mainstream and even, ironically, conformist. For better or worse we did this: we made smoking a joint, having casual sex, getting a tattoo, reading your horoscope, wearing jeans, dancing on your own as the spirit moved you, sporting an unconventional hairstyle and communing with nature all things which, if you didn't do them, made you seem somehow suspect.

But, inevitably, every force generating an equal and opposite reaction, with a fearful whooshing sound and a great sucking in of air, the pendulum – having reached as far as it would go towards a liberated Age of Aquarius – swooped down in the opposite direction. Once dismissed as too old, staid and boring, Richard Milhous Nixon rose from the dead to pluck back the American Presidency in 1969. Already the tables were turned: having felt itself on the brink of chaos (not altogether unreasonably as Joan Didion's 1968 report on the state of the Hippy Nation in San Francisco 'Slouching Towards Bethlehem' makes worryingly clear), America's 'Silent Majority' now saw Nixon's age and staidness a positive where, back in 1960 against the fresh faced Jack Kennedy, it had seen a negative.

The backlash against youth, and against the live and let live liberalism which so many of us Baby Boomers had enthusiastically embraced, had begun. From Nixon via Reagan right up to George W. Bush's disastrous start to the 21st century (literally, precisely making every wrong move) the entire pendulum swing to the right, and the awesome rise of the neocons must be seen as a reaction against that swing towards liberation/chaos which the youthful Boomers had (for the most part) participated in so enthusiastically, throughout that state of grace/gracelessness which was the second half of the '60s. Whether we went too far or not far enough isn't the point: Oldies, and even some of our own generation, panicked at the prospect of what we had unleashed and took flight into the opposite direction – towards some mythic, old-time stability and a desperately yearned for old-fashioned constancy. And this flight shaped much of history through the end of the 20th century and into the start of the 21st.

And this too – this swinging back of the pendulum with such awesome force and such breathtaking blinding of foresight – might arguably be thrown contemptuously in the lap of the Boomers. Had we been not quite so laid back, not quite so let it all hang out, not quite so . . . exuberantly youthful in that golden age of youthfulness which was the second half of the '60s, might the reaction against us and our decade have been quite so up-tight, blinkered, knee-jerk, reactionary and ultimately destructive?

It was one thing when the Oldie conservatives like Nixon,

Reagan, Thatcher, Dick Cheney, Donald Rumsfeld, Richard Perle et al hurled 'The Sixties' back in our faces, but it was even more painful when one of our own – George W. Bush, born 1946, the first year of the baby boom – spent his eight years in the White House systematically demolishing any vestiges of '60s liberalism which, against the odds, had survived the long march of the Oldie neocons. Not only one of us by birth, W had by many accounts lived the sex, drugs and Rock 'n' Roll party-on Boomer lifestyle throughout the '60s and into the '70s before turning full circle and, with some born-again help from Billy Graham, reformulating himself into the perfect anti-'60s crusader.

Had it been simply a matter of one party too many? Certainly this seems a reasonable presumption. And certainly W was not the only Boomer who couldn't cope with the let it all hang out route to the pursuit of happiness. But on the other hand one can't help but wonder if, perhaps in addition to W's inability to temper freedom with a pinch of self-control, there was not also, as in the case of so many of these '60s turncoats, a hint that W's problem – the real chip on his shoulder – was that he had never actually been invited to the party in the first place? Certainly we can't imagine W at Woodstock. Certainly W had always occupied a zone of uneasy, unsustainable ambiguity: too square to be one of the hip, too party-on and out of kilter to fit comfortably within the establishment into which he had been born. Was there, one wonders, some sexy Hippy chick at some party who spurned the drunken advances of this rich kid Texan Harvard boy? Some sexy Hippy chick (sorry to lay this on you lady, but this question needs to be asked) who ultimately bears responsibility for the invasion of Iraq, the destruction of the world economy and the failure to begin to tackle the problem of global warming before it was too late?

Thankfully we can now leave it to W to ponder his own strange, convoluted, clearly troubled history – and to do so back in Texas where, fingers crossed, he won't be able to screw things up much more. But now we Boomers face another existential challenge in the form of America's first *post*-Boomer President. First the police start looking younger every year, then you realize – with a start – that your doctor is considerably younger than you are. Then, if you live long enough, that moment comes when even the President of the United States isn't as old as you are. No doubt it's tough for every generation but for us Boomers – the generation of youth – it really is hard to take. There is no denying it now: we, who were once the epitome of and the standard bearers for youth, are now old. For some forty years we have been working night and day to shore up the ever harder to maintain myth of our eternal youthfulness, but now thanks to Barack Obama (born 1961, the year I started high school for heaven's sake!) this project is no longer sustainable. It is the end of an era: we Boomers are now officially past it.

So have all the social and cultural upheavals brought about by the post-war baby boom now come to an end?

Not quite. For there are still an awful lot of us Boomers, and our demographics and our Grey Power are formidable.

Ironically, so too is the power of the myths we helped to create about the significance and the inherent value of 'youth'. Thus, even while in many Western countries the number of actual teenagers is dwindling rapidly and may soon become just a trickle, the myth that 'youth culture' is still the driving force of our world remains broadly unchallenged. For just as we Boomers contrive to convince at least ourselves that, whatever our age, we're still teenagers in spirit (for we are indeed the first generation in the history of the world that never grew up) so too those in marketing, advertising, product development and cultural theorizing carry on with a model from the '60s, which presumes that youth culture and only youth culture is where whatever's happening is happening. (Overlooking even the fact that the last thing today's adolescents want is to be thrown into the ghetto of 'teenage' and target marketed to as 'youth'.)

But the ultimate problem is factual rather than mythic and theoretical: not all that many of us Boomers have so far had the good grace to die off, and the demographics of our final act on life's stage are truly scary. The real youth of today and tomorrow will face a stark choice very soon: either exterminate all these Boring Old Farts, or struggle 24/7 to keep them in the medical and nursing care which we Boomers seem to feel is our due for introducing the world to 'The Twist'. (Which, in truth, was the accomplishment of pre-Boomer Chubby Checker, born 1941.)

Want to know what the not too distant future will be like? Everywhere you look there will be old peoples' homes filled with old dears tapping their Zimmer frames to 'Can't Get No Satisfaction' while showing off their withering, drooping tattoos. And then, at long last, the final curtain. From about 2020 onwards crematoria will cover the planet – the unprecedented growth in funerals marking the Boomers' last economic contribution. Sixty, seventy, maybe even eighty years of socio-cultural, psychological and existential turmoil – and all, ultimately, because Hitler invaded Poland – finally resolved. Then and only then can our descendents (already labeled the 'Lost Generation') get on with their lives, and get on with the awesome task of saving the planet from the Boomers' unprecedented and terrifying carbon footprint.

Chapter 2

Coming Home

Charles Sydney Polhemus returned from Europe, the war finally over, in 1945. It had been the first time he'd left America, possibly even his first time out of New Jersey. He had 'prayed every day I wouldn't have to shoot anyone' and, his prayers answered, he had seen no significant military action.

Crossing the English Chanel about a week after D-Day, then traveling across France, he allowed himself to be talked into celebrating reaching the Rhine with a glass of beer. (When his teetotal Methodist mother heard of this she had reportedly taken to her bed in despair that her eldest son had 'gone to the Devil'.) But Charles Polhemus' celebrations had been brief: a 'Dear John' letter received the next day informed him that his hometown sweetheart back in Neptune City, New Jersey, had found someone else. Contrary to his normally frugal character (and certainly unaware of any Wagnerian symbolism) he threw his gold engagement ring into the Rhine.

The Neptune City, New Jersey, USA to which Charles Polhemus returned was little changed from the one he left behind some three years previously. A double misnomer, this community of some two or three thousand souls was actually a town rather than a city and, located about one mile from the sea, wasn't quite the Roman god's watery domain.

While Neptune City's Main Street – Corlies Avenue – boasted a couple of multistory buildings, and while a right-angled, numbered grid of streets suggested that the town's founding fathers had anticipated a certain degree of urbanity, in truth, Neptune City had developed mostly as single story 'bungalows' – typically, rectangular in shape with the smaller side, featuring a porch, facing onto the sidewalk and the road. Compared with the neighboring seaside resort towns of Asbury Park, Ocean Grove, Bradley Beach, Belmar and Avon – down the 'shore' where, according to Tom Waits, 'everything's alright' – Neptune City had quite a low population density. Yet its homes were, nevertheless, tightly packed together compared to the even less populous 'suburbs' which would soon mushroom up on the once agricultural land to the west of Neptune City.

Born and raised in a two room 'shack' on the corner of Corlies Avenue and South Main Street (later, the same corner where his younger brother Doug would have a Gulf gas station), Charles Polhemus – 'Charlie' – had attended Neptune High School just a stone's throw away from his home where, over six foot tall, he excelled as a basketball player and was (according to women of his age one would encounter, years later, in the supermarket) 'the best dancer in town'.

Back from the war, having survived it and with a little money in the bank, he bought himself a second hand but slightly flash car (a 1939 Plymouth with an extra, showy 'over-rider' bumper fitted; the same car Philip Marlowe would drive in the 1946 film of *The Big Sleep*) and a half share in a corner shop in the heart of Neptune City – just across from where his parents, now a step up from the 'shack', had bought themselves a bungalow.

In Philip Roth's *Sabbath's Theater*, the narrator Sabbath and his older brother Morty grow up in the years before WWII on McCabe Avenue in Bradley Beach, about a twenty minute walk from the 'shack' where Charles Polhemus, my father, was himself growing up at that time. Although slightly younger, Jewish (as opposed to my father's strict Methodist) and in Bradley Beach rather than Neptune City, the life of these two fictional brothers would have been similar to that of my father and his younger brother Doug. A life where most people knew one another. Where you could walk to the bank, the corner shop, the beach or to visit in each others' homes. Where you might sit on the porch watching the world go by whilst sipping a cold root beer and, on a Saturday night in summer, music blaring from a radio or a jukebox, despite what the Methodists might say, there could be dancing in the street. This was a world where men like Sabbath's uncle Fish sold vegetables on the street from a push cart, where pretty much anything an ordinary person needed could be bought just down the street (or by mail order from the *Sears, Roebuck and Co. Catalog*). Crucially, unlike the less populated, sprawling suburbs, which would start to push back inland in just a couple of years, this was a world on a human scale where for most people it was nice but not actually essential to have a car.

One Sunday morning in 1945, as he had done every Sunday morning since returning from the war, Charles Polhemus, together with his parents and his brother Doug (also just returned from the war, the Pacific in his case) went to the Memorial United Methodist Church over on West Sylvania Avenue. As the regular minister was on his summer holiday, the service that day was conducted by the recently retired Rev. Joseph Wardell Chasey who, once the Methodist Bishop of New York State, had recently moved down the shore to the upmarket neighborhood of Interlaken just north of Asbury Park (Rev. Chasey having done very well with his Bell Telephone shares bought soon after the company was formed, and held onto through the depression when many less secure would have had to sell up).

Accompanying Rev. Chasey were his wife Carrie and his younger daughter Margaret – known as 'Peggy' – who was in her final year of a liberal arts education at Douglas College in northern New Jersey. Blonde, attractive, bright, Peggy Chasey had the year before met and fallen in love with a young teacher at her college, who was Mr Right in all regards except one: he wasn't Methodist. Submitting reluctantly to her father's wishes (and, arguably, tragically because, if the truth be known, she would carry a torch for this man throughout her life), Peggy Chasey said no to Mr Right and, now in 1945 sitting in the congregation of the Memorial United Methodist Church, her eyes met the young, handsome, ex-GI Charles Polhemus who, while working rather than middle class like herself, was Methodist to his core. The couple were married in the same Church (the bride's father presiding) and I, the eldest of what would be three children, was born October 11 1947 – the second year of the baby boom in America.

For the first four years of my life my parents and I lived on Oak Terrace, a few blocks away from the church where my parents had been married and, in the other direction, a few blocks from my father's corner store and his parents' bungalow. 19 Oak Terrace was also a bungalow, also a rectangle with its shorter side fronted by a porch and facing onto the sidewalk and street. Although my memories of this period are dim, if not actually non-existent, tiny 2"X 2" B&W photos suggest a happy, All American, late 1940s family.

While hardly luxurious, at least in retrospect, the bungalow at 19 Oak Terrace would seem to have offered a reasonable life for a young, post-war couple: the mother able to push her child's pram to the shops, the bank, the hairdresser or to visit with a relative or neighbor. Children and teenagers could have a level of independence without any need to get their parents to drive them everywhere. If, unlike my teetotal parents, an adult wanted to go for a few beers in a bar, he (perhaps not she but my father's Aunt Charlotte told me privately that she enjoyed a cocktail at 'The Green Parrot' on Highway 33) could have avoided drinking and driving by simply walking home. By today's standards, Neptune City and thousands of other small towns like it scattered across America, were ecologically and sociologically sensible communities. The intriguing question then is why, as my family would do in the early '50s, millions of young American families turned their backs on towns like Neptune City – the home towns to which these GIs had triumphantly and optimistically returned after the war – and gravitated to new, land-hungry suburbs?

The obvious answer to this question is that, given the ever swelling ranks of the Boomer babies, there simply had to be more and larger homes and it was probably cheaper and more straightforward to spread out beyond the gridded town limits rather than to rebuild higher within existing communities. So, like a lot of things, this suburban sprawl (which in the 21st century – the gas running out – disadvantages America with what looks increasingly to be a dysfunctional infrastructure) is the Boomers' fault.

But there are other factors to be considered. Firstly, it could be said that, even before the outer spread of the suburbs, America's small towns – its fundamental social unit since its founding – were in decline. The key problem was what was happening on and to Main Street USA: as in the case of Neptune City's Corlies Avenue. As well as serving as the heart and central focus of those who lived in the town, Main Street USA was also the highway used by others to get from A to B. In Neptune City's case, its Main Street, Corlies Avenue, was also the final half mile of Route 33 which runs all the way across the state to the capital Trenton. This would be great for Uncle Doug's gas station on the corner of Corlies and South Main Street, but it simultaneously turned Neptune City's heart into a thoroughfare – in the process, slicing the whole town in half; making it a bit of an ordeal to amble from the barbershop over to the bank and have a nice chat with whoever you ran into on the way.

And, across America, long before the GIs had started to return home and the baby boom kicked off, Main Street USA, as well as functionally dividing rather than unifying each community, looked shabby and aesthetically dispiriting. Unlike in Britain and Europe where telephone and electricity companies would more often than not be obliged to take the more expensive option of burying cables underground, small town America always bristled with slightly off perpendicular telephone poles and main street was usually no exception. Nor was it seen as properly American for town planners to make any effort aesthetically to coordinate and control the look of its town centers which, accordingly, were only rarely glimpsed in the paintings of Normal Rockwell, who could more easily accommodate his cozy American Dream in nostalgic interiors or idyllic natural settings.

What you had instead, to take Corlies Avenue as an example, was a bank which rose two or three stories high with an impressive stone facade on its front while, on its sides, presumably in anticipation of the multistory structures which would be built to either side, its walls were naked, cheap looking bricks – giving the impression of architectural fraud and deceit. And, as the years rolled on and it became increasingly clear that this bank would never, ever have any company or support on either side, this lone building became a poignant symbol of the long gone dreams of Neptune City's future.

Architecturally, even in the immediate post-war years before the shift to the sprawling suburbs of greater Neptune would forever destroy Neptune City's future as a town center, the mostly one-story buildings which jostled for position along the length of Corlies Avenue were what we would today describe as post-modern in their inability to coalesce into some sort of single aesthetic pattern: here a traditional style barber shop unchanged for fifty years, there a dry cleaners effecting an air of modernity, here a would-be grand bank, there a pool hall (yes, right here in Neptune City) with tattooed, no good punks leaning on their bikes outside, here a police station and jail badly in need of a new coat of paint. The only consistency in the regular but slightly akimbo spacing of the telephone poles.

Increasingly dysfunctional owing to ever more, ever faster through traffic, ugly, hodgepodge, aesthetically unappealing, small town America's Main Street ceased to be a place which could be celebrated by a Norman Rockwell or any of his advertising illustrator imitators – and, in a very real sense, despite its lingering iconic resonance, became largely invisible in America's vision of itself. My father had grown up right there on Corlies Avenue, he must have known every inch of this center of his town, but with a second child on the way and - having sold his share in the corner store because, he said, he didn't want to be involved with a shop open on Sundays - a new job driving a truck for the Keebler Biscuit Company, he seems to have had little hesitation about turning his back on his community and heading out a few miles inland to what, at the time, was mostly small vegetable farms (New Jersey being 'The Garden State') or uninhabited, unused, left-to-nature land.

In the great American tradition, my father, my mother and I were – literally – heading West. Frontier explorers. With less than half the population density of the old communities like Neptune City, the new suburbs in greater Neptune and elsewhere across America heralded the first Space Age: the GIs who had mile by mile reclaimed the territories of Europe and the Pacific, now, with their wives and growing families, laying claim to bits of land they could call their own. Space. MySpace. It might, in my father's words, be only 'postage stamp size' but it would be *his own* postage stamp sized bit of space, of territory.

When you look at Neptune's suburbs on Google Earth today what you see is some pretty big postage stamps with mostly one floor, low level but long buildings – the long part of the rectangle now, luxuriously, running parallel with the road – positioned with plenty of lawn to the front and the back. Multiplied by millions of similar suburban dwellings across America – most initially fueled by the demographic time bomb of the Boomers – this exodus from the cities and the towns spread an entire country out horizontally as had never happened before. Elbow room. Space for the kids to grow up. But all of it, as never before in human history, making an entire, vast country dependent upon the motor car and affordable gas. (England's earlier development of suburbs in the 19th and early 20th centuries being structured around and deriving from the spread of the train and the underground railway.) But the black gooey stuff was just bubbling up from the ground in Texas and California in the '40s and '50s, so no worry.

The return of the GIs, the economic prosperity and the baby boom might have resulted in a town like Neptune City building upwards with multistory dwellings, replacing the often jerry-built or ramshackle bungalows; in the process finally realizing the urban vision of Neptune *City*'s founding fathers. But that would have gone against the grain of the national mood.

The late '40s/early '50s were the golden age of the

Western, with films like *My Darling Clementine* (1946), *High Noon* (1952) and *Shane* (1952) not only demonstrating notions of rugged individualism and self reliance, which surely clicked with the soldiers come back from foreign parts, but also projected these values against a backdrop of seemingly limitless space. By the late '40s that other American bible, *The Sears Roebuck Catalog*, for the first time included page after page of denim clad 'cowboys' and 'cowgirls' who proclaim 'Yippee!' The astounding success of the 1955 film of the musical *Oklahoma!* drove the point home: real Americans, heroic Americans needed land to roam free – if not the Great Plains or the Rockies, then at the very least your own backyard where you could, like cowboys, fire up the barbeque and cook some real American meat.

Back in 1947, on Oak Terrace, all this momentous transformation of America and of our lives as Americans was still to come, a fantasy just taking shape. My mother pushes me in my huge pram to the shops to buy dinner, over to my grandparents, perhaps to get rid of me for a few hours so she can go and have her blonde hair permed in the Veronica Lake style she favored at that time. Or we might go off to watch the boys playing baseball on the vacant lot. Years later with, I always thought, worryingly, just a touch too much twinkle in her eye, she would time and again tell the story of how one day a baseball hit high and wide landed just inches away from my pram. 'Could have killed you', she would add. Was the boy who hit the near deadly baseball the nine year old Jack Nicholson, who was growing up a few blocks over from Oak Terrace? Unlikely to be the three year old Danny DeVito whose family owned, or would go on to own, the dry cleaners and the pool hall. Anyway, I survived the baseball and the, some might think, cramped and old-fashioned lifestyle of Neptune City.

Within just a few years, all of us – Jack, Danny and I – and our families had left Neptune City. (Nicholson's family being rather unconventional, in that his 'mother' was actually his grandmother, his 'sister' in fact his mother – all of which my father told me long before Jack apparently knew it himself.) As a result, that Small Town America which GIs like my father had fought to defend and then triumphantly returned to, went into decline – one from which it will probably never recover. (At least not until the oil really does run out and, no longer able to get the kids to school, their food from the supermarket, a future generation of Americans might conceivably rediscover the practical and social advantages of small town life.)

In the late '50s/early '60s I attended Neptune Junior High School, at the time located in the old Neptune High School building to which my father had gone, across the street from 'the shack' in which he and his brother Doug had grown up. Twice a day my mother would run me the couple of miles to and from the school in her embarrassingly old and dilapidated car – we now, inevitably, having become a two-car family. This journey took us the length of Corlies Avenue which, with each passing year, became less of a town center where people went for a haircut, to the bank to top up their savings account, to pick up a couple of chops from the butcher, and became more and more a last refuge for those who had missed the boat on the American Dream. Failed or failing shops (some of them, no doubt, once a thriving part of Neptune City life, others just chancing what could be made of very low rents) littered the street – the stone fronted bank, now featuring a drive-in facility off to its still vacant side, looking ever more absurd and sad with each passing year.

The only members of my family who stayed on in Neptune City (Uncle Doug having married and, on the profits of his thriving gas station, moved to a particularly upmarket suburb) were my paternal grandfather Russell Sage Polhemus and his older sister Charlotte. One of my childhood heroes, a bit of a black sheep, rumoured occasionally to be found in The Green Parrot bar over by the hospital on Highway 33, strangely sophisticated and stylish for our family, Great Aunt Charlotte had by this time retired from her job as a fashion buyer for the prestigious Steinbeck Department Store in the still grand city of Asbury Park. A victim of that other great post-war demographic blip, the shortage of marriageable young men after WWI, Aunt Charlotte had never married and now, perhaps due to reduced circumstances, maybe from a sense of family responsibility, possibly just seeking companionship, lived in one of the two small bedrooms in Grandpop Polhemus' bungalow on 9th Avenue in Neptune City.

Grandpop's wife Nancy Allgor Polhemus, my father's mother, a country farm girl famous in her youth for walking some ten miles to church and back every Sunday, died in the early '50s only a few years after seeing both her sons leave home for the newfangled suburbs. At the funeral, tears streaming down his face, Grandpop exclaimed to my father, 'Charles, it's a terrible thing. First my dog dies and now my wife'. When his sister Aunt Charlotte died in the late '50s (my getting the bed she died in causing many a nightmare) Grandpop carried on alone in his bungalow.

A man who believed that the secret of a long life (and it must be admitted he lived into his 90s, surviving both his children as well as his wife) was to expose oneself to fresh air as little as possible, Grandpop Polhemus ventured from his bungalow only on Tuesday and Thursday evenings when he would have a meal with, in turns, our family and then Uncle Doug's. After I got my driving license in 1964 until the time I went off to college, I would go to collect him. Given that the windows and doors were rarely if ever opened, and given that Grandpop's life was measured out in Montecristo (but not real Cuban) cigars, I would hope to get in and out as quickly as possible. Outside on the porch, each and every time, he would hand me a dollar (not, in fact, sufficient for this purchase even then) and suggest I go over the street to what had once been my father's corner store and get some ice-cream. 'What flavor?' I would ask, knowing full well the answer. 'Cherry vanilla, Briars Cherry Vanilla' would be his suggestion, 'everyone likes that', when, in truth, no one in either family except Grandpop much cared for cherry vanilla – thereby ensuring that the old guy would consume close onto a gallon of the stuff every week.

At dinner, if you passed Grandpop a serving plate of, say, peas, he would want to know if they were Birdseye because 'they freeze them straight from the field', or whatever was the tag line of the current TV commercial. This was because, as disinclined to sleep in his bed as to take a bath, Grandpop would spend his nights resting in his Lazy Boy recliner and watching three old TV sets at once, all on the same channel, his great and terrible abiding fear being that two sets might cease to function simultaneously – a fear which was not all that unrealistic back in the early days of TV but which, now in the '60s reliability having improved, was arguably a little over the top. Breakfast, his only sustenance apart from Tuesday and Thursday nights eating out, was always Nabisco Shredded Wheat – full boxes stacked against one wall, empty boxes stacked on the wall opposite, a little table, a chair, a bottle of milk, a bowl and a spoon in between.

It was a similar story on the dinning room table: unopened boxes of Montecristo cigars (gifts for his birthday, Father's Day or Christmas – it was never a problem knowing what to get him) at the far end, a small pile of the twist string openers from the cigars, a mountain of the cellophane cigar wrappers and, finally, a carefully arranged stack of the empty boxes. A sensible, orderly (but not, it must be said, very clean) man, Grandpop thought it a waste of time taking down and then putting up again his Christmas decorations. So, even in July, the stuffy, hot, airless bungalow was festooned with strings of old Christmas cards – layered up and up in a sort of archaeological stratification – and, if my father had not insisted upon taking it away, last year's long deceased Christmas tree.

Such was Grandpop Polhemus' life in Neptune City, after the rest of the family had died or moved away to the suburbs. Near the end of Philip Roth's *Sabbath's Theater*, on a whim, Sabbath visits his hundred year old Uncle Fish, who is also living a lonely and less than spic and span existence about a mile away from Grandpop's bungalow, in Bradley Beach. Fish's place is two stories high, and although he does not really sleep much he does go up to bed at night. He tells Sabbath he's out of cereal (an eventuality which, due to careful stockpiling, would never befall Grandpop) but does make his own lunch every day: a lamp chop, a little apple sauce with maybe an orange for dessert. Of course there are no Christmas decorations, Fish being Jewish. Also, unlike Grandpop Polhemus, Fish would have a shower occasionally.

In an old sideboard which used to belong to his family (his parents both now dead), Sabbath finds a box marked 'Morty's Things'. Unlike Sabbath and my father and uncle, Sabbath's younger brother Morty didn't survive the war – shot down over the Pacific. At the bottom of the cardboard box Sabbath finds the officially folded flag which had draped his brother's coffin. For some of us the obvious yet all too easily forgotten truth is that a great many GIs never made it back to their home towns and many of those who did, unlike my father and my uncle, were deeply scarred psychologically if not physically. Such GIs had had their *High Noon* showdown and most of them, like Gary Cooper's Marshal Will Kane, had lived up to the terrible challenges of their time, their war. They had done what a man's got to do. Now that war was over and for the survivors it was time to move on to a new – and who could possibly doubt it? – better life for themselves and their growing families. Now was the future, an American, suburban future.

Chapter 3

Suburban Life

We know everything we need to know about Tony from the way he grabs that ticket at the tollbooth: like it's his and his alone and, come what may, even if it's just a New Jersey Turnpike ticket, one of life's perpetual little annoyances, something way beneath a mafia don like him, he aims to keep it that way. Out of the Lincoln Tunnel, the original backdrop shot of the Twin Towers later airbrushed out by history. The cigar: there will be three, exhaled clouds of smoke from the bear-like chest of, arguably, the most famous of all fictional Baby Boomers, Tony Soprano. Newark Airport – always, for me, a reminder of flights between there and London when my mother was dying of leukemia. Then we see the extraordinary, other-planet-like, noxious wastelands of 'The Garden State'.

Old, decrepit Newark. In *Sabbath's Theater* our narrator explains how the Jersey Shore accommodated north New Jersey city-dwellers into its original WASP communities: 'If you were a Jew from Jersey City you went to Belmar, if you were a Jew from Newark you went to Bradley [Beach]' – my hometown Neptune City's easterly neighbors. Tony, Italian, instead of the Jersey Shore, opted to move his family to the grand, elegantly landscaped suburbs of northern New Jersey – like Roth's central character Seymour 'Swede' Levov in *American Pastoral*, who gives up on the family glove factory in Newark to take up the good life in another of New Jersey's most upmarket suburbs. For 'The Swede' the good life proves not to be so good. For Tony, I guess it depends on how you look at it.

Both men, at least at times, yearn for 'the old neighborhood', and we clock Tony's inner city office on the sidewalk outside Satriale's Pork Store flashing by on the right. The rapidly merging white lines on black tarmac urge us on and brilliantly quicken the pace – the semi-detached hinterlands of urban decay becoming old, pre-war, two-story suburbs. Almost home now. But just before we enter the leafy glade of serious money, just on our right, only eight frames of it yet the familiarity always grabs and stays with me all the way up to the slamming of the car door: in that second or so of film we see the sort of humble, working/lower middle class, boxy, post-war suburban house millions of other American Baby Boomers and I grew up in. It's there a moment and then gone as Tony glides by on his way to the American dream/nightmare. What we have just fleetingly glimpsed is the most important building in 20th century, post-war America.

Grand, palatial homes landscaped into the countryside like Tony's go back at least to the villas of his ancient Roman ancestors. In *Mad Men* Don Draper's suburban pile in Westchester County, serviced by train right into the heart of Manhattan, would have been built long before the Second World War – its classic, New England traditional style jealously imitated, never achieved, in millions of post-war suburban homes. But that humble 'ranch style' house we glimpse before entering Tony's world was in its time – the late '40s right up to the early '60s – something new, something which would change the world.

In 1947 (that year again) the building firm Levitt & Sons began constructing some two thousand rental homes on what had previously been a potato farm in Long Island. Mass produced in a step-by-step process reminiscent of an automobile assembly line, these new, nearly identical dwellings proved instantly popular with recently returned GIs and their growing baby boom families, and 'Levittown' as it came to be known was an instant success. Two years later, their rental home project complete, Abraham Levitt and his sons switched to building slightly larger, more modern houses which GIs – now with secure mortgages thanks to the 'GI Bill' – could afford to buy. The 'ranch' style house, which would be duplicated thousands of times across the length and breadth of Levittown, was 32 ft long and 25 ft deep – about the size of the lower middle class suburban home which Tony passes before he turns into his own upmarket neighborhood.

Long, low to the ground, with minimal exterior (or interior) decoration, this 'ranch' style home became the standard architectural model not only for Levittown, Long Island (and then also three other Levittowns in Pennsylvania, New Jersey and Puerto Rico) but for the great majority of all the suburban homes which mushroomed up across America in the late '40s and into the '50s. As with cars in the course of this decade, the ranch style's long, low lines (originally a logical response to cheap land prices in the American West) seems to have clicked with the aesthetic gestalt of this decade when, suddenly, the high rise grill of my father's 1939 Plymouth or a home which was high rather than wide, seemed all wrong, undesirable, passé. And, mythically, iconically, what more perfect home for a would-be cowboy – all the former-GIs just back from doing what a man's got to do – than a 'ranch'? Yippee!, as they exclaimed in the *Sears & Roebuck Catalog.*

My parents, however, settled instead on the less popular 'Cape Cod' style which featured a slightly higher pitch to the roof, with a dormer window and a tiny, purely decorative porch in front, a cladding of unpainted shingles, shutters with a sailing ship motif and a separate (but stylistically identical) garage set slightly back, to the left side of the house – where there was the 'side door' into the kitchen which, in real life, was the main way in and out of the building. The choice may have reflected my mother's ancestral and ideological roots: New England was both her family home and, as a liberal arts student in college, her template for civilization. And it may also have reflected my father's own 'clam digger' ancestry, symbolically maintaining his link to the Atlantic even while, in truth, he was now moving a couple of miles away from it. No architect was required as, typical for the time, the plans were bought by mail order – possibly from Sears, Roebuck and Co. It was built by two of my mother's father's brothers (a carpenter and a mason) and paid for with a GI Bill secured mortgage.

If you follow Route 33 west from where it starts (the point where it butts into South Main Street, the site of 'the shack' and then Uncle Doug's gas station) about three miles inland – about a mile past Fitkin Hospital (now The Jersey Shore Medical Center) – you see Tilton Place which, thumbing its nose at the right angle, would-be urbanity of Neptune City, angles off from the highway at a jaunty forty-five degrees. Just over from this intersection (unfortunately not far enough to avoid the incessant traffic noise of the highway) is 423 Tilton Place where my parents bought a plot of land of about 70 feet long by 100 feet deep, on which they built a home measuring roughly 40 feet long by 27 feet deep. At the time, in 1951, there were a couple of other, older, two-story homes already on Tilton Place but the rest, including 423 when it was purchased, was wasteland with a thin, sporadic covering of bushes and the occasional undistinguished tree.

In photos the brand new Cape Cod style house seems

alien and out of place: the front and back yards unnaturally flat, without vegetation, set in scrub land punctuated merely by the odd, scraggly tree and stretching for as far as can be seen. The community life of Neptune City must have seemed far, far away – especially to my mother who, without a car of her own and not knowing a soul who lived in the few existing homes in the area, with no shops or other amenities within walking distance and her husband out driving a truck all day one week then all night the next, it must have seemed impossibly isolated.

And it *was* impossibly isolated. Unlike Oak Terrace, Tilton Place had no sidewalk. And why should it? For where would you walk to? In the early '50s, from 423 Tilton Place you could see a couple of houses over on the other side of Highway 33, but there was no crossing light and, even for an adult, crossing this increasingly busy highway would have been risky. Anyway, unless they happened to go to your church, how would you know these people who, without some such point of contact, might as well have been Martians?

In the years which followed our 1951 move out west to Tilton Place and the budding suburbs of greater Neptune, gradually, year by year, each plot of land was bought-up and built upon – both on Tilton Place and adjacent Maple Street which, also on a jaunty angle off Highway 33, ran parallel behind it. Growing up, I would build tree houses on the vacant properties adjoining ours only to see bulldozers arrive to knock them down. But at least now there would be other kids to play with.

Behind, and over to the side of our back yard, was the back yard of the Yanonnes who lived in a new ranch style house on Maple Ave. Born up in New York City, Fay Yanonne was Jewish; her husband - the delightfully nicknamed Yo - Catholic. They would, despite Fay's yearning for at least one offspring of her own gender, eventually have five boys. The eldest of these was Gary who was my age, and together with a few other neighborhood kids we would play Wiffle ball in the Yanonne's backyard. Designed specifically not to travel very far (an invention whose time had come with the spread of the suburbs), a Wiffle ball is made of plastic with holes in its sides to increase its drag. Unfortunately this deliberately un-aerodynamic design was not always sufficient to prevent the ball from occasionally landing in the adjoining backyard of the Thompsons, who were not the friendliest people on the block. A policeman, Mr Thompson had erected a double-height chain-link fence and, within that, a formidable hedge. If, your heart pounding with nerves more than effort, you managed to scale this fence and find a boy-sized gap in the hedge, inevitably, like magic, a powerful spotlight would come on and Mr Thompson (strangely, seemingly always in uniform) would apprehend and then frog march you home to complain to your old man who, clocking the uniform and mindful of Mr Thompson's status as a law enforcement officer, would apologize, promise it wouldn't happen again and then, after Mr Thompson had departed, declare the man a complete jerk.

Basketball and barbeques worked better than baseball in the backyards of these new American suburban homes. But the real function of the vast, mostly unused spaces, at least in Neptune in the early '50s, was to provide space underground for each family's dry well. Lacking waste pipes connected to a public sewage system, the dry well served to disperse the waste produced by the American suburban family.

The problem with this, however, was that when a certain critical population density was achieved – the baby boom quickly exceeding the mythical 2.5 children family limit – the system failed and one by one each household had its shit coming back. A local government based initiative for the laying of sewage pipes (seen by my father and the town's Republican politicians alike as un-American and totalitarian) not on the cards, the immediate solution was for each family periodically to pay for a tanker truck to come and suck out your dry well. When this failed, like George Washington, my father took an axe and chopped down the tree (in this instance apple rather than cherry), which he had lovingly and proudly planted in the center of the backyard and which now looked to be on the verge of producing the odd apple but which, located above the dry well, was seen by my father as the cause of the problem. Unfortunately, it was not. Now the backyard was just lawn (except, off to the side, connecting the house and the garage, a white picket fence in the center of which was a trellis covered in roses – but in time this too would have to go in order to accommodate parking a second car for my mother). And still shit happened.

The next step – repeated in each and every backyard in my neighborhood, no doubt across most of the new suburbs of America – was that great holes were dug (often by hand, by the old man, occasionally with neighbors looking on and offering advice) and cinder block dry well extensions built. And then there were extensions added onto the extensions. From a sociological perspective this was all for the good with Protestants, Catholics and Jews, with ancestries going back to such diverse places as Italy, Germany, Ireland, New Zealand or, as in my father's case, the Jersey Shore itself, finding common cause in the face of imminent disaster thanks to the dry well crises. But however much it was discussed, however many more cinder block extensions were built, the problem refused to disappear.

Shit happens – as American suburbanites learned the hard way in the 1950s. And so, inevitably, to my working class Republican father's consternation, the government finally admitted defeat at the hands of nature and decreed that sewer pipes would need to be laid and each household charged according to the length of its property. The length of the property? Outrageous! Suddenly all those long, low houses didn't seem such a great idea. It was in this way that 1950s America, begrudgingly and never fully, realized that its suburbs produced waste and that said waste would have to be dealt with, exported somewhere else. Not until the 21st century (and, again, begrudgingly and for most never fully) would it be appreciated that the other essential waste product of the suburban lifestyle – the carbon emissions from its unending car journeys – would prove even harder to flush away.

Beyond streets like Tilton and Maple which, optimistically, had been laid out and surfaced before the war, there were still in the early '50s small farms which, one by one, were now bought up by developers. The first stage was to construct a couple of model homes: variations on the 'ranch' theme, sometimes a 'Cape Cod' or 'Colonial', often a 'split level' construction (which typically had a lowered garage and, above it, half a staircase up from the living room, bed and bathrooms).

Especially in the summer, city dwellers – known by the locals, for reasons I never understood, as 'Bennies' – would visit these model homes and, hubby eventually worn down and defenseless against a vision of the horrors which would befall his dear children if they were forced to grow up in the city, would sign on the dotted line and resign himself to a life spent commuting up to New York. But the breathtaking, futuristic yet scenic new New Jersey State Parkway would be completed in 1957 and, provided the traffic wasn't too bad, one could be doing a reverse Tony Soprano and shoot into the Lincoln Tunnel before you knew it. And so like magic, sometimes within just a couple of months, what had been a farm became a landscaped suburban community with aesthetically pleasing (but gas guzzling) curved streets arching off as far as the eye could see.

The resulting influx of city-dwellers shifted the demographics of Neptune away from its WASPish beginnings towards a more eclectic spread, including Catholics and Jews, some of whom, heaven help us, even voted Democrat. Or at least that was how my father saw it – in time, this demographic transformation of 'his' town (so different from the Jersey Shore described in *Sabbath's Theater* with its almost exclusively Jewish perspective; and what of the likes of Jack Nicholson's family?) would prompt him to threaten moving us all to North Carolina where, as demonstrated by Billy Graham choosing to live there, God was feared by good Protestants, no one drank alcohol and people didn't run around 'half naked', as they increasingly did even in the new A&P supermarket in Neptune. For years the *National Geographic* map of North Carolina was menacingly pinned to the colonial pattern-papered wall of my parents' bedroom but, perhaps because my father felt he had a responsibility to stay near and care for Grandpop, perhaps because my mother was the real power in the family, we carried on at 423 Tilton Place.

While a substantial number of Catholics and Jews - urban born 'Bennies' lured by gleaming Formica kitchens and the prospect of sizzling meat barbequing on the open prairies of their very own ranch - might be new to the leafier, once agricultural now suburban areas of greater

Neptune, 'colored people' as they were then called (white people being 'flesh' color according to the packs of crayons) had long lived in Neptune but, of course, not in the new suburbs. There was not a single black family living on Tilton or Maple when I left to go to college in 1965 – probably not even by the time I graduated in 1969. No one went around saying that it was a 'white only' neighborhood or sounding off in a racist way, but if some black family *had* moved in such apparent nonchalance might have been revealed to be a paper thin facade. Nor, as far as I can remember, were there any black people in the '50s and early '60s living in Neptune City. Instead, all the 'colored people' lived over on the other side of Corlies Avenue in the more urban concentration around Springwood Avenue (not, unfortunately, anything like as picturesque as its name suggests) and, ironically, in Whitesville (the area having originally been established by a farmer named White).

To a white kid growing up in Neptune City and then the new Neptune suburbs, attending Sunday School at Hamilton Methodist Church which at the time had no blacks in the congregation, going to an all white grade school, it came as something of a shock to arrive at high school and find that well over a third of the students were black. While later years would see racial tensions in Neptune High School erupt into violence, during my years there (1962-1965) no such thing occurred. On the other hand, however, it must be said that few friendships crossed racial lines and all hell would have broken loose if an interracial relationship had formed. No doubt there is still a long way to go but the progress made in America regarding race within one generation – yes, that of the Boomers as it happens – is truly remarkable. In 1950s America it would have seemed far more likely that Martians might invade, than that we would ever have an Afro-American President.

But even if in the '50s and '60s there was little sign as yet of the new suburbs in Neptune becoming racially mixed, big, profound changes – of worldview as well as of demographics – were underway. Unquestionably the single biggest and most pressing change was the mind-boggling, upward demographic explosion of the baby boom – intensified further by the influx of new families who, once just 'down for the summer', had now decided to give up on the city and buy their own 'ranch'. The backup resulting from the overflow of the dry wells was only the start of it.

Could the schools cope? One solution was to introduce 'split sessions', whereby one year you would go to school only in the morning (but starting really early) and the next year only in the afternoon (but finishing later than would traditionally have been the case). In this way the same grade school building could accommodate twice as many pupils. The other solution was the construction of a huge new, sprawling high school. Unlike the old school which had proudly risen up several floors, with a huge ornate staircase at its core, like the new suburban homes and the modern more streamlined cars, the new Neptune High School would be a low slung, incessantly horizontal affair which seemed to go on and on forever – especially if you were racing to get from, say, the hallway outside the metal shop classroom (where my locker was located) and the art department which, according to Google Earth, are some 0.17 miles apart as the crow flies.

Situated on a new, wide, straight road set at a right angle to Highway 33 – Neptune Boulevard – the new high school was the first stage in the creation of a new town center which, in time, would also include a post office, a library, a junior high school and a town hall. Built largely on landfill, this new town center with its gleaming, low-slung, modern-style buildings was obviously intended as a replacement (nearer the geographic heart of greater Neptune) for Corlies Avenue which, as we have seen, ceased to be a convivial main street as, year by year, it became more of a highway cutting through Neptune City and dividing it in two.

Given this historical precedent, one might have thought that Neptune's town planners would have seen the advantages of orienting Neptune's new center around some sort of car-free pedestrian plaza. Having had the pleasure of sitting, sipping Campari & soda in wonderful, ancient (and some more modern) Italian towns, watching young and old alike pouring into the piazza at dusk, seeing people mingle, chat, show off their clothes, flirt, shop, drink and, in due course, settle down for a meal in one of the many restaurants which front onto the square, I can just about close my eyes and imagine something similar happening in a pedestrian piazza built (with the freedom of constructing on land which was virgin and empty) at the heart of a new, improved Neptune.

Instead, Neptune's town planners of the late '50s and early '60s – captivated by the lure of a 100% motorized future; unable to see any downside to a life lived completely within the cocoon of the automobile – opted for a wide 'boulevard' with each public building stretched out along its length having its own separate car park and with no significant public spaces for people to interact. Moreover, they created a town center which functions and is only populated by day. Devoid of cinemas, shops, bars and restaurants, there is no reason for anyone to come here after school and office hours. And so Neptune, like most suburban communities throughout America, then most suburban communities throughout the Westernized world, decided it didn't need a social heart, a place where its inhabitants could come together as a community. No, if you wanted that sort of thing, try the mall.

But that would require a bit of a wait, since malls as we know and love (?) them today would need a chance to evolve. Before the mall with its contained, security-checked, air-conditioned ersatz version of the piazza or town square, came the shopping center – often, originally, in quite humble form. But that isn't to say we were in any way nonchalant or unimpressed by its invention. Far from it, this was a marvel and, to us, a far-out vision of the future. In the mid '50s a tiny 'shopping center' was built on

Highway 33, about a quarter of a mile from my family's home at 423 Tilton Place. A rectangle only about 150 feet long, with floor to ceiling windows and glass doors fronting onto a parallel park parking lot, the 'Garden Shopping Center' was considered so remarkable that a postcard (which I still have) was produced to celebrate it. There was a drug store, a 'Variety' shop which, if memory serves, sold mostly things for sewing and dressmaking, maybe a dry cleaners. In theory one could have walked from my house to this new miracle of modern design – and I can half remember doing so, or maybe going on my bike – but the lack of sidewalks, the traffic on Wayside Avenue where there was no crossing and the general lack of pedestrians in the neighborhood discouraged this: you felt odd, old-fashioned, out-of-place, suspicious walking somewhere, anywhere in the new suburban America. (For more on the stoicism and triumph of the American pedestrian see Geoff Nicholson's delightful *The Lost Art of Walking: The History, Science, Philosophy, and Literature of Pedestrianism.*)

Further afield, in what had presumably been an undeveloped part of Neptune City, perhaps by the mid-'50s, an A&P supermarket arose to herald a brave new world and sound the death knell for local butchers, greengrocers and 'general stores' (although the local corner shop which my father and his partner Tommy had opened after the war would struggle on, without my father, well into the '60s by opening long hours including on Sundays).

Again, as with the Garden Shopping Center, the A&P was a boxy, metal and glass structure with a flat roof, but the shiny new A&P was on a much bigger scale, as was the parking lot which surrounded it. I can recall the excitement of being pushed around this vast space in a shopping trolley – surely one of the great, unsung inventions of that time, essential to the concept which lay at the heart of this new shopping experience: the idea that you would shop once or twice a week (rather than daily as previously, before refrigerators were commonplace), sling everything (including your Baby Boomers) into the trolley and then take all your shopping home, in your car, in brown paper bags.

I remember too that the A&P had a self-operated machine which, a small piece of magic, ground the coffee beans you had chosen and deposited the pulverized product of this process directly into a little paper bag. I can even recall my mother telling me that before becoming a chain of supermarkets A&P had specialized in tea and freshly ground coffee. There were also wooden barrels of wonderful pickles with tongs and waxy paper bags to hand. But what I remember most of all was the sleek, space-age modernity of a building which wasn't made of wood, had a huge flat roof and, with its glass paneled front, seemed to have no barrier between inside and out. Like everyone else in America in the '50s I couldn't wait for the future to arrive and now, with the opening of this amazing new building, it was here for all to see.

In time the A&P supermarket would become one 'anchor' at one end of an enormous 'L' shaped shopping center, but by this time it had changed its name to, I think, Foodtown (what a great name and how ironic that, now that towns were being replaced by the endless suburbs, the concept of the town would be redeployed as a place where food rather than people lived).

But now this supermarket, which at its birth had seemed so gigantic, was dwarfed by the length of the long, thin rectangle of the futuristic, space station-like structure to which it was attached. Where the two arms of the 'L' met there was a sort of department store called '2 Guys' – proclaimed in huge, red electric letters which towered above the long lean horizontalism which lay to either side of the sign. I remember buying my first LP $33\frac{1}{3}$ stereo (!) high fidelity (!) record in 2 Guys: Dave Brubeck's *Time Out* with its oh so cool modern art painting on the cover. Excitedly putting it on the stereo (!) at home, it seemed to have the world's longest drum solo with ta-ta-tum ta-ta-tum repeated into infinity. My father suggested that the record was faulty. I protested 'no dad, this is Modern Jazz', but eventually we took the thing back and 2 Guys exchanged it.

With the arrival of this enormous, supremely modern Neptune City Shopping Center in the late '50s, it seemed that the shopping experience just couldn't get any better. But, unbelievably, it could and it did. In 1960, Monmouth Mall opened near Eatontown, which is only about six miles from our home on Tilton Place. This, however, is as the crow flies and a trip to this capitalist cathedral and mind-boggling miracle of 20th century design seemed to take hours each way. Partly this was due to my mother (who now had her own car of course) being an extremely slow, cautious and hesitant driver ('age before beauty' she would mumble, as cars overtook us or refused to slow to let her onto a highway). Partly because, at one particular bend on the twisting back road we took, there was a little eroding hillside from which protruded pieces of sandstone, which my brother and I would throw into the trunk – pieces of sandstone which, after enough trips to the mall, become the decorative border of a flower bed in our front yard.

The final reason for the duration of this trip was that we would usually take a detour to stop off at the cemetery, where mother's father the one time Methodist bishop was buried. Unlike the flat, bleak, featureless expanse of the Glendola cemetery where my paternal grandmother lay, this cemetery was rather grand with gently rolling hillsides which looked out onto attractive countryside. Brother Joe and I would fetch some water in a bucket from the tap while mother trimmed back any weeds, arranged the flowers or wreath she'd brought and, more often than not, shed a tear for the man who had ordered her not to marry her dashing Mr Right, the man who believed that FDR not Hoover had bought America to the brink of catastrophe, the man who had hoarded his AT&T stock throughout the depression when, probably, many of his parishioners struggled giving enough to the church to pay his salary, the man who had ordered his family to leave a cinema because a delay in starting the film meant the ending would have come a few minutes after midnight and therefore on a Sunday and the man who, strangely, had once disappeared for a week to the Bahamas (his wife and family only discovering his whereabouts on receiving a postcard).

So for me Monmouth Mall and death were always subconsciously intertwined, but even this could not dull my sense of wonderment in the face of a sublime modern miracle. Not only was Monmouth Mall on a scale which beggared belief (and which reclassified Neptune Shopping Center as embarrassingly provincial) but, rather than a line or an 'L' of shops which simply fronted onto a parking lot, Monmouth Mall had at its heart – unlike the now suburban sprawl of Neptune – an enclosed, public, pedestrian space where human beings could mingle, gawk at each other (and there were always lots of sexy girls I couldn't help but notice), show off their new clothes or hairstyles, maybe even (if you could lose your mother and kid brother for a moment) get to know each other. Here was life.

And, sadly, here too was death, and not only my own subconscious associations with my grandfather's grave. For the triumph of design and commercial evolution which was the Monmouth Mall was also the death of the old, once unbelievably grand and sophisticated, department stores which had arisen and grown – to great gasps of astonishment in their time – in the late 19th and early 20th centuries.

Within the catchment area of Monmouth Mall the primary focus of this new threat was the commercial district at the heart of the Jersey Shore's great seaside resort city of Asbury Park, in particular Asbury Park's supreme retail achievement, Steinbach Department Store, where my great aunt Charlotte had once worked (and I'm sure excelled) as a fashion buyer. In my youth Steinbach was seen as too upmarket for my family, except perhaps in exceptional circumstances. But it was always there, towering – all five floors of it - majestically above the rest of this grand and prosperous city by the sea, as a symbol of what might be yours if you moved up in the world.

But now, after the opening of Monmouth Mall, Steinbach was itself moving *down* in the world. Indeed, it would finally close the doors of its grand Asbury Park department store in the '70s – a huge old building which, like a ruin from some ancient world, sat there as an embarrassing reminder that a once golden age was no more. Its commercial center devastated by the coming of the suburban shopping malls, its tourist income sagging as people opted instead to jet off for their holidays to Florida or somewhere exotic like the Bahamas, Asbury Park was no longer the imposing, fashionable resort it had long been – once confident enough even to laugh off that irritating line in 'At Long Last Love' by Cole Porter and famously sung by Sinatra who, a Jersey boy, should have been ashamed, which unfavorably compared 'only Asbury Park' with the

Old World splendor of Granada. Race riots in the '70s were, arguably, the final nail in the coffin. Asbury Park was down for the count.

Except that in 1973 a baby boomer (born 1949) from nearby Freehold New Jersey brought out a record entitled *Greetings from Asbury Park*, which featured on its cover an old postcard image of the once majestic resort in its heyday. With his 'E Street Band' Bruce Springsteen had been having a little local success and was eking out a living playing clubs like The Stone Pony in Asbury Park. Interestingly, indeed ironically, the existence of clubs like The Stone Pony only came about because of Asbury Park's decline as a commercial and resort center: cheap rents and a general air of decay sowing the seeds of SOAP (the 'Sound Of Asbury Park'). Certainly one couldn't imagine the likes of a rough and ready, slightly dodgy looking rock 'n' roller like Springsteen resonating lyrically and symbolically with a still prosperous, still smug, still respectable Asbury Park in its prime.

It seemed that Asbury Park, despite the collapse of its commercial center, despite the decline in its tourism and despite its race riots and lingering racial tension might just – with a little help from The Future Of Rock 'n' Roll – shape-shift itself into a new kind of successful, reasonably prosperous resort: one where instead of elegant, restrained ladies showing off their fancy bonnets in the Easter Parade on the boardwalk, rough and tough, street cred, blue-jeaned rock and rolling Baby Boomers like Bruce could get down and boogie. But sadly this rebirth – which briefly in the '70s proposed old, down-at-the-heels Asbury Park as the world capital of Rock – would prove to be unsustainable. (At least in the decades immediately following on from Asbury Park's recreation as a musical mecca.)

We will celebrate The Boss and SOAP further in the chapter on 'Rock 'n' Roll', but to carry on with the story of Asbury Park we must move on to a more recent, sadly foreboding and downright disturbing vision of this once grand resort, in the form of Tony Soprano's fitful dreams. The first of the New Jersey mafia don's Asbury Park dreams is set on the resort's famous boardwalk – the huge expanse of decoratively slanted boards as wide as ever (now in its emptiness embarrassingly so) but populated neither with ladies parading in their Easter finery nor jive-ass rockers doing their thing. There's just Tony and, instead of the shops selling traditional fancy wrapped salt water taffy, an impromptu (unheard of in the old days of my or Tony's youth) rack of dead fish for sale. And (for nothing is impossible in dreams, especially those of a nervous gangster) one of these fish speaks and does so, prophetically, with the unmistakable voice of Big Pussy – who will soon be sleeping with rather than impersonating the fish.

A different dream in another Sopranos episode bodes even worse: here Asbury Park's once postcard perfect seafront is populated only by zombie gangsters. Over in The Casino (where once Tony or I would have fed nickels into one of those mechanical grabber machines, in the perpetually unfulfilled hope of snagging a cool portable radio, and where a beautiful old-school merry-go-round offered the chance of a gold ring), now windswept, broken-windowed, puddled with old rain water, Paulie Walnuts and our (and Asbury Park's) old friend Steve Van Zandt sit playing poker. A shot is fired. Murder and mayhem ensue. Blood trickles into the puddles of dirty rain water. Tony wakes up, Asbury Park doesn't.

Not at any rate for decades to come. I last visited Asbury Park in the mid 90s when, following on from my mother's death, father having died a decade previously, my brother, sister and I cleared out and then sold the family home at 423 Tilton Place. Needless to say, this was a difficult time emotionally and visiting the once indescribably exciting Asbury Park and seeing it in what seemed beyond doubt its own death throes, made it even more so.

Yet even then, even in the midst of this ruinous evidence of decay, it was hard to believe that a place with such brute iconic power, a place of mythic history twice over, could just fade away forever. And now, in the 21st century, Asbury Park is slowly but surely demonstrating that, like Mark Twain, reports of its death had been an exaggeration - with new life being gradually breathed into the boardwalk, the beach, the old Convention Hall and even the once crumbling Steinbach Department Store which has been reborn as upmarket apartments. And, as fate would have it, this rejuvenation is happening at precisely the time that the American landscape has become littered with 'dead malls' and, as 'peak oil' approaches, we await the day when the once futuristic suburbs like those of Neptune (rather than compact cities like Asbury Park with railroad connections and a new-found sense of community) face a problematic future.

Chapter 4

Modern Times

It's 1960 . . . Richard Nixon is battling John Kennedy for the White House – with help (not enough, as history will prove) from Don Draper and the other *Mad Men* at The Sterling Cooper Ad Agency. I'm in my first teenage year and in need of a new suit, so my father takes me to Fisher's on Springwood Avenue.

For my father's generation – after, as before World War II – a good, desirable suit used a surplus of fabric and lots of gratuitous buttons to signal luxury and success: extra wide lapels, big shoulders, baggy trousers, double-breasted. But in the '50s (influenced by 'Cool Jazz' and the new styles of Italian menswear) an opposite, 'modern' look began to emerge: trim, pared-down, minimal. By the early '60s, even in Neptune, it was impossible for a guy to look hip without a single-breasted suit with narrow lapels, tight trousers, an 'Ivy League' button-down collar shirt, a straight, pencil-thin tie (cut square at the bottom rather than, heaven forbid, pointed), a plain, silver tie pin (exactly the same width as the tie and worn no more than 3 inches up from the belt) and a pair of loafers (optionally ornamented with a shiny dime lodged in the strap over the arch).

Like so many things, this 'modern' (or 'modernist' or, in Britain, 'Mod') style was born in the '50s within the emerging world of 'Cool' Jazz. Its startling, double-take shock of the new is described perfectly by Joe Goldberg in Gene Sculatti's delightful book *A Catalog of Cool*:

There were several stores along Broadway displaying these wonders. The hippest of them all but, sadly, a world I never made was Phil Kronfeld. In the conformist Fifties, Phil Kronfeld used to show a suit in his window that looked like a Lenny Bruce parody of the regimental banker's grey flannel. It was grey, all right, but not the dark grey, as light as your mother's hair, and it was single-breasted, in a time when double-breasteds were still the thing. Most outrageous of all, it had one button. One button! Do you understand what that means? Can you visualize how deep the cleavage went, how much of your solid-knot tie it showed? [Sculatti (ed.), 1982, p. 4]

By 1960 this modern style of menswear had made its way from Broadway and the new Jazz clubs of Manhattan all the way to Neptune, New Jersey. But my father (whose own appreciation of Jazz reached nothing more contemporary than Louis Armstrong) didn't know this. To his dying day my father was handsome, well-groomed and exceptionally 'dapper' (using a word to which he was partial) but the less-is-more 'Mod' thing never impacted on his sartorial consciousness. Accordingly, my younger brother Joe and I attended church, and any other rare occasion which called for 'Sunday Best', dressed in suits so voluminous that both of us could easily have fit into just one with room to spare. Now, however, as the older sibling and a teenager, much influenced by Modern Jazz and the style of the hipper male teachers at school, I was determined to stand my ground. (Hip teachers like Mr. Foster Diebold: unquestionably the coolest person ever to teach English Lit - who, as well as wearing suits so sharp you could cut yourself on them, also drove a sports car. A sports car which, strangely, someone blew up with a bomb one evening - the mangled wreckage prominently exhibited in *The Asbury Park Press* the following day. Yet, as if this sort of thing happened all the time, even in Neptune, following only an absence of a day or two, Mr. Diebold returned to Neptune Junior High with an air of nonchalance worthy of James Bond or Don Draper at his best.)

Back in the days before shopping malls transformed the American consumer experience, the usual place on the Jersey Shore to buy a suit would have been Steinbach, or one of the other large department stores in the center of Asbury Park where the goods on offer tended towards traditional, classic quality rather than avant-garde street cred. Had my father opted to take me to one of these stores I expect I would have emerged dressed like Bing Crosby rather than, as I hoped, a member of The Modern Jazz Quartet. But these stores were expensive and Fisher's on Springwood Avenue was known for its bargains. My father liked a bargain. And, to be fair, it should also be said that, while dated, my father's own sense of style had a flair and working class edge which he might have found lacking in the bigger, middle class department stores.

Like most of the Jersey Shore's towns, Asbury Park is sliced in half by railroad tracks which run north and south, parallel with and about a mile back from the sea. The east half of Asbury is all neatly gridded streets down to 'The Circuit', which encircled the first and second blocks back from the boardwalk and where, *a la American Graffiti*, a lot of gas was used in the pursuit of love, sex and the flaunting of automotive design. In the early '60s, this eastern slice of the city (where the big department stores were) was grand, prosperous and exclusively white. West of the tracks however, streets get narrower and instead of being based on an urban, right-angled grid, all jumbled up. More importantly, at least back in 1960, the tracks also marked a division of class and race. Blurring the boundary between Asbury and Neptune, this neighborhood west of the tracks was where the 'colored folks' lived - their community focused on Springwood Avenue, which had long since lost the rural and picturesque connotations of its name.

Although only a mile or two from my home, this was a neighborhood I saw only rarely and fleetingly. As a kid I'd collected old newspapers and magazines from our neighbors, and when these threatened to take over the garage my father would help me load them into the car and we'd go together to the 'Scrap Yard', which was located in the 'Colored' neighborhood. First they would weigh the car loaded down with all the newspapers, then we would unload, then they would calculate the difference and I'd come away with a few dollars in my pocket.

More than this, however, I'd come away with my mind jostling with vivid images. Black dudes in sharp suits hanging around a street corner – their postures laid-back yet precise. A group of young, sexy women in tight-fitting dresses with gravity-defying bouffants and extraterrestrial make-up outside a bar. Dingy liquor stores and lovingly painted churches. A tired mother laden with grocery bags shepherding her children home – all in old but beautifully cared for, freshly cleaned and ironed clothes. An old, white-whiskered drunk propped against a wall. Poverty and Cadillacs. Sounds of shouting and mesmerizing music I didn't recognize. Everything all mixing together, cheek and jowl - so different from my own neighborhood where little happened on the street and each family lived out their isolated lives within a fenced-off rectangle of land.

Fisher's Department Store, situated at the heart of this black neighborhood, on Springwood Avenue itself, was a wonderfully ramshackle place with boxes and bags of stock crammed into every inch of available space. If there was carpet on the floor it was threadbare. If there was the occasional mannequin it had a broken nose or was missing an arm. Mostly there were just jumbled racks and towering piles of clothes or shoes, and it always amazed me that anyone knew where anything was, but they always did. Also, luckily for me, they knew exactly what was 'in' and what was 'out' – no doubt resulting from taking scrupulous note of their black customers' shifting trends.

Nevertheless, the salesman who came up to serve us – white, Jewish, old enough to be my grandfather, dressed in a style which was far from cool – didn't inspire my confidence.

'We're looking for a suit for my son here', explained my father.

'No problem', replied the salesman, 'I've got just the thing'.

Sizing me up with his eye, rummaging around amongst the store's seeming anarchy, he returned in a remarkably short time with exactly the suit I was looking for – one remarkably like that described so enthusiastically in *A Catalog of Cool*. My eyes lit up. My father, however, was clearly not impressed.

'You and I sir', the salesman said turning to address my father, 'we like a fuller cut. But this will be right for your son'.

Not waiting for my father's reply, I went to try it on. It fit like a glove. A tight glove. It was cool. I had to have it. But my resolve would be tested to the limit. It was bad enough modeling, turning this way and that, fully aware of my father's penetrating gaze tracking over every inch of me. But then, his coup de grace: focusing on the tight cut of the trousers at the crotch he loudly commented, 'Everyone can see everything you've got'.

Nothing could have mortified me more. I didn't want my father to know I had a cock, let alone allude to its existence in public. A couple of years before, when the physical education teacher had instructed us boys to buy an athletic support, instead of conferring with my 'old man' about this the way I expect other boys instinctively did, I'd chosen to walk miles to a drug store unfrequented by my family in order to make the purchase clandestinely. Now, despite all this effort, my sexual being – that common denominator of masculinity which I shared with my father but so desperately wanted to avoid acknowledging – had ceased to be a secret.

I wanted to shrivel up and disappear, but I also wanted that suit. I REALLY WANTED THE SUIT. And I said so. Smiling, a glint of respect in his eye at my perseverance, my father gave up the fight and I entered The Modern World in a suit which, while no doubt a whole lot cheaper and less well made, was pretty much the same style as that worn by Don Draper in the opening credits of *Mad Men* which, in its graphic reduction of jet black and pure brilliant white – cuffs, tie, lapels all as bare to the bone minimal as a Mondrian – so perfectly captures the insistent modernity of the year I entered the world of cool school style and the year the original series of *Mad Men* is set: 1960.

It would be a mistake, however, to assume that the modernism which so pervaded, energized and defined the late '50s and early '60s – the Boomers' childhood years – always and inevitably equated with minimalism. One has, for example, only to look at the astonishingly over-the-top car designs of this era – the soaring fins, the sci-fi tail-lights, the extravagant use of chrome – to appreciate that the era's stylistic expression of the modern embraced *more* as well as less; to appreciate that the modernism which so enticed us was much more than simply a look, a superficial style, an aesthetic, a fashion. For at the heart of this attraction to all things modern was an all-pervasive worldview – one which loathed the established, the traditional and the timeless, and exalted in transience, change and progress. Ultimately, at the most fundamental level, this worldview was focused and founded on a particular perception of history and of time (one which also, simply by its absence, fundamentally defines our own, present *post*-modern age in the 21st century).

We may think that the notion of time as a progressive and progresssing line – an arrow shot from the past into the future – is natural and universal but, like all perceptions of time and space, it is the product of particular cultural and historical circumstances; perceptions of time and space being key components of what Peter L. Berger and Thomas Luckman memorably termed *The Social Construction of Reality*. For tribal, traditional peoples, time spirals, shoots off here and there, nestles comfortably into the familiar, boomerangs back upon itself in endless looping repetitions. And change, as the label 'traditional' indicates, was seen throughout the vast sweep of human history as problematic; something to be feared rather than celebrated.

But at some point in European history, probably the Late Middle Ages, perhaps driven by the dramatic population decline resulting from various plagues, the growth of upward social mobility led to a change in the perception of change itself. In what Durkheim would have seen as the 'collective consciousness' being shaped by 'social facts', this new class who had themselves personally experienced change as a positive – those who we would today call middle class – came to formulate a new worldview which saw time as a more linear dimension and, most importantly, saw change as progress and something to be celebrated rather than feared. Eventually this worldview would be termed modernism, and it is this celebration of change and this equation of change with progress – the presumption that anything which is new is, indeed, inevitably improved – which, as fate would have it, reached its ultimate mass realization at precisely the time when the Baby Boomers were growing up.

At the heart of modernism, its driving force, is optimism and there was plenty of it about at this time – in part because the lifecycle development of the Baby Boomers was fueling the capitalist economy as never before. Any young person growing up today will find it extremely difficult to understand just how easily optimism came in the late '50s and in the first part of the '60s – especially (but not only) in America. Again, it is a simple matter of the collective consciousness being shaped by social facts: there could at this time be little doubt that the vast majority of Baby Boomers would have better, more prosperous lives than their parents. The economy was booming and every day science and technology provided new examples of their magic – a sorcery which at the time seemed to have no downside whatsoever. Everything, indisputably, appeared to be in a state of constant and inevitable perfectibility: things really could only get better.

In the 21st century, when we are perhaps more inclined to presume that the best has already been and gone ('the '60s must have been so cool', students say to me enviously), to presume that science and technology have brought at least as many problems as gains and when logic points to future generations having a much more difficult time surviving let alone thriving, the naive optimism of the late '50s and early '60s seems frankly absurd. But not only did such optimism exist, it united even mainstream conformists and the most alternative Hipsters. Like 1960's newly elected next President John F. Kennedy, the most avant-garde artists and Jazz musicians – even the Beats *On The Road* in their gas guzzling machines – eagerly awaited a new, improved tomorrow.

And so whenever *tomorrow* became manifest it was enthusiastically, unthinkingly welcomed and embraced. Like some invisible yet undeniable, omnipotent yet benign tsunami, The Future swept through Neptune, New Jersey as it had or would through every town and city in America. And, here and there, it left visible, concrete evidence of its existence and its unprecedented promise: Foodtown, the New Jersey State Parkway, television, bold, clean, no fiddly stuff graphics on signs and advertisements, glossy colour magazines, cars with fins and tail-lights from outer space, one button suits, girls in bikinis on the beach, mascara, bouffant hairdos, Rock 'n' Roll, McDonald's, girls who (reputedly) did it, Carvel Ice Cream and, there, just on the corner by the intersection of Corlies Avenue and Highway 35, The Neptune Diner.

Sitting in the Neptune Diner with my high school friend Leland, drinking coffee and eating mile high vanilla cream pie, consoling ourselves on our failure to pick up any girls after hours of cruising round and round 'The Circuit' in Asbury Park, it would never have occurred to me that the sexy modern design of this diner had a history which predated the '60s – *our* decade. For naive teenage Baby Boomers like me – dismissive, even hostile to the past, keen only on peering into the future – the rounded chrome corners, wide plate glass windows and, inside, the floor to ceiling, wall to wall covering of stainless steel, were just another example of what was unique and special about this our shiny youthful decade.

Ironically, it was beyond our modernist mindset that such modern design itself had a past – one which went back not only to before the last war but right back at least to the 1920s when, another great and terrible World War fought and won, that optimism which underlies and powers Modernism first found widespread stylistic expression in America:

It [the 1920s] was a time of great change, extreme experimentation and diverse styles. Gradually, people began to realize that they didn't care to put up with what had been comfortable for their parents or grandparents. They came to dislike walls encrusted with elaborate plasterwork and carved wood ornaments that would better serve on wedding cakes . . . Modernism called for a total break with the past – no looking backward for design precedents. Designers tried to create contemporary styles to go with the new pace of living. To do so, they drew upon the example of machinery, where the design was purely functional – automobiles, airplanes and ocean liners . . . This extreme functionalism was readily applied to architecture. [Gutman and Kaufman, 1979, p. 36]

And as Richard J. S. Gutman and Elliott Kaufman go on to demonstrate in the book from which I've just quoted, *American Diner*, aside from the skyscraper, it was that unique and wonderful American institution the diner which came most perfectly to express this new modern aesthetic: streamlined, decoratively bold but uncluttered, mass produced in factories, without a trace of wood or other old-fashioned natural materials, clean and religiously functional.

All of which was such a delight to young Baby Boomer

modernists like Leland and myself, as we sat comparing the wobble of our slices of ultra aerated vanilla cream pie to that of the ample, white nylon encased backside of our waitress who, heavily mascaraed, bouffanted, her rhinestone encrusted glasses hanging on a chain around her neck, would go on to star in so many Tom Waits songs. But even beyond the waitress's swish swish sashaying bottom, and the Rock 'n' Roll possibilities of the little jukebox at the end of each booth, what was so appealing about this and other diners was the way in which every square inch of space had been thought through, planned and designed. In this sense the Neptune Dinner was a sci-fi spaceship which, fortunately, had landed on the intersection of Corlies Avenue and Highway 35.

The arrival of the first McDonald's in Neptune (on what had been wasteland, well away from the old community focus of Neptune City, intended only for customers who came by car) brought a new level of modernity. While the Neptune Diner's building had been mass produced in futuristic style, the restaurant itself was unique to Neptune, right down to its name. At McDonald's, on the other hand, the whole operation – from the building to the menus, from the precise cooking process to the exact way of addressing customers – was mass produced somewhere else and then franchised out in identical form to every town in America. This arrangement is an accepted part of life today, but in the early '60s it was remarkable and revolutionary (preceded only, in my experience, by Howard Johnson's which, by virtue of its placemats printed with maps showing the location of hundreds of identical restaurants, allowed my mother to plan family trips across great swathes of America to the mile, and without fear of encountering the culinary unknown).

It must have been a Tuesday night, because for our first family visit to McDonald's we had Grandpop with us. My memory is of the famous 'golden arches' reaching a great height and extending out far into the parking lot. But my suspicion, based on photos of typical McDonald's of this period, is that this memory has more to do with the depiction in TV commercials at the time rather than reality (if this is true, it is an interesting commentary on how, already in the early '60s, reality was being shaped more by television than by direct experience). While I was marveling at the iconic arches, Grandpop became very agitated in demanding that his hamburger be very well done. It may have been to get his own back on his constantly demanding old man, or it may just have been a sincere underestimation of the possibilities for individualization built into this new system, but his son, my father, told him that 'Here you get it the way it comes'. A few minutes later we sat in the car and, in hushed silence, even Grandpop silenced for once, tasted the future.

But it was another franchise new to Neptune – Carvel soft ice cream – which at the time seemed far more revolutionary and modern. For with Carvel, not only was the architectural structure and the edible product mass-produced somewhere else, but this soft ice cream which spiraled towards heaven on top of your cone was itself – in the nature of its very substance – the stuff of modernity.

Just opposite the little Garden Shopping Center, across Highway 33, it appeared one day as if by magic (or, on reflection, with one in every town, would this not have been the perfect means for extraterrestrials to take over America?). Even more than the Neptune Diner or McDonald's, while tiny, the new Carvel was a startlingly modernist structure: an entirely glass and steel building which cantilevered forward and, in doing so, presented skywards two enormous stainless steel ice-cream cones which, in the proud and provocative angle of their presentation, resembled (or was this just me?) a pair of gigantic, futuristic, stainless steel bazooms. But even this was as nothing compared to the marvel of the product itself which, employing a new alchemy, took the non-stuff of elemental particles (or so one presumed) and transformed them into a magic elixir, a substance of pure pleasure worthy of the gods. This was not, one thought, *iced cream* – something ultimately from cows – but rather, much better, the stuff of enchanted, futuristic dreams.

Even more important than its transubstantiation of non-stuff into stuff, this was an *extruded* stuff which could become any shape (or any colour) you wanted it to be. Like molten metal, plastic, breakfast cereals or concrete, soft Carvel ice-cream, pushing its way out of the machine, submissively conforming to the shape demanded of it, was (and hopefully still is) infinitely flexible, infinitely transmutable. Once upon a time, in the old, boring, distant reality of the past, shape, colour, pattern had all been entailed by the innate qualities of the natural substances from which things were made. A clever furniture maker could bend a piece of wood, slowly, carefully, to form the curve of a rocking chair, but there were always limits and, ultimately, the nature of the wood or any other traditional material determined what could be made from it.

Steel and glass led the way in the first great reshaping of the universe way back in the Industrial Revolution, but in the 1950s and early 1960s everything seemed suddenly to be within the domain of the extrudable and that which could be converted from one thing (something which in the mind's eye of the average person wasn't even really a 'thing' at all, just chemicals) into something entirely different. Something – as had already been demonstrated at Disneyland, a new kind of fabricated reality – out of nothing, *Ex nihilo*.

And the something created by this modern alchemy could be whatever you wanted it to be. Take the case of that iconic '50s and early '60s substance Formica which, if you wanted, could be supremely futuristic with atomic, amoebic, parabolic or any other space-aged design. Or, if you preferred, magically, this new substance could become 'mahogany', or 'marble', or any other 'real' material you might choose it to be. At Neptune's DIY heaven, Channel Lumber (one of the new huge box buildings which materialized over on Highway 35 in the early '60s) could be found all the limitless possibilities of Formica laid out for all to see – layered up in an infinity of racks which took up a whole, huge aisle all on their own, each lovingly encased in clear plastic protective covering.

The choice was yours. An interesting irony this: we rightly see the '50s and the early '60s as the era of ultimate conformity – with even the exceptions to this rule (the Beats, the Bikers, the Hipsters) demonstrating just how overwhelming must have been the stifling weight of the conformity which prompted their extreme rebellion. And surely this is true. But at the same time one must also acknowledge the fact that the '50s and early '60s saw the birth of unprecedented consumer choice, diversity and heterogeneity within the mainstream as well as within the eccentric, rebellious fringes.

Such individual choice was obviously the driving force behind the supermarket: a nearly infinite constellation of types of cereal from which to choose rather than, as previously in the corner shop, just a handful. And in Channel Lumber it wasn't only the Formica for your kitchen countertop which offered a seemingly unlimited range of choice for your home. How I used to marvel at the stylistic range of the little screw-on plates which covered the electrical switch and socket boxes in suburban American homes. There were the standard off white 'cream' plastic plates, with which our own home at Tilton Place had originally been equipped, but there was also the (to me) excitingly futuristic (think diner decor) option of dazzlingly undecorated, gleaming stainless steel. This, however, was only the beginning: 'wood effect' (or even, possibly, real wood itself), sculpted into all manner of unlikely shapes offered Old World Louis XIV gilded possibilities on the one hand and, on the other, New World 'Colonial', which one felt would have been George Washington's choice had he lived in 20th century suburban America. But it didn't even stop there: 'Ranch' style electric switch plates could symbolically transport your New Jersey (or wherever) suburban box into the Wild West. Or, something vaguely rustic and Mexican, could position it south of the border. Electrical plates shaped like pink flamingos or Elvis were also available (and how one kicks oneself now, for not having bought and preserved them for posterity).

That personal freedom first outlined theoretically in The Constitution was now available in practice at your local supermarket, at DIY emporiums like Channel Lumber and at Howard Johnson's with its 28 flavors of ice cream. The big department stores like Steinbach in Asbury Park had offered some choice, but such stores always limited the possibilities according to their own definition of 'good taste' — such 'direction' being expected of them. That would have been the job of my great aunt Charlotte in the women's fashion department there — sorting the wheat from the chaff. But now shops like Channel Lumber abdicated from this responsibility to guide the consumer to the 'right' choice. Now, so long as it didn't catch fire and burn your house down or give you an electric shock, the consumer could have any imaginable style of plate to cover his or her electrical boxes. Achieving a real democratization of style, Channel Lumber said 'If you want it you can have it, and far be it from us to tell you what is 'good' or 'bad' taste. Here you the customer really are always right.' (So it will be the Elvis electrical plates then).

This freedom of choice was inherently modern, but frequently (and more often than not when it came to the appearance of the suburban American home) the style option chosen was one which harked back to a reassuring past rather than boldly looking forward into an ever more futuristic future. For the really interesting thing about design in America in the '50s and early '60s was the extent to which 'real people' almost never opted for 'modern' design in their own homes. I can't remember a single house on my block where the new completely or even predominately triumphed over the old. A 'modern' style sofa (as eventually appeared in my family living room) often reflected not taste so much as the fact that it was a great deal cheaper than traditional styles and, in our case, acquired for a mere carload of Green Shield Stamps. Modernity was fine for public buildings, but when you went home at night you wanted the old world, the tried and tested, the cozy, comforting and safe.

We see this dichotomy, this schizophrenic split, in Don Draper's 1960 life in *Mad Men*. Don's sharper than sharp, supremely minimal suits – with that razor-edge slash of white cuffs and collar – we've already mentioned. There's also Don's extremely less-is-more office and, of course, the squeaky clean glass and steel skyscraper in which he works. And let's not forget his Modern Jazz loving, determinedly bohemian, in the groove, conspicuously copacetic mistress. But back in Don's suburban home it's a very different story: old style, naturalist wood cladding, soft drapes in traditional windows, frilly lampshades, patterned wallpaper, cream not white trim. And within it all, also perfectly retro-styled, Don's wife Betty who, a Grace Kelly clone, wears flowing, flowery dresses, not too much make-up and her hair so natural-looking that only her hairdresser knows for sure.

In Don Draper's 1960 suburban home all is tasteful, feminine, reassuringly classic and traditional – but for the electric lights and the TV set (which, when not in use, as was the case with almost all TV sets at this time, is discreetly hidden away in a mahogany cabinet which resembles an old-fashioned sideboard) it could be *18*60 in this reassuringly timeless home. And this is of course exactly how Don wants it: his entire life is a balancing act between the future and the past – a balancing act which he hopes will bring a steady-state sustained stability and easy equilibrium but which, unfortunately, is in reality the precarious, death-defying balancing act of the circus acrobat performed day after day after day.

In Federico Fellini's 1963 masterpiece *8½* it is interesting to note that, at least as far as the women are concerned, the polarities of Don Draper are reversed. Of course, Marcello Mastroianni's central character Guido is, true to the Italian style, at least as modernist and minimal in his own appearance as Don Draper is in his. But, unlike Betty Draper, film director Guido's wife (played by the breath-taking Anouk Aimée, who dangerously unhinged my seventeen-year-old self and troubles my sleep to this day) is also a miracle of modernism: trim, stark, white linen trouser-suited, tightly cropped hair and a pair of jet black, chunky, almost square, cubist, plastic glasses. Instead, it is Guido's *mistress* – froufrou, frilly, frivolous, curvaceous, Old World feminine – who seems to have stepped out of a previous century, and who supplies a reassuring yet enticing retro fix for our anti-hero hero.

The need for just such reassurance was also to be found in the homes of millions of early '60s American families – homes, like the one I grew up in at 423 Tilton Place, which stylistically demonstrated a hesitation, a dis-ease about completely, unreservedly, leaping headfirst boldly into the Brave New World which beckoned and bewitched as never before at the start of the 1960s. Yes . . . but. Best to embrace the new but to preserve some section of your life (your home, your wife, your mistress) within the timeframe of a reassuring (imagined) past. And so it came to pass that Chanel Lumber sold an awful lot of 'ye olde world' mahogany veneers, 'Colonial' light switch covers and wallpapers worthy of long dead European monarchs.

This stylistic inclination back towards the past shouldn't come as that much of a surprise. As Gutman and Kaufman tell us in *American Diner*, precisely the same thing happened during the first flowering of Modernism in America back in the 1920s:

But though a few fashionable and fashion-setting clients bought the new modern furniture, the majority of Americans were still fearful about experimenting with the sacred domain of their own homes. For quite a few years, most people continued to fill their houses with the same old mohair-covered, over-stuffed suites of furniture and the same fussy decoration. Modernism's most important early appearances, therefore, were in public spaces – hotel lobbies, railroad stations, offices and commercial buildings.' [Ibid.]

And this duality – this schizophrenia – carried on even throughout what one would have thought was the ultimate flowering of the modernist spirit in the late '50s and early '60s. Not that you would know it from flicking through any book on the design of that period: for the curators of design collections and custodians of good taste, have thought it best to remove my family home (and those of pretty much everyone else who shopped at Channel Lumber) from history. But while these reassuring pockets of tradition lingered on (and on and on), one beacon of modernity penetrated even the most traditionally draped of windows to dazzle with its brilliant sparkle: the futuristic sci-fi vision of guilt-free, casual, thoroughly *modern* sex.

Chapter 5

Sex

Famously, in 'Annus Mirabilis', the poet Philip Larkin argued that sex began in 1963 – sometime between the lifting of the ban on the publication of *Lady Chatterley's Lover* and The Beatles' first LP. Of course, the very existence of the baby boom generation tells us there must have been a fair bit of hanky panky – what Ray Charles called 'Making Whoopee' – going on immediately after the war. And, as everyone in Britain knows, during the war the American GIs were 'over paid, over sexed and over here'.

When, in 1969, I told my parents I was going to Britain to work as an archaeologist, my father, who had been stationed in England during the war, took me aside and cautioned 'the English don't have proper plumbing and the women have very low morals'. I figured I could cope with the primitive plumbing. The point about English women having low morals only increased the incentive provided by a *Playboy* magazine article on 'Swinging London' and

Michelangelo Antonioni's London-set, sexually provocative film *Blow-up* (1966).

One's parents' sexuality is a country one never wants to visit, but I've often wondered just how first-hand had been my father's experience of English women's supposed moral laxity. And had things remained properly chaste back on the home front when my mother, the Methodist Bishop's daughter, met her Mr Right? Surely, as war raged and life seemed – and often was – so very here today and gone tomorrow, who could possibly blame anyone from that era for living in the here and now?

However, despite this, we understand what Larkin was getting at when he wrote that sex began in 1963. The early '60s saw a new wave of sexual possibility breaking over much of the world. Medicines had conquered once deadly venereal diseases like gonorrhea and syphilis, while IUD and oral contraceptives offered reliable, convenient (and invisible) birth control: for the first time in history banishing the twin practical perils of promiscuity. And just as importantly, slowly but surely, a new, more open, less inhibited pro-sex attitude was emerging at the start of the '60s. True, there had always been a few oddball pioneering proponents of more liberated attitudes towards sex on the fringes but now, in line with a freer portrayal of sex in magazines and films, there was a shift in the mainstream as well.

Long swept under the carpet, sex was becoming visible, a subject for discussion, something which was increasingly acknowledged as a fact of life in the real world. Maybe not in my family: I remember while driving back from a weekend at Aunt Ruth's hearing the announcer on the car radio say something about 'unwed mothers', and when I asked about how this could be my mother saying 'God sometimes makes a mistake' (how very bizarre to go so far as deny God's infallibility – surely a theological keystone of Christianity – in order to avoid discussing sex), and then father saying 'you don't need to know about these things; it would never happen in our family'.

On the highly self-censured TV of the time married couples (rather strangely one always thought) slept in separate, single beds. But photos in *Life* magazine of Marilyn Monroe or Jayne Mansfield with their breasts bursting from their ultra low-cut dresses or itsy bitsy teeny weeny yellow polka dot bikinis, gave the game away. Lying in bed in an excited state, trying to get to sleep, a teenager like me feverishly imagined that there were people out there doing *'it'* at that very moment in time (while not actually having a clue as to exactly what 'it' was or how 'it' was done).

In fact I think Larkin got it a few years late. In about 1960 my round of collecting old newspapers to sell on for recycling began, to my great delight, to net the occasional issue of *Playboy* magazine. Safely back in the family garage, I would hide each issue deep amongst the stacks of old newspapers. If my memory is correct, 1960 is also the year my neighbor Freddie invented masturbation and, kindly, passed on to me knowledge of this revolutionary invention (really, he should have patented it, would have made him a fortune). Unsure that I could find a safe place to keep my treasured copies of *Playboy* in the house (and certainly not in the bathroom where they would have been most useful) I would study each issue the same way that, say, a medieval monk might have studied the Bible, committing to memory every tiny detail which could provide inspiration later.

Naturally this included each heavily air-brushed, pubic hair concealing centerfold (it came as such a shocking, almost off-putting surprise years later when a real live girl did, finally, let me get into her panties, to discover a forest of untidy hair). I also treasured and stored in my mind many of the ads which – the creative gems of Madison Avenue's hippest and no doubt best paid *Mad Men* – connected up the dots between the sex and the consumerist world within which this new sexuality – casual, promiscuous, fun, recreational and without romantic complication – could flourish.

Famously, the centerfold lovelies were 'The Girl Next Door'. This was said to be Hugh Hefner's Big Idea and the key reason for his magazine's success. For me, however, these girl next door rosy-cheeked cheerleader types held little interest. I have always presumed that this is because I was raised a strict Methodist, and constantly urged in my formative years to find myself 'a nice Methodist girl' – a determination always to do the opposite of what my parents wanted shunting my desires further afield; ideally, as far away from 'The Girl Next Door', Tilton Place, Neptune, New Jersey, America, perhaps even planet Earth, as possible. (A painful but enlightening revelation coming a lifetime later, in therapy, when I finally grasped that always to do the reverse of what your parents wanted is never to experience free will. And, even more worrying, that in doing so I may have been acting out the repressed desires which my parents themselves yearned to act out but could not.) But Hefner was also raised a strict Methodist and, unless we are to presume that his Big Idea was purely a business tactic, which seems improbable given his unceasing energy in this quest, he must himself have had the hots for, indeed, been obsessed with, The Girl Next Door.

Strange how we tend to think of human sexuality as that part of our lives where we are most 'like an animal', instinctual and straightforward, while being constantly confronted with evidence that our sexuality – most of all that dark and yet often strangely illuminated territory which is sexual fantasy – instead constitutes that part of human behavior which is most complex, semiologically deep and indicative of the unique, profound and ultimately unknowable nature of human consciousness. There is so rarely in human sexual desire a simple, universal X > Y cause and effect equivalent to, for example, the immediate and unwavering stimulation of all male gorillas when catching sight of the particular shade of pink of the female gorilla's backside when she is on heat. We humans and our desires are so much more complicated and culturally, even individually varied than that and, although it seemed so much more straightforward at the time, this was true even in the early days of the sexual revolution when the battle lines between the forces of repression and, on the other hand, the forces of sexual liberation seemed so clear-cut and indivisible.

While Hef's strict Methodist background appears to have triggered in him desires which compelled him to search out a previously denied eroticism at the very heart of small town, Norman Rockwell style, All-American America, my own response to Methodist sexual inhibition was an obsessive yearning for The Exotic Other and The Bad Girl who, dripping with make-up and peroxide, unlike Hef's squeaky clean, scrubbed, natural looking Girl Next Door, looked like a Bad Girl. But, happily, she too could be found in *Playboy* – in the photo features which, for example, recorded for posterity and wide-eyed innocent kids like me the great party scenes at the Playboy Mansion. Of course you didn't see even these Bad Girls actually 'doing it', but you knew for sure that they did. And, what's more, you knew they did it casually, nonchalantly and without the sort of romantic entanglements and relationship angst and disappointment which, as you grew older, you sensed to be the sorry plight of virtually all the so-called 'happily married' adults you observed in real life.

Surely Hef and the Bad Girls at the Playboy Mansion had found the secret which would make it possible to avoid all the adult dread, discontent, disappointment and disenchantment which, the older you got, seemed more and more to define and condemn adult life in the prosperous, superficially serene suburbs of Eisenhower's and then Kennedy's America. Surely this revolution of casual, unencumbered, easy sex, as well as getting us laid, a means as well as an end, would open the door to a better life all around – a well-balanced, satisfying, positive way of life which, no longer eaten away at by the parasites of inhibition, jealousy and repression, would resemble nothing less than the sane, sensible, rational yet sexy future which science fiction had excitedly proposed for some time.

In this sense, the way of life which *Playboy* sketched out for us every month was supremely modern. Yet, strangely, interestingly, Hefner – exactly like Donald Draper and the other *Mad Men*; like pretty much everyone except me who shopped at Chanel Lumber in Neptune – had an (at best) schizophrenic relationship with modernism. Instead of a sleek, floor-to-ceiling glass-walled penthouse filled with the latest Scandinavian furniture, Hef treated himself to (and, if we are to believe the hype, rarely left) his Playboy Mansion – which he filled with (and with no hint of irony, irony never being a strong point of Mr Playboy) chandeliers and (apparently genuine, and why not?) medieval suits of armor. Aside from the state-of-the-art stereo equipment and the huge cinema screen which magically descended from the ceiling, the original Playboy Mansion in Chicago (in the '60s second only to the White House as an iconic American residence) resembled one of those rooms upstairs in the Philadelphia Museum of Art or The Cloisters in New York, where Old World artifacts and even whole buildings have been shipped from Europe and painstakingly reassembled in the still wet-behind-the-ears, eternally pubescent USA.

While Hef's monthly 'Playboy Philosophy' conjured up a (quite reasonable, usually consistent, occasionally brave) vision of a futuristic future, liberated from old-fashioned beliefs and moribund inhibitions, the visual message of the Playboy Mansion (the original, in Chicago) was as old-fashioned as it was possible to be in the second half of the 20th century. Here was retro which harked back not, say, to the Art Deco of the early 20th century, the Art Nouveau of the late 19th century or even the Colonial style of the 18th century, but which was literally and unapologetically *medieval*. (The more recent Playboy Mansion West moving forward only slightly in history with its 'Gothic-Tudor' styling.)

And can a man who smokes a pipe, wears pyjamas, drinks only Pepsi, fancies rosy-cheeked cheerleaders and has a 'mansion' full of medieval armor really be cool? (Cool being the most important thing to be in the first half of the '60s - as, indeed, it would appear to remain to this day given that one can now acquire a degree in and make a good living from 'cool hunting'.) Yes: at least until the second half of the decade when us Baby Boomers took charge of the sexual revolution and stripped of their medals all those who were deemed to be insufficiently 'alternative', we did indeed see Hef as cool and we did indeed count him as a hero.

For it was Hugh Hefner who most clearly and energetically sought to answer that BIG QUESTION with which events confronted us in the early (and some would argue, also the later) part of our shiny, promising decade of the '60s. Namely, now that science had for the first time in history resolved the practical problems of promiscuity – disease and pregnancy – could we not adjust our emotions, our behavior and our institutions so that we could enjoy a casual, angst free, life-enhancing sexuality? Could we not, in other words, discover and enjoy a *modern* kind of sex?

This was the question which confronted us in the '60s and, at least in the first half of the decade, it appeared to be *Playboy* Hef and his party guests at the Mansion who had not only drawn up the blueprints for this new, liberating, cool, modern sexuality but who, month by month, issue by issue, successfully put their theories into practice. The apparently undeniable evidence put before us in *Playboy*'s glossy pages was that jealousy, inhibition and repression could be decoupled from human sexuality and shunted into the sidings of history.

Certainly that is what we believed at the time. It came as something of a shock, therefore, to hear Barbi Benton (Hef's girlfriend from 1969 to 1976) say in a 2003 BBC TV documentary entitled *Sex Empire*:

I broke up with him [Hefner] two times before the final time – partly because of his philandering. At some point you just say 'I can't take it any more. I'm mad as hell and can't take it anymore'.

This was surprising because the impression some of us had in the '60s was that Hefner and his cohorts had broken through the old barriers of jealousy and deceit, to step into the modern 'open relationship' age in which rational, sensible people conducted their sexual explorations and erotic experiments openly, hiding nothing from their partners and, having slain the old, antiquated green beast of jealousy, shouting encouragement from the sidelines and never, ever, like some nagging wife of premodern times, getting 'mad as hell' over some 'philandering'. And would Hef, one wonders, have also gotten 'mad as hell' if Barbi or his other girlfriends proved themselves to be philandering playgirls?

It would be sad to think that Hef never practiced what he preached. Certainly at the time, excitedly perusing our copies of *Playboy* in the first half of the '60s, a great many of us took it as given that, between the backgammon games and cinema screenings, Hef and his coterie were themselves practicing a new, liberated, open and honest approach to sex. Presuming that we had seen the future and that it did indeed work, encouraged, urged into battle, a huge number of us Baby Boomers would go on to fight the good fight of the Sexual Revolution in the second half of the '60s (and beyond). In time, by the late '60s and into the '70s, we Boomer Hippies may have come to dismiss, mock and criticize Hef (sexism, objectifying women, capitalist greed, failure to protest loudly enough about Vietnam and having short hair being just some of his sins) but, whatever his faults, we felt sure that he had successfully answered the big question about sex for the modern age in the affirmative, and in the process had provided a model for sexual liberation which we could carry further.

While *Playboy*'s vision of new and improved, casual, modern sex was more widely known, many of us at college in the second half of the '60s (the sort who carried around bulky copies of *Being and Nothingness* in the hope that it would impress the opposite sex) also saw Jean-Paul Sartre and his partner (not wife) Simone de Beauvoir as demonstrating the possibilities of 'open relationships'. However, recent books such as Carole Seymour-Jones' *A Dangerous Liaison* suggest that things were far from smooth and were instead decidedly angst-ridden for Sartre and de Beauvoir – and even worse for the many young partners they exploited and then casually tossed aside. But again, historically, as in the case of Hefner, we had no inkling at the time that not even such super brains and logical thinkers as these French existentialists could modernize themselves and their emotions, so that they became angst free sexual adventurers.

While that fascinating threesome of de Beauvoir, Sartre and Hefner (just imagine them plus the odd bunny or two on Hef's revolving round bed with matching ceiling mirror) appeared in the '60s to offer real life confirmation of the workability of the new model of modern sexuality, fictional characters in the cinema and literature seemed to be having considerably less success. Both Marcello Mastroianni's journalist Marcello in Federico Fellini's *La dolce vita* (1960) or the same actor's film director character Guido in *8½* (1963) strive tirelessly for modern, casual, permissive sex, but both end up sinking under the weight of their very old-fashioned deceit and jealousy. *La Dolce Vita* in particular, right down to its chillingly ironic title, is arguably the bleakest vision of modern life's existential emptiness ever created in the cinema. And the failure of modern, casual sex clearly lies at the heart (or lack there of) of this existential emptiness.

Michael Caine's cheeky, cocky, constantly fornicating *Alfie* (1966) seems at first glance certain to demonstrate the easy-picking delights of casual sex, but he too comes a right cropper: in the end brought low by the prospect of facing his own mortality without a loving, caring partner. Even the completely played for laughs *What's New Pussycat?* (1965) finds it impossible to reconcile Peter O'Toole's fashion journalist's seemingly insatiable philandering with his love for his fiance Romy Schneider. If the big question was whether modern emotional coolness can triumph over old-fashioned jealousy and deceit, then *What's New Pussycat?* (the title originally coming from the message on Warren Beatty's answering machine) and other films of the '60s seemed doubtful at best about the answer.

In literature things were no better. Philip Roth's Portnoy (1969) spirals into madness in his insatiable search for pussy – an obsession which first grabs him up in adolescence like Dorothy's tornado and, we can only hope, will finally set him down in peace in his old age. John Updike's Rabbit (1960) runs and runs, ricocheting back and forth between the responsibilities of fatherhood on one hand and his hunger for pussy on the other; never finding a resolution between his sexual desires and his social role – nor even between his philandering and that would-be, essential honesty of which, at least at times, we think him capable. Such conflict is, of course, as old as humankind but, during the '60s, encouraged by how science had tackled the practical perils of promiscuity, we had this idea that we could crack this old chestnut once and for all – crack it as had never happened before in human history. The real life characters of Hefner, Sartre and De Beauvoir appeared to demonstrate that it could and should be done. A wide range of fictional characters on the other hand suggested it was an impossible dream.

Only James Bond seems to have resolved the seemingly irresolvable, and perhaps therein lies his magic and lasting appeal. The love and death of his new wife Tracey in *On Her Majesty's Secret Service* (1969) aside, Bond never allows himself deep emotional contact with anyone (until he falls head over heals for Vesper Lynd in *Casino Royale* – one of the key features which signal that this 21st century Bond as portrayed by Daniel Craig has moved on from the increasingly unbelievable character as portrayed in the '60s and '70s).

The emotional coolness and personal detachment of the earlier Bond always seemed central to the notion of modern sexuality – and central to the character (or, if you will, lack thereof) of the early '60s' two greatest playboys, Bond and Hef (the later only marginally less fictional than the former). Both ideologically and stylistically, here too was the starting point for the 'Sexual Revolution': casual, uncomplicated, cool sex cocooned within a futuristic world of shiny sports cars, groovy home stereos, Modern Jazz, cocktails shaken not stirred, urban sophistication and exotic jet travel. And from the perspective of the early to mid '60s, in fact right up until 1966, this emotionally minimal, less is more, modern 'Sexual Revolution' seemed as inevitable as it was irresistible.

But, later in the '60s, when the Baby Boomers (by this time nearing if not already having achieved the end of their teens) got their hands on this revolution, it took some radically different turnings – turnings which neither Bond nor Hef might have foreseen and, as the ultimate exponents of capitalist materialism (despite even the appeal of all those bra-less tits and spray can fit hipster-jeaned Hippy chick butts) surely would not have been entirely comfortable with. For by 1966 and 1967, politicized by Vietnam and the personal immediacy of the draft, often turned-on and dropped-out, many of the Boomers had given up the easy-going cool capitalist hedonism of the early '60s and joined the 'counterculture'. Generally, these 'alternative' Hippy Boomers were all in favor of a more liberated approach to sex – the Sexual Revolution would continue – but it would (at least in theory) be decoupled from the materialistic, 'plastic' context and styling which *Playboy* (and Ian Fleming) had clearly always considered an essential part of the package.

Instead of cool, modern, capitalistic sex *a la* Hef and Bond (and, as seen more recently, Don Draper of *Mad Men*) the Boomer Hippies proposed something set apart from the marketplace and, if possible, while retaining the notion of casual promiscuity by all means, injected with a bit of warm, brightly (but naturalistically) colored, positive counter-cultural vibes. And so it came to pass that cool, glossy, emotionally detached modern sex metamorphosised into casual but caring *Free Love*.

'Free' to distinguish it from the essentially prostitutional exchange of sex for money which, as throughout human history, had powered the first half of the Sexual Revolution. Now, good, right-on, counter-culturally approved Hippy chicks would be expected to put out for no bread (but it must be said that, from the perspective of a Hippy guy with little if any bread to his name, it sometimes seemed that the guys with the biggest stash, the grooviest pad or the flashest car did still get laid the most).

'Love' because some semblance (or at the very least, a simulacrum) of emotional, romantic attachment would now replace that emotional detachment which had once been a defining feature of modern sex: the counterculture, with a linguistic creativity and flexibility worthy of Don

Draper, having invented a revolutionary 'Love The One You're With' Instant (but also instantly removable), No Mess - No Fuss - Reusable - Rechargeable - Emotional & Caring - Not Just A Physical Thing - Bonding Device (patent pending). And moreover, and crucially in terms of this era's historical significance in the broadest terms, this New Improved Sexual Revolution became the driving force – for many of us, if we're honest, at least at times, the engine – of political dissent, protest and the questioning of materialism: *Make Love Not War*.

Thus, while the Sexual Revolution was one single wave which swept from the early '60s into the '70s and, for some, way beyond, it took on profoundly different characteristics in the two distinct halves of this decade – a bifurcation which resulted from the increasingly politicized Boomers (the males of whom, it should not be forgotten, were personally threatened with the draft and potential annihilation in Vietnam) taking control of this Sexual Revolution and making it their own in the second half of the decade. Hef may have given us Boomers our first taste of the sexually liberated Promised Land, but our Age of Aquarius was going to be very different from the goings on in the Playboy Mansion.

From the perspective of the Hippies, Hef and his bunny girls were 'straight', 'capitalist pigs' and, worst of all, unforgivably, 'plastic'. The view from the Playboy Mansion on the other hand would have seen the Hippies as 'scruffy', 'worthless layabouts' and, worst of all, 'uncool'. From 1966 onwards ('66 being the crucial, pivotal year of this crucial, pivotal decade) a would-be Hippy like myself, even though hand-reared, so to speak, on *Playboy*'s pioneering glossy take on sexual liberation, had to shift gears quickly: becoming overnight even more secretive and furtive about the odd issue of *Playboy* than in the days of concealing these from one's parents.

In a matter of only a year or so one went from seeing *Playboy* as the vanguard of the revolution to seeing it (belatedly for some of us) as the enemy. The aesthetic and ideological split was clear; chalk and cheese. Yet, despite everything, there was always an undeniable common ground: sexual freedom. And, if the truth be known, there were some of us male Hippies who found ourselves less turned on by the Hippy girls, who refused to wear make-up or sexy footwear, shave their body hair or even use deodorants, than we were by the glossy, 'plastic' 'Playmates' we furtively glimpsed in *Playboy* when our Hippy comrades were elsewhere fighting the revolution.

But Hef, while unquestionably a liberal, seemed increasingly not to be 'one of us'. He didn't seem too bothered about getting himself and the bunnies down on the barricades to protest against the war. He continued to delude himself concerning the importance of The Almighty Dollar while, as the Beatles had pointed out, all we needed was love. And, to be completely honest, being practical about it, guys like me could only mingle with the likes of *Playboy* Bunnies and the Playboy Mansion's Bad Girls in our masturbatory dreams while – can you believe it! – real live Hippy chicks would smoke a joint with you and then, as casual as could be, inquire 'You wanna make it?' And that would be that: the sexual revolution having been won without a shot fired.

In the autumn of the crucial, pivotal year 1966 I was an anthropology student at Temple University in Philadelphia. One day, soon after my arrival in the city, I plucked up the courage to go into a 'Coffee Bar' located near the main campus on Broad Street. The place was almost empty except for two young women – both with long straight hair and wearing excitingly tight hipster-style jeans and t-shirts. One girl's t-shirt proclaimed 'Make Love Not War'. Although only half way through my personal metamorphosis from cool Jazz Hipster to long-haired, Native American headband-wearing Hippy, the two girls gave me a smile when I came up to the bar and ordered my coffee. Encouraged by this, suddenly, strangely bold, I asked the one in the 'Make Love Not War' t-shirt if she practiced what she preached. 'Do you live far from here?' she wanted to know.

Back at my place, as casual as could be, Make Love Not War peeled off her clothes and, with a smile, lay down on my narrow bed. I couldn't believe my fate: all those years of fantasizing about casual sex and here it was lying naked on my bed and playfully, encouragingly, oh so invitingly, smiling up at me. Thanks to a lovely woman I'd met and fallen in love with the previous year, at a different college, I had finally (and very satisfyingly) lost my virginity.

But monogamous sex within a long-term loving relationship was clearly not going to help the cause of the Sexual Revolution to which, since the earliest days of secretly stashing my *Playboys* in the garage amongst the newspapers, I'd sworn my allegiance. I too removed my clothes and lay down next to Make Love Not War. We kissed. We touched each other. It was great until it became all too clear that, despite her best efforts, I was never – not in a thousand years – going to achieve an erection. 'Not to worry', Make Love Not War reassured me while, with an easy but I couldn't help thinking, in truth, disappointed smile (we had, after all, come some three stops on the Broad Street Subway and now she would have to reverse the journey) she put her clothes back on and then, with a wave, was gone.

I had utterly and completely failed the revolution. The most ultimately groovy, supremely liberated, politically and physiologically perfect Hippy chick had just a brief moment ago been lying absolutely starkers on my bed and I had let the movement down – failed, literally, to rise to the occasion. Dejected, distraught, defeated, I stared blankly out my kitchen window, and it was only after a few minutes that I realized the woman who lived across the little alley which separated our brownstone buildings was washing her dishes and staring back at me. 'What's wrong? You look terrible', she asked. Having spoken with her before, enjoyed her company when chatting between our respective windows – and perhaps because I knew she was studying to be a doctor – I blurted out the whole, sorry, tragic tale. 'Come over for a drink', she proposed.

Rebecca was about 22 to my (just) 19 years. She was Jewish, curvaceously, delightfully curvaceous, full of life and, after leaving me alone with my glass of wine for a few minutes, was now stood leaning against the frame of the living room door wearing a pink baby-doll nightie. We made love (yes, the right word for it) on the sofa, then on the floor. After some excellent food and wine we again made love on the bed and, splashing a great deal of water about in the process, in the bath. 'Doesn't seem to be anything wrong with you' was her professional diagnoses. Twenty-five years later, in London, a sexual therapist I'd visited hoping that he would 'cure' my impotence – which persisted whenever my theoretical intentions to advance the good cause of the Sexual Revolution overshadowed my actual, impulsive, straightforward desires – concluded 'I think your cock has more sense than the rest of you'.

I was not the only young adult in 1966 delightedly signing up for service in the cause of the Sexual Revolution. All over America and, indeed, all over the Western world, there were millions and millions of us Baby Boomers falling over ourselves with excitement at the prospect of doing just that. 1966 was the year when the tropical storm of the steadily growing and increasingly unstoppable Sexual Revolution collided with the equally unstoppable demographic tsunami of the Boomers' explosion into young adulthood, and the inevitable sexual explorations which that would entail. Factor in the whirlwind of panic and protest which was sweeping through American Boomers at the prospect of the draft (a jump to 400,000 US troops in Vietnam in 1966) and you have the makings of the perfect storm. And then some. The times they were a changing and - as would be evident for all to see by 1967's 'Summer of Love' – one such change was that the Sexual Revolution would now be under new management, Boomer Control.

We Boomers loved the idea of ourselves as sexual revolutionaries – and even more the Boomer-centric notion that (as with everything else which happened in the '60s) this was something entirely and uniquely of our own making. All of which was great for our egos but it also meant that the weight of history was on our shoulders and, at least in our eyes, ours alone. The upshot of this was that, despite our fun-loving and laid-back image, we Boomers would have to put a lot of work and perseverance into 'our' revolutions. Even the fun bits: never quite the carefree lark some might have imagined, from the start this 'Sexual Revolution' of ours came with more responsibility than liberation.

Like Crusaders headed for Jerusalem, we had to do what a man (and now also a liberated woman) has got to do. Namely, we must seek out sexual possibilities in all our waking hours and when those opportunities came we must do *it* every chance we got. That is, we must have sex with as many people (especially strangers) as possible. And we must do *it* as often as possible – tiredness, indifference, revulsion and jealousy not being suitable excuses for a true Sexual Crusader.

When doing it we must also avoid if possible the 'missionary position' (the normal and, presumably, only position known to our parents) while, at every opportunity, engaging in the newly invented (our invention, obviously) oral sex. We must stop using words like 'penis' and 'vagina', and get down to the nitty-gritty of it with words like 'cock' and 'pussy'. We must get sex out of the bedroom and do it in ever more novel locations: the kitchen table, the living room floor, in public places, in nature, in front of the White House if we could get away with it (for we had also invented the notion - or so we thought - of sex as a political act).

We should do it with all races, ethnic groups and nationalities – provided, obviously, that they had long hair, didn't wear a uniform, didn't support the war, weren't racist and were not 'up-tight'. If possible we should do it with more than one partner at the same time and in full, honest view of as many on-lookers as could be contrived. We should do it here and now and with the one we're with – rather than 'save' ourselves for some hypothetical future time which, given the bomb and the stupidity of politicians, might never happen. We should never be up-tight and never, ever jealous. Condoms should be avoided as they were 'plastic' and not 'natural'. We should do it on drugs whenever possible. Guys should always get it up: to fail in doing so would be to let down the revolution. Girls should never say 'no': to do so would be to let down the revolution.

It was all a great deal of responsibility. Indeed, when you think about it in retrospect, it was a lot of *work* and required the kind of discipline which, in any other context, would have been seen as positively Puritanical. Productivity was important: more sex with more partners in more unusual positions and situations. It was a good idea to quantify this productivity and keep a record of one's efforts in the cause of the Sexual Revolution – the more internationally minded amongst us, for example, keeping a running tally of nationalities; a sort of United Nations of sexual conquest (the problem always being the difficulty in knowing what should and what could not be counted as 'sex').

But as well as quantity the Sexual Revolution was about quality, and for us Boomer Hippies this focused on the matter of replacing stealth and deceit with openness and honesty in sexual matters. The old world we were fighting against was held together with lies – be they the body count from Vietnam or the husband who secretively slings his shirt into the washing machine so his wife will not see the lipstick on his collar. We knew we couldn't do anything about the '11 O'clock Lies' (as we called the news), but we thought it entirely doable to conduct our own private lives – including our sex lives – in a way which was straightforward and devoid of deceit.

There was a great deal which was both ridiculous and

worthy only of derision in the Hippy Boomers' Sexual Revolution (a whole army of us more often than not in dire need of Dr Portnoy's couch), but this striving after honesty succeeded more than many people might think. The openness and lack of duplicity with which Captain America and his new found friend conduct their one night stand at the Hippy commune in *Easy Rider* being a moment in that often uneven film which seems to ring true. In real life I expect there are a great many of us veterans of the '60s Sexual Revolution who can look back on all sorts of sexual shenanigans and goings on – all conducted within the context of 'open relationships' – without recalling any outright deceit beyond the occasional white lie of 'That was great!', when in truth it wasn't. This I think was a considerable and not to be underestimated achievement.

On which point (that of honesty being the best policy) let us jump-cut through history to the Oval Office of the White House, where the first Boomer President is in the company of a young intern named Monica Lewinsky and reaching for a cigar. Of course one will never know, but it has always been my guess that, like me and millions of other Baby Boomer crusaders of the Sexual Revolution, Bill Clinton has always been propelled on not simply by a lust in his loins but a sense of duty, responsibility and obligation. 'Mustn't let the side down', Bill thinks as he ponders the erotic possibilities of his cigar. Must keep at it and keep it up for the sake of history and posterity. Like me, Bill felt he had to do his bit. He was in a word *driven* –

driven on not only by simple carnal lust but by an ideological commitment to slay the old gorgons of repression.

One also guessed that between Bill and Hilary there had long been openness and honesty – for surely Hilary Clinton is no fool, and surely this sort of thing had been going on for a very long time. One would also like to think that this wasn't a one-sided deal, and that our Bill had overcome his own masculine jealousies such that he could and did handle it if the tables were turned, and it was Hilary doing the playing around. But then came 'I did not have sexual relations with that woman' and all this paled into insignificance, for this surely marked the moment at which the Boomer Sexual Revolution's dream of a future in which deceit rather than sex would be taboo came tumbling down.

Of course long before Bill (or was it America?) let us down in 1998, the broader, less ideological objectives of casual, modern sex had already been dealt a hammer blow: A.I.D.S. having demonstrated that the breaking of the once seen as inevitable, God-given linkage between promiscuity and dangerous, life-threatening disease had been but a short-lived and exceptional window of opportunity rather than, as we thought in the '60s, a permanent feature of our sci-fi future.

So was the whole Sexual Revolution which began in the '60s and which, at least for a time, became a central tenet of the typical Boomer lifestyle and worldview, just a waste of time? Worse still, was it the end of civilization? Was it our Sexual Revolution which, in going way too far, triggered that moral and political backlash which from Reagan and Thatcher to W and Sarah Palin (and beyond) desperately yearns for some mythic golden age before the '60s when everything went to hell?

One hopes not but only history will tell. Certainly at its most excessive and obsessional it's hard to take the '60s Sexual Revolution – and those of us who got caught up in it – seriously. We tried to swing the pendulum so very far in the direction of total and totally uninhibited sexual freedom . . . But then consider how far in the other direction it had swung in the world we had been born into. The fact that today's new generations seem so ignorant of and disbelieving in the unhealthy repressions of the past – while generally also looking with incredulity at my generation's absurdist experiments in 'liberation' – would appear to suggest that the pendulum now rests in a healthier, saner, less extremist territory.

Of course some of us veterans of the Sexual Revolution (ignoring Dr Portnoy's pained expression) wonder if this current lack of extremism and obsession – this absence of being constantly and perpetually driven – isn't perhaps a road to boredom? But that's for the next generation to work out for itself. For us veterans, now in our 60s (who ever would have thought it?), hopefully content with a good TV documentary on lemurs in Madagascar and a cheap but cheerful bottle of red, there are still the memories which occasionally pop into the head like bubbles breaking the surface of a glass of champagne:

- My Hippy girlfriend and I having sex on acid in Philadelphia and, afterwards, both of us exclaiming 'That was amazing!!!', before wondering if we'd even had sex at all or whether this memory of fantastic sex had been some sort of shared hallucination. Then concluding, sensibly, that it didn't matter a damn one way or another.

- That other Hippy girl in Philly (this also around '67) who had two names – one for her 'good' self and one for her 'bad' self – and who was fan-fucking-tastic on a 'bad' day.

- The beautiful fiery-haired Welsh woman in London (this would have been around 1971), who wanted to loose her virginity with the help of myself and her nymphomaniac sister in a threesome.

- The seven British strippers who kindly sat on my face, each in turn, in a scientific experiment to see if I, blindfolded, could tell one from the other – me scoring 100% by the way.

- The three gorgeous, exotically adorned Italian women who arrived at my London flat with their body-piercer, a generous supply of ecstasy and their own strap-on dildo.

- The Norwegian woman sat next to me on a 747 flying back to London from my father's funeral in New Jersey who, as we were starting our descent into Heathrow, turned to me and asked if I would be so kind as to play with her pussy and bring her off, if possible, just as we were touching down. And who gave me a friendly Scandinavian wave in the airport when I spotted her heading off for 'Connecting Flights' – our little romance (and, yes, that is the right word) short and sweet, and leaving only a positive feeling.

How I hope that when my time has come, and I'm dying of a heart attack or been hit by a bus or whatever, that I have the presence of mind just to kick back and let these treasured, totally guilt-free, memories run through my head like a PowerPoint presentation.

Chapter 6

Drugs

It's really late – so late that there is only the occasional passing car and not a soul to be seen. And this on Broad Street, the main north/south thoroughfare of downtown Philadelphia. It's 1967 and I'm walking home with my flatmate and friend Andre – a budding, promising classical guitarist and avid player of the ancient Chinese game of Go. I'm studying anthropology at Temple University, near which we have spent the evening and from where we have about a half-hour walk home straight up Broad Street. We're carrying two big grocery bags, which are full to brimming over with twigs from which the leaves – marijuana – have been removed.

To be precise, Andre is carrying both big bags, as I am hoping that should the police stop us I can avoid rotting in prison for the rest of my life on the grounds that I'm just an innocent bystander. The fact that I've got waist-length hair, hip-hugging flairs covered in 'peace' symbol badges and am all too clearly a no good, degenerate, Commie-loving Hippy is something which I'm trying to keep from my mind. As we walk along, Andre and I chat about the meaning of life and struggle to affect as casual a demeanor as possible. At one point we glance back down Broad Street and realize that, as in some warped fairy tale, we have left a trail of marijuana twigs behind us.

A trail which any even half-witted cop could easily have followed right back to the terraced house across from the university campus where this great adventure had begun. The details of how this had all come about – 'We're nice, well behaved, hard-working, middle class students, officer', the explanation taking shape in my mind's eye as we reach the half-way point home and get excessively nonchalant when a police car cruises past – are not clear now, and may well not have been even back in 1967. Somehow Andre knew this guy who was studying Jazz guitar and financing his studies, as one does, by selling dope. And we've gone down to this guy's apartment, which is near the campus, and the entire floor of the place is ankle deep in marijuana leaves and twigs – like autumn leaves to be raked up from a lawn.

It's all too much for this one guy to cope with, and we're offered a bag of twigs each if we will lend a hand and help with stripping away the leaves and bagging them up. Like old time agricultural workers we roll up our sleeves, fortified with sips of the tea which our new-found friend is boiling-up from the twigs. Although I'd smoked the occasional joint since arriving in Philly (kids today might find it hard to believe, but there had been absolutely no drugs in my high school) I'd never before drunk tea made from marijuana. I presumed it wouldn't be very powerful but, when the room began to spin like Dorothy's in Kansas, and when the great – seemingly increasing rather than decreasing – drifts of leaves and twigs began to be blown about by strange cosmic winds, I started to think otherwise.

At one point, needing a break from the hard slog of agriculture, we went out to a nearby Jazz club. As a young teenager back in Neptune, New Jersey who yearned for all things Beat, it had been my dream to escape to New York City where I would hang out in little Jazz clubs where black Jazzmen grooved and white chicks dressed all in black with cool haircuts beckoned. Now, for the first time, I was in such a world and, appropriately, stoned out of my mind.

Our friend the dope-dealer and would-be Jazz guitarist knew everyone, so we got in free and were given prime seats right at the front where some white sax player was wailing. And here's the thing: when he would swoop up and down or left and right with his shiny, sparkling, effervescent horn, instead of the smooth, continuous movement one would normally expect, the path of the dazzling saxophone was caught up in little time-lag eddies, with the result that what one saw at any given second was a stacking up and superimposition of the moments from before. Wow!

And there were Beat Girls with long, ironed-straight blonde hair wearing low-slung jeans tight over their hard little butts, grooving on the Jazz. But our agricultural responsibilities obliged us to leave when the set ended, and we returned to the apartment to continue stripping the leaves and bagging them up. This went on for hours — during which time yet more marijuana tea was drunk, the room spun (but slowly and not unpleasantly) and the drifts of marijuana banked up against the walls and around the door frames, like snow in deepest winter.

And then, miraculously, suddenly, all the pungent leaves were bagged and stacked-up like some supermarket special offer display, Andre and I were thanked, given an enormous, overflowing bag of twigs each and, eyes still wide at the way moments and movement were strangely layered into a single Einsteinian instant, began our long trek home through a black North Philly ghetto which only a few years before had erupted in a race riot. When we finally did make it back to our apartment on Alleghany Avenue our affected nonchalance evaporated immediately and Andre and I both began shaking all over (and, it must be said, not in a cool Rock 'n' Roll way). Kindly, despite my cowardliness in refusing to carry one of the bags, Andre generously handed one back to me. Despite the late hour, we sat up a while longer sipping some more marijuana tea and making plans to, on another occasion, invite the two Hippy chicks who lived on the first floor up to share our DRUGS.

When looking back on this incident – so many years ago yet so fresh in my mind – I'm struck by how absolutely terrifying it all was. Neither Andre nor I were, or saw ourselves as, the sort of kids who did this kind of thing. Had one of those passing police cars stopped to check out these two white Hippy freaks, trudging through a rough black neighborhood in the middle of the night and carrying two big brown shopping bags (when, in those days, no shops stayed open all night), our apparently promising young lives would no doubt have been sent plunging into the abyss. So why subject oneself to such a stressful, paranoia-inducing ordeal?

The Hippy chicks' recent arrival in our apartment building did provide part of the answer to be sure. As with 'Can I buy you a drink?' in the mainstream world, 'I've got some mind-blowing weed, want to come up for a joint?' was always – or at least one always presumed it was – the ice breaker, the entry point, the lubrication to get from A (non-sexual situation) to B (sexual situation). Alternatively, and this too had some truth to it, one's interest in and sheer determination as regards marijuana – pot, weed, Mary Jane, reefer, tea, loco weed, dope, grass, herb, ganja, bhang, hashish, etc. – was that without it one's capacity to see and call oneself 'alternative', possessing a metaphorical shape other than 'square', might well be called into question. Our heroes, the Beats and the Jazz musicians had all loved their dope, and who were we latter-day would-be Hippies to dispute the centrality of drugs to the huge and increasingly undeniable counterculture which, fueled by the baby boom generation's coming of age, seemed set to change the world in the later part of the '60s?

So the pursuit of sex and authentic subcultural identity certainly played a part in getting budding Hippies like Andre and me to risk all for two overflowing supermarket paper bags of marijuana twigs. But perhaps we're coming at this from the wrong angle. Looked at from an anthropological perspective, the taking of mind/perception altering substances, far from being exceptional in the human species, is actually much more common than it is unusual.

Perhaps simply possessing a time-traveling, hypothetical, 'what if', past, present *and future* human consciousness (a consciousness which, amongst other things, knows not only that I am but that one day I will not be) is reason enough for wanting to escape into another mindset? For surely a consciousness of the type uniquely possessed by our species (a consciousness acquired as a by-product of tool making and other endeavors which require hypothesizing a possible future resulting from present actions) is a terrifying burden at least as much as it is a liberation. Or, arguably, like someone with a flash sports car, if you possess something with the complexity and possibilities of the human brain is it not altogether natural to feel like taking it out for a no holds barred test drive? Maybe we Hippies – like the Beats, the Jazz musicians and millions of tribal peoples from the earliest days of our species – took drugs because human beings just like taking drugs.

Perhaps drug taking – especially when that alternative narcotic of religion fails to provide full existential satisfaction and reassurance – is a human default position?

It might also be pointed out that the particular reality within which people lived and we Boomers grew-up in the Eisenhower post-war years was unusually rigid and existentially unsatisfying and that, therefore, there was a heightened, above average, desire – even, arguably, a need – for escape to some alternative, more flexible reality which offered greater creative and personal potential. The identikit, suburban boxes stretching over the horizon of post-war America divided reality up into tiny 'postage stamp' plots, within which the 2.5+ nuclear family was isolated as families had never been previously – old friends and the extended family at least a car journey (a problem in a one car family) and possibly even half a continent away.

And then there came television. The Baby Boomers were the first generation to grow up with TV – with *I Love Lucy*, *The Adventures of Ozzie and Harriet*, *Howdy Doody* and so forth – setting out the parameters of a strange yet seemingly ultra normal B&W world, where amusing little problems popped-up only to be amusingly resolved within handy half-hour time slots. Nothing really horrible ever happened (except to bad guys in *Dragnet*) but then, equally, while a kind of contentment reigned – one not unlike that surreal contentment depicted in the opening shots of David Lynch's *Blue Velvet*, but in B&W – neither was there unrestrained joy or, indeed, deep rooted, resonant, life changing feeling of any kind (with the single exception of Kennedy's assassination and then, on live TV a few days later, the killing of his assassin: a televisual shock only out-shocked by 9/11).

In the 'real' lives of the suburban families like mine who watched this early TV, parents argued, people had heart attacks and died, some kid riding his bike on the highway got hit by a car, your cat got run-over, your mother developed an unmistakable sadness which suggested some terrible disappointment with how her life had panned-out, people lost their minds, a neighbor who had borne five boys in a row took to dressing-up the youngest of these as a little girl. And the interesting thing was that, rather than thinking 'These TV situation comedies just aren't like real life', you wondered how and why it should happen that the block you lived on – and only the block you lived on – failed to fit within the template of 'real life'.

Perhaps it is just looking for an excuse but, when the 'reality' within which you grow-up is itself so unreal and cathode ray thin, it is arguably no surprise that getting off your head and pushing hard on the envelope of reality should have such a strong appeal. This would seem especially evident when considering the enthusiasm which we Boomers brought to taking and experimenting with what we saw as 'our' drug – the one which would forever be equated with the Hippies of the late '60s, LSD; a mind-blowing, miraculous chemical which instantly replaced a

B&W and grey, completely predictable universe as inhabited by the likes of *Ozzie and Harriet*, with one so bursting with colour and inventive possibility that even the submarine which you called home would be a groovy electric yellow. But however mischievously appealing, this thesis that *I Love Lucy* obliged an entire generation to neck vast quantities of LSD has only limited application because, as so often in this history of the Boomers, the truth is that the real pioneers of 'Acid' had all been born long before the baby boom happened – and had themselves grown-up in a world where reality had yet to be confined within thirty-minute TV storylines.

In 1939 the Swiss chemist Albert Hofmann (born 1906), hoping to discover a respiratory and circulatory stimulant, synthesized LSD-25, a derivative of lysergic acid which is a precursor of the (often deadly, often hallucinogenic) ergot fungus. Attracting little interest, Hofmann only returned to his discovery in 1943 when, after accidentally absorbing a minute amount through his fingertips, he experienced 'remarkable restlessness' and 'an extremely stimulated imagination'. Deliberately taking 250 micrograms (a huge dose of this incredibly potent substance) a few days later, Hoffman had the world's first bad acid trip but, despite believing himself to be possessed by demons and that sort of thing, he would go on in his autobiography *LSD: My Problem Child* to describe what the world came to know as 'acid' as 'a remarkable but not unpleasant state of intoxication . . . characterized by an intense stimulation of the imagination, an altered state of awareness of the world' and a 'medicine for the soul'.

Dr Timothy Leary (born 1920), a lecturer in psychology at Harvard University between 1959 and 1963, together with his colleague Dr Richard Alpert (born 1931), believed that LSD-25 and other 'psychedelic' drugs could have beneficial, therapeutic qualities if administered under the right circumstances. Clinical trials carried out by Leary and Alpert seemed to support this view, but as LSD and other psychedelic drugs began attracting too much publicity, even though still legal in the USA, Leary and then Alpert were dismissed from Harvard. After years of further experimentation on themselves and others at a mansion at Millbrook in New York State, these two once eminent university researchers would make more direct, populist appeals on behalf of the mind-expanding effects of this amazing drug. As Leary put it during the Human Be-in at Golden Gate Park in San Francisco in 1967: 'Turn on, tune in, drop out' – a suggestion which hundreds of thousands, if not millions, of Baby Boomers sought to put into practice. But following on from LSD being made illegal in America in 1966, Leary was convicted of drug possession and sentenced to twenty years in jail. While gardening in the grounds of his prison he escaped, went on the run and would come to be described by President Richard Nixon as 'the most dangerous man in America'.

Yet, as we now know, the American government had itself been experimenting with LSD long before Leary ever considered doing so. During the cold war, starting in the '50s but carrying on into the late '60s, the CIA became interested in whether LSD could function as some kind of brainwashing truth drug and/or a weapon. Apparently, without the permission of hundreds if not thousands of subjects – indeed, without even telling them that they had been given a drug – they gave doses of LSD to a wide variety of soldiers and civilians to see what effect it might have. Not surprisingly, completely unprepared for what was happening to them, many thought they were going mad. Some did go mad. One tried to kill himself, another jumped from a window and succeeded in doing so (although a subsequent exhumation of his body and autopsy suggested that he had in fact been murdered before being thrown out of the window).

The CIA also farmed out its psychedelic drug research to scientists like Dr. Leo Hollister at the Veterans Hospital located in Menlo Park, California. Under the top-secret MK-ULTRA project, Dr. Hollister and many others across America administered LSD and other psychedelic drugs to paid volunteers who were observed and tested under hospital conditions.

One of these volunteers was a young creative writing student at Stanford University named Ken Kesey (born 1935), who would soon find fame, fortune and literary acclaim as the author of *One Flew Over the Cuckoo's Nest*. Reasoning that lying on a hospital bed while being prodded and questioned by an endless stream of not all that quick-witted doctors and constantly having blood samples taken was perhaps not the most conducive environment for psychedelic experimentation, Kesey liberated (as we used to say) some Acid and other drugs when no one was looking. Thereafter there followed years of Kesey's more relaxed cosmic experimentation within his own home, in the company of his friends and, famously, on an old clapped-out 1939 International Harvester school bus while it traversed and in doing so transformed the United States of America forever.

With none other than Neal Cassady (born 1926, inspiration for supreme Beat hero Dean Moriarty of *On the Road*) at the wheel, Ken Kesey and his band of a dozen or so 'Merry Pranksters' set off from Kesey's home in La Honda, California on June 14, 1964. Painted all over in mind-boggling, brightly colored, grab your sunglasses, like far out man, swirling patterns, with 'Furthur' (yes, two 'u's) the destination given on its indicator board, wired inside and out with microphones and speakers (which played back – but with a time delay – all that was picked up by those microphones) and with gallons of LSD laced orange juice stashed in its makeshift fridge, Kesey and his Merry Pranksters traveled through the deep south, up to New York City (where they would meet with Jack Kerouac, Allen Ginsberg and where Kesey's new book *Sometimes a Great Notion* had its launch), over to Timothy Leary's Millbrook center for psychedelic research (where the noisy, party-on proto Hippies would not be welcomed with any great enthusiasm) and then back again to California. As is well reported in Tom Wolfe's *The Electric Kool-Aid Acid Test* and in Paul Perry's *On The Bus*, a great deal of the time during the course of this pioneering expedition was spent with one and all completely off their heads on Acid and, surprisingly, miraculously all things considered (would you really want a sleep-deprived, stoned Neal Cassady at the wheel of your bus?), without loss of life.

On returning to California, Kesey and his ever-growing band of hangers-on would begin their 'Acid Tests', party with the Hells Angels and generally set the stage for both the 'Psychedelic' and 'Hippy' revolutions. While 'Furthur' had been wending its way back and forth across America in 1964, blowing minds as it went, I was in my junior year of high school in Neptune, New Jersey – where now and again fellow students would get themselves killed in car accidents when driving back from NYC (where at that time the drinking age was only eighteen) loaded on booze, but where the closest you got to illicit drugs like pot was through reading *On the Road*. Seen as something of a far-out, weirdo, beatnik eccentric in my high school days, I think if anyone had any demon dope to peddle I might have known about it. And 'Acid' was something your dad checked the level of in the family car's battery.

But then, within just a couple of years, everything changed. By the 'Summer of Love' in 1967, if not before, what seemed like every Baby Boomer in America started doing drugs; dressing and acting like some deranged Merry

Prankster. Overnight we became the people our parents had once warned us about. The Sexual Revolution had a lot to do with it. The war in Vietnam did too. But so did drugs – and most importantly, that new, futuristic drug LSD which, ignorant of history as usual, we believed was 'our' own unique creation. Indeed, I doubt that I was alone in knowing almost nothing about pre-Boomer recreational drug use (with the exception of knowing how heroin had been the downfall of many Jazz musicians). For example, however embarrassing to admit today, I had absolutely no idea that the band The Doors were named after Aldous Huxley's exploration of psychedelic drugs *The Doors of Perception* – a book which I had never heard of, let alone read, in the '60s. But then, sometimes it's for the best – and I have a hunch that Huxley would have agreed – just to find things out for yourself.

So . . . It's 1967 and Fab Freddy the whiz-kid of Temple University's Philosophy department has some Acid and wants to know if my Hippy girlfriend and I want to come out to this place he knows in the countryside and try it.

It was a lovely, crisp, bright autumn day – on a sort of commune in the countryside about an hour's drive outside Philadelphia. Two Hippies with hair down to our waists and patched, tight on the behind bell bottom flairs, Lindy and I marveled at the tiny little square of paper – could this really be Acid? – before gulping it down with the others in our band of adventurous countryside counterculturalists. After a while, feeling a little more confident with the rush and swirl of reality, we ventured off on our own into the woods which surrounded the farmhouse which served as our group's base of operations.

Here, surely, was the Garden of Eden – the lush forest stretching as far as one could see. There were dark bits where the sunlight failed to reach, ultra bright bits where it did and every colour imaginable in the places in-between. We held each other and kissed – witnessed in my mind's eye by a camera circling around us; time freeze framed. But as is so often the case in any would-be Garden of Eden, there was a problem. Actually two problems. Firstly, all this reality crashing into us was worrying as well as exhilarating and I for one (Protestant presumptions that every silver lining must surely have a cloud built into me from birth) looped a horror movie through my head where the sweet Hippy couple can never find their way back to the farmhouse and spend eternity wandering further and further and further and further into the ever darkening ever darkening ever darkening ever darkening forest.

More immediately worrying, periodically slicing viciously through the stillness and near soundlessness of sunlight dancing amongst the trees, there was the sound of gun fire. Yes, gunfire! For, as had been commented upon back at the cozy farmhouse, this was the first day of Pennsylvania's deer hunting season and, judging by the number of explosions coming from all around, every hunter in the state was out there and determined to kill something. My worry was that a dead Hippy or two would prove even more tempting than venison stew. But the periodic shots were clearly far away and Lindy and I continued our exploration of Eden.

But then there came a much closer and far louder crr-aackkk of gunfire

and

time

went

into

ultra

slow

motion

as

the

bullet

entered (much less painlessly than one might have previously imagined)

my

back.

Or so it seemed to me. At any rate, time certainly did go into ultra slow motion. I'd recently seen a film – I think, *Doctor Zhivago* – where there is a scene in which someone is shot in a wood which suddenly seemed remarkably similar to these woods in which Lindy and I were now tripping. The thing is that in this film you *hear* the single shot which kills our hero but you don't *see* its effect – the death by gunshot is purely auditory. The question now was whether the same thing could happen in a wood about an hour outside Philadelphia on the first day of the hunting season.

I didn't want to freak out Lindy and so, instead of proclaiming that I'd been shot, I turned as calmly as possible to present my back to her, and when she didn't scream 'Oh my god you've been shot – there's blood all over your back!' I felt some level of relief. But then, I'm thinking, 'She's tripping, maybe she's preoccupied elsewhere'. And then, 'Maybe she sees I've been shot and – like in the war movies where the guy's legs have been blown clean off or there's a huge hole where his guts should be but his buddy holding him says 'You're gonna make it' – Lindy is trying to spare me the fact that I've been shot and don't have a chance in hell of surviving even the next five minutes.

What was going through my mind is this: I've never in all my nineteen years been shot so, ergo, I don't actually know what it feels like. Maybe it hurts a lot less than one imagines? Here you will note an interesting effect of LSD: at least in my experience, it causes one to question those standard issue, one size fits all assumptions which normally whisk us through everyday life.

In the French philosopher Maurice Merleau-Ponty's *The Phenomenology of Perception* (almost as weighty as Sartre's *Being and Nothingness*, if you're thinking of lugging it around to impress people as I used to do) the author meets a German WWI veteran identified as Patient S who has a large shrapnel fragment lodged in his head and who, while superficially functioning in a way which might be described as intelligent and reasonable, shows signs of a certain unwillingness to accept without questioning those everyday presumptions which are normally taken as obvious, water-tight and beyond need of challenging – an unwillingness which those who have taken LSD may recognize.

For example, Merleau-Ponty and Patient S are sitting in the latter's basement flat in Berlin. A window high up on one wall looks out at pavement level and when a shapely, stocking-clad pair of women's legs pass by both men look up appreciatively and Merleau-Ponty says something like 'Good looking woman'. Patient S, however, clearly a more rigorous philosopher, isn't having any of it: 'How can you be sure that was a woman and not just a pair of woman's legs?' he quite reasonably wants to know.

Likewise, tripping in the woods outside Philadelphia in 1967, I, just as reasonably, was unwilling to make the presumption that the fact I wasn't curled amongst the leaf-litter in mindboggling pain didn't prove beyond doubt that I had not been shot in the back. Not wishing to push Lindy too far in her clearly heroic determination to shield me from the tragedy of my young death, I said nothing as we made our way back to the farmhouse. Thankfully, Fab Freddy was right there as I emerged from the dense forest and, the whiz-kid of the philosophy department and an existentialist, I knew I could trust him to tell it to me straight no matter how distressing: 'Only a metaphysical flesh wound' was his eventual opinion, after inspecting every inch of my back with great care for what seemed like hours.

A common presumption is that while on an acid trip one hallucinates things which come from out of the blue and which are not real. At least in my experience this is not an accurate description of such an event. If anything, the reality experienced by the tripper is *more* rather than less real than that experienced by someone who is not tripping. In everyday life we are constantly filtering-out huge chunks of reality as 'normal' (and not requiring our attention) while configuring those bits which do get through according to programmes which we have learned from birth – thereby participating in what the American sociologists Peter L. Berger and Thomas Luckman memorably termed *The Social Construction of Reality*.

In the process, as well as experiencing only a small fraction of the reality which in reality confronts us at any moment, we, more often than not, see, hear, smell and feel that which we *expect* to see, hear, smell and feel. For example, when we look at an expressionist painting in which someone's face has been painted with a green hue, we think this is the painter playing with reality when, in fact, the painter – overcoming his or her own programmed expectations – has accurately depicted the fact that, for example, a green lampshade or some stained glass in the window of a Parisian bar, has transformed 'flesh' colour into green.

All of which was well appreciated by William Blake (who provided Aldous Huxley with the title of his book and who clearly had no need of ingesting psychedelic substances himself) who noted:

If the doors of perception were cleansed everything would appear to man as it is, infinite. For man has closed himself up, till he sees all things through narrow chinks of his cavern.

These filtering and configuring programmes which limit and distort our experience of reality are necessary to get us through everyday life – without them life would just be too much and it would be a strain getting anything done and focusing on whatever task we have in hand. A clock ticks. A truck drives by on the street outside the house. There's a little draft coming in through the window. Someone, many buildings away, is playing some pop song you might recognize if it impinged on your consciousness, but it doesn't. Your leg muscles are a bit sore from the long walk you took yesterday. In about half an hour you will need to go for a piss and there is some pressure building up in your bladder. Your stomach is not altogether happy about that curry you had earlier, but it's nothing to worry about. There is a slight smell coming from the dustbin in the kitchen, the remains of the fish you had yesterday. Also from the kitchen, there is the sound of the refrigerator's motor clicking on. So it goes.

All this is real and is going on out there in the real world around you and in the real world within you but, at least at this moment, none of it registers on your consciousness monitor and you are able to concentrate on watching the news on TV while, simultaneously, wondering whether you should go to your high school reunion and if you paid the gas bill.

This filtering system is extraordinarily complex and unquestionably one of the great triumphs of human development: rather like our equally extraordinary immune system it, day by day, month by month and year by year, builds up a data template of what is 'normal' and can therefore be ignored (the traffic outside the house; in the case of the immune system, a healthy red blood cell) while instantly raising the alarm when something not fitting the existing template comes along. In our immune system this might be a new bacteria or virus. In the case of our reality filtering system it might be a distant, not very loud dripping of water which suddenly reminds us 'I forgot to turn off the bathtub tap!' (what is so fantastic about this system is that, if measured objectively with some sort of metering device, the sound of the car going down the road outside the house might be many times greater than that of the drip, and yet we ignore the former while 'hearing' – of course we actually hear both sounds – the latter).

For some reason incredibly minute quantities of LSD interfere with or even switch off parts of this reality filtering system, with the result that what seems like (but probably isn't literally) *everything* floods in – sounds, smells, colors, touch sensations, proprioceptive (inner body) sensations, long repressed emotions all break through the dam of consciousness.

If you like a neat and orderly, zipped-up tight model of reality, this is all a highly disturbing, disorientating and, no doubt for some, dangerous experience. On the other hand, should you fancy a peek beyond the narrow chinks of the cavern, it can be an exhilarating and revelatory mind trip – offering, with luck, when the ordeal is over, a more flexible, open-ended but still functional and efficient grasp of 'reality'. This is no doubt what Ken Kesey and his other 'astronauts of inner space' sought to explore when, having returned to San Francisco from their epic travels in August 1964, they initiated their 'acid tests' to bring the wonders of psychedelia to a wider group. By the end of the decade there were hundreds of thousands, maybe millions, of us 'Freaks' and 'Hippies' – the Boomers now also most definitely 'on the bus' – determined to carry on with the psychedelic revolution and swing fully open those old, creaky doors of perception.

It's Spring 1970 and I'm on what would today be called my 'gap year', living in Oxford, England, squatting in a nice old terrace house (soon to be demolished to make way for a new library) with a bunch of Catholic ex-monks (a long story) together with (after some love-the-one-you-are-with-escapades) my Hippy girlfriend Lindy who you've already met. There's some smoking of dope most evenings – especially entertaining on the one night a week when the new *Monty Python's Flying Circus* is on the telly (definitely best watched with a bunch of stoned, recently defrocked Catholic monks who might well be expecting the

Spanish Inquisition). On the negative side it is a bit of a bummer that, whenever he gets really stoned, one of the former-monks becomes obsessed with the idea that his girlfriend's sweet little black cat is possessed by the devil – but so far the rest of us have been able to prevent the brutal extermination of this house pet.

One morning, pleased with ourselves for (apparently) succeeding in convincing him that the cat should be given an exorcism rather than exterminated, Lindy and I make up our minds to take the Acid tabs we had been saving. Having done so, we then decide to have a bath together – bathing naked as the waves of hyperreality edge closer to the shore of our consciousness. This plan is working splendidly: the warm water and the encounters of our naked flesh pointing inexorably in the direction of what promises to be mindboggling sexual congress. But just then, taking note of the little portable radio left by one of the previously-mentioned monks on the table next to the bath, I reach over and switch it on. From its tiny, tinny speakers comes what, in time, Lindy and I agree are the (electronically distorted) sounds of (1) someone sighing and (2) an old door creaking.

Today in the 21st century, having lived in the UK for more than thirty years and having become the sort of middle class, middle-aged person who organizes his life around the programmes of BBC Radio, I might have guessed that these sounds were a Radio 3 broadcast of some peculiar, definitely minority-interest experimental contemporary music. In 1970, however, having hardly ever even heard BBC Radio, raised on American commercial radio stations which steered well clear of the complex currents of experimental contemporary 'serious' music, I (and, judging by the expression on her face, Lindy as well) presumed that the act of switching on this electronic device while tripping had caused some sort of rupture in the space-time continuum, and the subsequent depositing of ourselves and the contents of the room, including a bathtub full of (increasingly cool) water, into another parallel universe.

Although unusual and something which would take a little time getting one's head around, slipping into a parallel universe was not in and of itself something we Hippies would have described as a 'bummer'. So, settling back into the cooling water, we let the magical sounds transport us for what seemed like several days but was probably only several minutes. Suddenly the electronically manipulated sighing and creaking stopped and one of those old-time, Queen's English BBC announcers came on and told us we had been listening to the French 'musique concrète' composer Pierre Henry's 1963 composition 'Variations for a Door and a Sigh'. So, not a rip in the time-space continuum after all.

Relieved and disappointed in about equal measure, we returned to exploring each other's naked bodies in the bath. But somewhere in the back of my brain the fact that this composition was the work of a French composer was triggering alarm bells. Only a day or two prior to this Acid bath I had happened upon a newspaper headline which someone had left on the kitchen table, that told the chilling tale of how some famous French pop star had killed himself by attempting to change a light bulb while in the bath. Zap! Bummer, for sure.

And so all the pieces of this terrible (for Lindy and I were but young with our lives ahead of us) truth came rushing towards us with terrifying, inevitable speed and logic: the radio is an electronic device and, while in the bath and intertwined with Lindy's naked American Hippy body, I had touched it. Ergo (and surely all those weird noises should have alerted us to this fact, Queen's English announcer or not) we had been electrocuted and were now dead. If we didn't seem to be actually, particularly dead this was presumably because (1) in the last moments of one's life time can stretch out into near infinity and the act of dying had not yet caught up with us or (2) as all who describe death as a 'passing to the other side' are implying, things don't actually come crashing to a halt when you die: you just hear a bit of peculiar electronic music and then carry on much as before.

I explained all this to Lindy who, unfortunately, could find nothing to fault in my logic. We climbed out of the bath, dried ourselves off, dressed in our regulation issue hipster jeans and anti-war t-shirts, and went upstairs to ask the ex-monks (who were, by the way, also tripping and congratulating themselves on the successful exorcism of the cat) if we had indeed passed to the other side – like John

Cleese's unfortunate parrot. We explained about the bath, the Acid, the portable radio and the otherworldly sounds. Like their predecessors at, say, The Council of Trent which took eight long years to conclude that the Protestants were going to hell, our ex-monk housemates deliberated long and hard and with great seriousness on this most pressing (at least for Lindy and myself) of existential matters. After what seemed like considerably longer than The Council of Trent's eight years they all came to the conclusion that (this being a most contentious matter which, to date, neither the Church nor the great Western philosophers had really cracked) they couldn't be sure one way or the other.

While all this pondering of life and death had been going on, the sky above old, ancient Oxford had grown dark; night having fallen. No longer tempted by the flesh and having completely forgotten about eating, Lindy and I decided that we would venture out into the warm night of this learned (and it must be said snobbish) town. Outside all was quiet except that, almost imperceptibly but to our ears all too perceptively, there was a distant but distinct sound – a ringing which, we both agreed, as with Hemingway's tolling of the bell, was ringing for us.

Accordingly, for what seemed like a very long journey indeed, we step by step made our way towards the source of this ringing. Two out of their heads American Hippies circumnavigated the salubrious districts of academic Oxford and then penetrated deep into previously unseen working class 'townie' districts. Finally, the sound now loud and

360 degrees all around us, we found ourselves on the corner of a rather sad and somewhat dilapidated street, in front of a rather sad, somewhat dilapidated jewelery shop, which had a smashed window and an alarm that was flashing as well as ringing. A crime scene no less, and suddenly the place was crawling with smartly dressed British 'Bobbies' who demanded to know if we had 'seen anything'. 'No officer' I stammered – just in time holding back from explaining that, very probably having passed over to the other side after a foolish incident involving a bathtub, a portable radio and some sighing and creaking, we might not have been the best of witnesses even if we had.

Back home – having found our way like ancient mariners by staring long and hard at the wondrous night sky, whole constellations directing us on – we found that the ex-monks had all gone to bed ('crashed' as we used to say, the act of sleep being a more violent matter in those days). Now, sat alone, two (recently deceased?) human beings, we confronted each other and our predicament across the old, delightfully worn, wooden kitchen table.

I can't remember which of us cracked it but once we did the logic of it sat there like a great stone edifice which could not be dismissed with some flippant wave of the hand. Dawn was approaching, light gradually filling the room. Soon (we knew this from previous LSD all-nighters) the milkman would come. Or (and this was the fateful logic which sat there like some great stone edifice) would he? Here was the point: no sensible milkman would deliver milk to dead people, of this we were absolutely certain. And so, accordingly and with infinite patience, resolve and, yes, not inconsiderable trepidation (for we were young and with all of our lives ahead of us, and fearing that people would say 'stupid Hippies, taking drugs, killing themselves, and for what?') we waited with our spoons and bowls and box of Cheerios (for, despite ourselves, there were some American things which we American counterculturalists still clung to).

And we waited some more. And then, yes, we heard the strange purring, whirling sound those old British battery-powered electric milk floats made coming down the road. Like private detectives we crouched peering surreptitiously from behind the lace curtains. And, yes, I am pleased to report that, whistling as he worked, our milkman came up the path and left there by the door our two bottles of milk. Say what you will about drugs and American gastronomy, those Cheerios were the best breakfast there has ever been.

A year before this most satisfying and cosmic of breakfasts, Bill Clinton had lived in Oxford where, as we would learn years later – unlike the ex-monks, Lindy and me – he did not inhale (why not just say 'no thanks', Bill?). Arguably this not inhaling was a smart, foresighted move for someone who wanted to become the first Baby Boomer President.

But, frankly, it's a little strange because absolutely everyone back in the late '60s and early '70s presumed that, obviously, the legalization of 'soft' drugs was just a matter of time. At least in the circles in which I moved (Catholic former-monks included) it was extremely unusual to encounter anyone of the baby boom generation who didn't partake. Surely there must come a simple statistical point where the use of 'soft' recreational drugs was so widespread, so normal, so mainstream that it would be absurd to continue with laws which categorized all these people as criminals and thereby put too great a strain on the judicial and prison systems. Indeed, not only as regards drugs but much more generally, it seemed absolutely clear to us at the time that a more liberal, open-minded, consciousness expanding Age of Aquarius was just around the corner.

However, in another parallel universe founded on the views of a 'Silent Majority' – one which desperately yearned to turn back the clock to a halcyon and more predictable age, when *I Love Lucy* managed to resolve all problems without recourse to mind-altering drugs and to do so in B&W and within a thirty minute time frame – President Richard M. Nixon (the most dangerous man in America?) declared an all out 'War On Drugs' in 1971. To date (billions spent on it, hundreds of thousands if not millions sent to prison, international relations stressed to and beyond breaking point, the power of drug dealers growing greater year in and year out) it would seem that, like Vietnam, Iraq and Afghanistan, this is just another war which even America is unlikely to win. Ever.

Chapter 7

Rock 'n' Roll

It's 1967 and once again I'm walking up Broad Street in Philadelphia on my way home from university. No big bags of drugs this time and the sun hasn't yet set. On the west side of the street I encounter an enormous line of people – all black, all dressed to the nines – waiting to get into the big concert hall of which, previously, I'd not taken much notice. Catching the eye of an amiable-looking guy in the line, I ask what's going-on and he gives me a look of utter incredulity – as if I had inquired as to whether the world was flat or round. Other eyes widen and glances are exchanged. Finally, taking pity on me, without a trace of malice, he puts me right: 'You don't know? Ray Charles is coming to town!'

To this day it grieves and embarrasses me (all the more so given that I might have been the only white guy in the place) that I didn't even check to see if there were any tickets still left. Ray Charles had come to Philadelphia and

I'd not even clocked the significance of this event. To me in 1967, the name of Ray Charles conjured up only faint memories of rather schmaltzy ballads with lots of strings, songs like 'I Can't Stop Loving You' and 'Georgia on My Mind' which had featured in Charles' cross-over into the white 'Top 20' mainstream.

Shocking to realize now: back then in the '60s, a white kid from the New Jersey suburbs, I had absolutely no knowledge of the way that, starting in the late '50s with 'It Should Have Been Me' and the immortal 'What'd I say' (a riff which activated some fundamental cosmic rhythm that could kick start the entire universe), Ray Charles had shaped the direction of Rhythm & Blues and, in doing so, had set the stage for Soul and Funk. But I just kept on walking home, perplexed that all these hip looking black people were waiting in a line which curved almost all the way around the block, for a guy who did slushy romantic ballads with lots of strings which my parents might well have enjoyed.

Worse still, if it had been Aretha Franklin playing in Philly that night – despite the fact that she'd had a recent number one hit with R.E.S.P.E.C.T – I (and I can't tell you how much shame I feel in admitting this) wouldn't have had a clue who she was. This ignorance hinged on the fact that I had become a Hippy, surrounded by Hippy friends, and we had collectively cut ourselves off from the 'straight', 'plastic', 'capitalist pigs' world to the extent that, the news aside, we knew zilch about what was going on; ignorant even of the most popular music of the time.

In our younger days (that is to say, just a couple of years earlier) we Hippies might well have watched *American Bandstand* on the TV and, while it had always been a struggle warming to the ever-smiling and too all-American-boy Dick Clark who hosted the show, we might have clicked with and thrilled to the rare but (as history would prove) ever-lasting gems like, say, The Shirelles' 'Will You Still Love Me Tomorrow', The Marvelettes' 'Please Mr Postman' or Little Eva's 'Locomotion', which were featured on the show.

Now in 1967, however, even the name *American Bandstand* would have been too much to take (*Un-American Bandstand* we would have switched on enthusiastically) and so we deliberately cut ourselves off from such sources of Rock 'n' Roll information. Something which was particularly ironic in the case of *American Bandstand*, which was recorded right there in Philadelphia and which, in featuring the dancing of the kids from the largely immigrant populations that lived south of South Street where its studio was located, had made Philadelphia the dance capital of the world.

Being a Hippy accentuated my ignorance of popular culture but such self-inflicted blindness was only part of the problem. Post-war America had always been a mainstream culture, in which access to information about that which was beyond the norm was extremely limited. Obviously this was especially so in matters involving a racial divide. There were absolutely no blacks on TV other than sportsmen or musicians like Louis Armstrong with plenty of mainstream appeal. Or musicians like Ray Charles who, as I would learn in years to come, worked both sides of the fence – doing his funky thing in R&B while occasionally crossing over to 'Top 20' success with sweeter, whiter sounds. Perhaps things were different for Afro-Americans who, realizing all too well that there was little for them on TV, may have invested more time in searching out their own 'race' radio stations.

No doubt city-dwellers had opportunities to acquire information about what was going on in the wider world which those of us in the suburbs – cut off, in truth, from everyone and everything – did not. So, while I'm fully prepared to take the rap for my lack of knowledge about popular music in my Hippy days, I doubt that my ignorance concerning the true Rhythm & Blues origins of Rock 'n' Roll was simply a personal failing of my own making. While it is true that there were white kids like the young Elvis who kept on twiddling the radio dial until they found black gold, the odds were certainly stacked against most whites hearing and learning about what was going on in black 'race music'.

Today in the 21st century we have all sorts of radio stations, satellite TV channels and an infinity of Internet sites devoted to strands of popular music which are too obscure to feature in the 'Top 20' mainstream but, back in the '50s, when (predominately white) Rock 'n' Roll was establishing its identity as separate from its (all black) roots in Rhythm & Blues and other forms of 'race music', there were no such media alternatives.

The handful of TV channels, the 'major' record labels and the principle radio stations all catered to a mainstream white audience and saw no need to reveal what was going on in the tributaries which flowed into, or which ran parallel to, this mainstream. Indeed, it was in their interests *not* to provide such information and it was for this reason that, for example, one heard white cover versions but only rarely the original of the same song by an Afro-American artist. (Decades later you hear many of these black musicians – damn right – complaining on TV documentaries about how their own versions of their songs wouldn't get airplay once white musicians had covered them. Too true: but let's also spare a little indignation for the fact that whites like me more often than not had to make do listening to Pat Boone's rather than Little Richard's version of 'Tutti Frutti'.)

Accordingly, white American kids like me grew up in the '50s and early '60s with some awareness of Rock 'n' Roll, but absolutely no knowledge of the black Rhythm & Blues which – all the way back to the '30s and '40s – had not only pioneered but, in truth, fully explored and developed the possibilities of the music genre which '50s whites would herald as 'Rock 'n' Roll'; fully believing that here was something new, something invented by white Americans.

Which isn't to say that Afro-Americans were not welcome to join in – as evidenced by the success of black artists from Fats Domino to Chuck Berry, Ray Charles to everyone out of Motown. But it is to say that, even amongst those black musicians who crossed over into the mainstream, there was a tendency towards a softening, a toning-down and a smoothing-over of rough edges which, at the end of the day, meant that much of the gutsy brilliance and down and dirty energy (and often filthy lyrics) of Rhythm & Blues got lost in the translation. (But not, as it happens, in Britain where kids like those who would later form bands like The Beatles, The Rolling Stones, The Animals, etc. apparently found it easier – though still requiring diligence and perseverance – than we did in America to access the original black recordings. With the result that when the 'British Invasion' of America began in 1964, Rock 'n' Roll bands from the UK were essentially exporting back to America its own music – but a music which white Americans never knew existed. I can remember thinking it odd and extraordinary that a bunch of white kids from England – The Animals – would have written a song about a brothel in New Orleans.)

When Rhythm & Blues was rebranded as Rock 'n' Roll it not only traversed a racial divide but also a newly-created age barrier. What had been a definitively adult music in the hands of Joe Turner or Muddy Waters would, in the '50s, be repackaged specifically as a 'teenage' phenomenon. For the first time in history a genre of music was presented as suited to a specific age range – that post-childhood but pre-adulthood which Madison Avenue had identified as 'teenage' and in need of its own fashions, soft drinks, cereals, fast food, record players and, most importantly, its own music.

The need to clean-up the lyrics was the least of the difficulties in effecting this transformation. There was also the minor problem that all the leading figures of this new fangled 'teen' music were themselves already adults. Alan Freed, who many contend invented the term 'Rock 'n' Roll', was born in 1921. Bill Haley was just short of his thirtieth birthday when he and his Comets had their first number one hit with 'Rock Around the Clock' in 1954. The youngest of the lot, even Elvis Presley was out of his teens when his debut album appeared in 1955. All of which is clearly evident in 'teen' films like *Rock Around the Clock* or *Don't Knock the Rock*, when the 'kids' who leap up and start jiving are all too clearly fully-grown adults – especially the wide-hipped, curvaceous women dancers who looked a treat to my eyes but whose high school cheerleading days were obviously long gone.

My assumption had always been that this sudden blossoming of all things 'teenage' was simply a product of the coming of age of all the Baby Boomers. But this presumption just doesn't fit the demographic facts. The war ended in September 1945 and so the very first Boomers appeared in 1946, with more, including myself, popping out in 1947. But mainstream Rock 'n' Roll kicks off in the mid '50s when we Boomers were just children. When asked what he's rebelling against, biker, hell-raiser and would-be juvenile delinquent Johnny (Marlon Brando, born

1924) shrugs 'Wha ya got?' in *The Wild One* in 1953. That other iconic rebellious, angst-ridden teen, Jim Stark (James Dean, born 1931) goes off the rails in *Rebel Without a Cause* in 1955. On the female side, registering lower on the Richter Scale of angst and rebellion, *Gidget* (Sandra Dee, born 1942) discovers the joys of romance within California surfer culture in 1959, when the very first Boomers were only just becoming teenagers.

It is, therefore, something of a mystery that there should have been such a cultural focus – even an obsession – with all things 'teenage' in the '50s when, demographically speaking, there were not actually all that many of them about. One simple explanation is that, while few in numbers, these '50s teens – reflecting the fact that the American economy was then firing on all cylinders – had new spending power for cinema tickets, clothes, cars and records. The advertising and marketing industries were quick to notice and target this demographic and so, even though the great tsunami of the Boomer adolescents was still a few years off, anyone wanting to make a buck rushed specifically to direct their product towards this small but typically affluent teen market with money to spend.

As well as the spending power of the '50s teens, the sudden allure of all things 'teenage' in this era might, arguably, also derive from the fact that so many of the young adults of that time had themselves been robbed of their own adolescence by the war – the '50s obsession with youth reflecting a yearning to roll back the clock to adolescence on the part of an older generation which had been forced to grow up all too quickly. Whatever the reason, it was a brave (or maybe just crazy) song writer, musician or producer who dared to stray outside the territory of teen love and teen angst. Accordingly, the world was promptly drowned in a deluge of songs about teenage love (all, ironically, sung by adults – with the exception of Frankie Lymon (born 1942) who, with his fellow 'Teenagers', had a number one in 1956 with 'Why Do Fools Fall in Love?').

Hollywood too rushed in where fools once feared to tread, with such adolescent-targeted classics as *I Was A Teenage Werewolf* which came out in 1957. Like most of the teen-focused films of the '50s, *I Was a Teenage Werewolf* tells of a teenager gone bad who becomes a menace to society. Here is a clue to another, negative rather than positive, reason why the '50s had such a preoccupation with teenagers despite their comparatively small numbers.

America was in the grip of a moral panic – convinced that every teen was a potential if not an actual in-your-face, flick-knife-flicked juvenile delinquent. Sociologists argued endlessly about whether the problem was growing-up with absent fathers during the war, television, having too much money or comic books. Whatever the cause, here was something to keep adults from sleeping peacefully at night: fighting Hitler had been one thing, but if the enemy was right here in your own neighborhood – maybe even in your own home – then this was going to be quite a battle indeed. The 'generation gap' which emerged in the

'50s stretched across a no man's land of (mutual) fear and loathing.

And exactly the same thing was going on in Britain. As in America where the moral panic about '50s teenagers was always as much about class as age – kids from the wrong side of the tracks who, unlike their parents and grandparents, refused to defer to their 'betters' – the British '50s youth-culture panic focused on the working class Teddy Boys. Throughout the war the British working class had been promised a better, more egalitarian deal once Hitler was defeated, and post-war there was the expectation that even in class-ridden Britain things would change. Politically, to the establishment's great surprise, this expectation saw Churchill and his fellow Conservatives in the wartime National Unity coalition tossed-out and replaced by a Labour government in 1945.

One might have thought that would be the end of the story, but when a few upper class dandies started sporting a 'New Edwardian' dress style which harked back to days of aristocratic excess, something really strange and unprecedented happened: working class lads began to copy the same flamboyant, extravagant 'Edwardian' dress style (which featured extra-long jackets with flashy velvet trim). Aping their betters, refusing to stay in their place, these 'Teddy Boys' visually embodied that new working class assertiveness which had seen off the Conservatives.

And, they really were teenagers: Teddy *Boys*. To begin with, early in the '50s, the soundtrack for this new subculture was supplied by big band Jazz – the popular bandleader Ted Heath even bringing out a song called 'The Creeper' to celebrate the thick, crepe-soled 'Brothel Creeper' shoes the Teds wore with their long jackets and tight trousers. But then Rock 'n' Roll arrived from America and, terrified by the heady equation of uppity working class + teenagers + Rock 'n' Roll, the moral panic spiraled out of control.

Back in America the very same juxtaposition of wrong side of the tracks teens gone crazy on the jungle rhythms of Rock 'n' Roll focused on the 'Rockabilly' subculture now emerging from Memphis – as exemplified by the likes of Elvis, Jerry Lee Lewis and Carl Perkins. Again, as is evident in the case of Carl Perkins' 'Blue Suede Shoes', these were working class guys refusing to look like working class guys. And, extraordinarily given that this was happening in the American South, this new Rockabilly sound was a fusion of, on the one hand, white 'Hillbilly' Country & Western and, on the other, what was still being sold as 'race' music. Add in that scary new, hormonally unstable 'teenage' element – complete with the graphic sexual explicitness of Elvis' hip gyrations – and it is little wonder that preachers and civic leaders up and down the land began publicly smashing records and demanding 'Rock 'n' Roll has got to go!'

But it didn't. And therein lies a key defining feature of American and world history straight through into the 21st century. From the '50s on it would be 'youth' which, rightly or wrongly, was perceived as the cutting edge of innovation and change. From the '50s onwards – specifically from that moment when the teenage Elvis managed to do what would elude me and twiddle his radio dial onto some foot stomping, clap hands, sway your body, get down Afro-American music – the logic as well as the morality of segregation would steadily become ever more untenable. In a revolution which perhaps more than any other defined life in the second half of the 20th century, the triumph of Rock 'n' Roll signaled a new, unprecedented democratization of the arts: from the '50s on, elitist Culture (with a capital 'C') would be obliged to play second fiddle to popular culture – a popular culture which had as its heart the throbbing, pulsating rhythms of Rock 'n' Roll.

And you could dance to it. Well, some people could. In 1960, in my first teenage year, I went from my local, all white, within walking distance weather permitting elementary school to attend Neptune Junior High School which was housed in a rather grand but ramshackle building that had once been Neptune High School – a stone's throw from my uncle Doug's gas station on the corner of Corlies Ave and Main Street; the same site where, before the war, my father and his brother Doug had grown up in a two room building known (not all that affectionately) as 'The Shack'. In Neptune Junior High I came into contact with black kids – and kids of all races and ethnic backgrounds dancing to Rock 'n' Roll.

But, sadly, I never managed to overcome my inhibitions

and join them. Every lunch time, because there were too many of us Baby Boomers to fit in the cafeteria all at the same time, half of us would go to the school basketball court where Rock 'n' Roll 45s were played, and where most kids would hit the floor to dance. But not me. I would sit with my friend Scott way up at the top of the bleachers, where we would watch the proceedings and comment sagely on the decay, depravity and decline of Western Civilization. What I didn't know then (perhaps he didn't yet know either) was that Scott was Gay and was therefore unlikely to find all that enticing the idea of close bodily contact with girls. If truth be known, however, I on the other hand, found this prospect very enticing indeed but, not knowing how to dance, too shy to risk all with everyone watching, spent two years of lunchtimes sat at the top of the bleachers conferring and agreeing with Scott on the imminent decline and fall of Western Civilization (and, obviously, on the key role of Rock 'n' Roll in precipitating that decline and fall).

Back in elementary school there had been the occasional dancing lesson, but I found it hard to grasp even the basics of this strange ritual. How, for example, did one know if a particular record was appropriate for a feet-shuffling 'slow' dance or the jivier, circular swirling of a 'fast' one? I remember sneaking a look at the dance teacher's collection of 45s to see if this vital bit of information was marked on the record label, but to my amazement there was no such instruction. So, how did they know?

And I was at a further disadvantage, because most of my fellow students went to this same teacher's home for private lessons after school. I didn't want to do this: firstly because it seemed a waste of time and money to be doing something so normal, so mainstream, so what one was expected to do (and involving girls – yuck!) and, secondly, because (according to women my father's age one might encounter in the supermarket or after church) my father had been 'the best dancer in Neptune'.

Sitting with Scott at the top of the bleachers, looking down at the swirling, bopping bodies below, I was always aware that my 'old man' would have excelled at both basketball and dancing on this very same polished wooden floor. My father was a tough act to follow. More than that, I was going through a phase (one which, sadly, lasted for a very long time) of wanting to make myself the precise opposite of my 'old man'. If my father liked onions, I would refuse to eat them. If my father hated chicken, I couldn't get enough of it. If my father had loved dancing in his youth, I wasn't about to go anywhere near a dance floor. As I would explain to Scott (who was interested in classical music) this Rock 'n' Roll was just 'noise' and this so-called dancing was just . . . well, it certainly wasn't cool the way Modern Jazz was.

And yet, to be honest, the fact was that at the very time I was dismissing Rock 'n' Roll music and dance as unworthy of such a cool dude as myself, I was every lunchtime sat there mesmerized by the way the girls would swirl one way – their skirts flaring-up a bit – and then, suddenly – a magic, frozen moment in time, a beat skipped, as the transition was made – spun back in the opposite direction. Or, when slow dancing cheek to cheek, the way some of the flashier guys would bend their partners back and, once again a magic, frozen moment skipping a beat, hold this while meaningful glances were exchanged at close quarters as other dancers moved in planetary orbit around them.

Time and time again I would sit there calculating what song and which girl offered me the greatest opportunity for success – and, more importantly, the least chance of making a complete and utter fool of myself. But always, however many times and ways I sketched-out my route and line of attack, it was always just too far and too precarious a journey to get all the way down from the top of the bleachers onto the dance floor, to cross the floor in full view of everyone and then, as nonchalantly as possible, ask some fresh-faced thirteen-year-old girl if she would care to dance with me. And if she said no? Just imagine the ignominy of it. And if she said yes? Well then, yes, there was still the little matter of the fact that I didn't actually know how to dance.

In Neptune High (all sleek and modern, sprawling outward, equipped with two huge cafeterias and therefore no need for enforced lunchtime dancing), I steered my cool school eccentric Beatnik course against the winds of that Baby Boomer teenage Rock 'n' Roll revolution which, decades later, would be so exuberantly and fittingly celebrated in George Lucas' film *American Graffiti*. Not for me the Sophomore Hop, the Junior Prom and all that adolescent nonsense. Me, I was going to escape this sweet, syrupy, like totally uncool Rock 'n' Roll idiocy and – one day, one day – make that hour and a half bus ride up to New York City where I would live in a cool pad in Greenwich Village and hang out in obscure Jazz clubs where Beat girls in skin-tight Capri pants and short modern haircuts would give me the eye (and more) because they recognized that I wasn't one of those stupid jerky teenagers who danced cheek to cheek with his sweetheart at the prom to gushy pap like 'Teen Angel'.

As things turned out, I never made the scene in The Village but, as a Hippy in Philadelphia in the late '60s, I found that I wasn't alone in wanting to get some distance between myself and what we (ever so serious) Hippies saw as the meaningless commercial nonsense of Rock 'n' Roll. Accordingly, settling down for an evening with a few joints and, say, The Mothers of Invention's *Hot Rats* or some really far-out sitar stuff, we collectively entered a period of our lives when we managed extraordinarily well – all too well – to separate ourselves off from everything in contemporary popular culture bar a certain thin, ideologically tested strand of head-trip Rock.

So full of fear and loathing for the 'straight' world were we that – like abstaining monks and nuns – we denied ourselves TV (except for the daily flagellation of the news) and even the radio. Remember that this was a time before 'narrowcasting' cable TV, before TV or radio stations (or even programmes) which focused on minority musical genres and, however hard to believe today, the Internet wasn't even a gleam in any computer nerd's eye. If you wanted to know what was going on in music you could either watch Dick Clark's *American Bandstand* (which really was far too straight and cheesy for any self-respecting Hippy to contemplate) or you could just tune-in and drop-out to some cosmic vibe of your own making.

The media was far too mainstream and limiting in what it had to offer – in a way which younger generations today would find completely astounding. But we pig-ignorant, snobbish, elitist Hippies took a bad situation and made it even worse. Never in life, before or since, have I had such limited knowledge of what was going on in popular music as I did in the late '60s.

For me today, looking back, the greatest embarrassment – a crime really – was to have missed out on the rise of Soul, something which would never have happened in the UK where the ultra cool Mods grooved – and danced – to a hardly differentiated musical gradation which merged rather than segregated everything from Jazz to Ska, Rock to Soul. And where the trend-setting Mod 'faces' led, everyone else followed – with the effect that many American Soul musicians who were struggling in the US, ironically partly due to the 'British Invasion', managed to kick-start their flagging careers when they appeared on British TV shows like *Ready Steady Go!*

But even within that particular genre which we alternative types were forging and perfecting in the second half of the '60s – ROCK – without realizing it at the time we were taking away far more than we were adding. Hippy kids like me who had never made it to the Hop (or if they had, hoped this would remain a secret to be buried by the sands of time) saw Rock as an evolutionary step up from primordial, primitive Rock 'n' Roll – taking something which had been superficial and silly, and stripping-off its adolescent nonsense to make of it a hard and solid, serious and timeless perfection: in a word, a Rock. We thought we were doing the world a great favor by holding tight onto this Rock while ditching the 'Roll'.

The Rock which we Boomers nursed on its way in the late '60s brought the wonders of Jimmy Hendrix's reworking of the national anthem at Woodstock, the Wagner on LSD operatic grandeur of The Doors, the head-tripping complexities of 'concept albums' as pioneered by The Beatles' *Sergeant Pepper's Lonely Hearts Club Band*, the infinity of psychedelic permutations on offer within The Grateful Dead's fractal-like explorations of inner-space, and a lot else besides – taking a genre which had been content with an endless looping of the theme of teen romance and transforming it into one capable (even if only occasionally) of exploring philosophy, politics, ethics, the nature of human consciousness and the ontological condition (being *and* nothingness) of the likes of Suzy Creamcheese. But without the Roll, the Rock became something one sat and listened to. Like Descartes, we 'Heads' opted for the cerebral while (sex excepted) dispensing with the physical. In a nutshell, the problem with Rock minus the Roll was you couldn't dance to it.

OK, you could wave your hands around or jump about a bit, but in truth very few of us even did this. Watch the DVD of Woodstock where, a handful of happy Hippies cavorting about at the beginning and end excepted, what you have is half a million white people sat on their butts looking up at a stage. When, finally, Soul Funksters Sly and the Family Stone come on, we realize what's been missing: syncopation – that '**ugh!**', that slight but all important warping of the space-time continuum which, once Rock had arrived, would have to seek sanctuary in Soul and Funk.

And, of course, when Rock lost the Roll and went 'serious', as well as the loss of get down and boogie syncopated rhythm, a certain rough and ready, let's put the show on right here, just do it, licentious, illicit, wrong side of the tracks, down and dirty, black leather-jacketed, party-on spirit also departed from the now comatose (if not deceased) corpse of Rock 'n' Roll. The future would be 'serious' and 'progressive'; cerebral and trippy (and, let's be honest, middle rather than, as originally, working class).

How extraordinary and downright ironic that, despite decades of whitening-up, commercializing and sanitizing, Rock 'n' Roll, against all the odds, kept on flashing-up the occasional brilliant, priceless gem – Booker T & the M.G.'s'

'Green Onions', The Beach Boys' 'Good Vibrations', The Rolling Stones' '(Can't Get No) Satisfaction', The Beatles' final flourish of 'Get Back' – which showed how that fortuitous union of the original rural Blues and syncopated, driving, dance-orientated rhythm which began way back in the '30s could still get it on. But then – and here's the truly ironic bit – the sweaty beast with two backs which had powered all that rocking and rolling and rolling and rocking, was finally obliged to grab its clothes and run out the door by that 'alternative' 'counterculture' which preached 'let it all hang out'. We thought we were perfecting Rock 'n' Roll into Rock – making something hard, impermeable and eternal – but in truth we were ditching for good any chance of good rocking tonight.

For good? Fortunately the cavalry was on its way.

As we began to explore in previous chapters, in the mid '70s, Asbury Park, New Jersey – once a grand and exceedingly popular seaside resort – was in a sorry state. It still possessed a huge, wide boardwalk, enough salt water taffy to destroy the teeth of a small country's entire population, mini-golf, peddle-boats in the shape of swans, a Fun House complete with a giant mechanical gorilla, 'The Longest Bar in the World' (my friend Leland used to claim that it started in Asbury and then went underground to Newark), 'The Circuit' around which hot-rodders cruised as in *American Graffiti* and, most importantly, a functioning 'Fireball' pinball machine. But as more and more people in the '70s wanted and could afford air travel for their holidays, traditional seaside resorts were suffering and Asbury Park was no exception. In addition, crucially, Asbury Park experienced frightful race riots in 1970 – and these continued to taint the image of this would-be carefree, fun resort for years to come. Also, of course, it didn't help that the world economy was going down the toilet as a result of the oil embargo.

But every cloud has a silver lining, as they say. Plunging rents meant that some old building, like that which would house the live music venue The Stone Pony, could be rented for next to nothing, and a shabby, going to seed air of desolation is always a good breeding ground for down and dirty Rock 'n' Roll. The penny finally dropped in 1973 when Freehold born local Bruce Springsteen called his debut album *Greetings From Asbury Park*. Here was a place – where better than a down at the heels, seen better times seaside resort? – where old-school Rock 'n' Roll could feel right at home, could cut loose as if 'progressive' rock had just been a bad dream. Could put the show on right here.

In 1974 music critic Jon Landau pronounced 'I saw rock and roll future, and its name is Bruce Springsteen'. Not Rock, please note. Landau was very specific: here in his banged-up leather jacket was the future of Rock *'n' Roll*. And note also that this time around – for the first time – the future of Rock 'n' Roll was in the hands of a Baby Boomer, Springsteen having been born in 1949.

In 1974 I was living in London and when I went to see

the newly released film *American Graffiti* I came out of the cinema cursing myself for, blinkered by a misplaced understanding of the nature of cool, having missed out on so much great rocking and rolling. At this time there was a '50s 'Americana' revival thing going on in London – hamburger joints with gleaming jukeboxes blaring Rock 'n' Roll, a shop in Covent Garden called 'Flip' was doing a roaring trade in vintage clothes from the USA. Like others in London still dazed and confused from the after effects of Glam Rock, this all seemed fresh and fun to me and I started wondering if my teenage self back in Neptune had not been more pretentious than hip to have rejected out of hand all this great stuff.

My English girlfriend of many years, Lynn Procter, was keen to see America for herself and we formulated a plan to go for a holiday in Asbury Park, New Jersey. When the US Embassy refused Lynn a visa and as I, no longer a graduate student, was having my own UK visa problems, we decided to get married. As a Hippy I'd always vowed that I would never do the square, just a piece of paper marriage thing but, after a suitably downbeat and off-beat ceremony at the Hampstead Registry Office which featured a plastic ring that had come in a box of cereal, we were off to the land where I and, more famously, Rock 'n' Roll were born.

Lynn and I stayed at the Pink Flamingo Motel in Asbury Park (where, a decade previously, I had succeeded in losing my virginity). It was July, hot as blazes and, if you used your imagination a bit, it was like stepping into the 'Greetings from Asbury Park' '50s postcard which was used on the cover of Springsteen's debut album. By day we would soak up the sun on the beach (where there were noisy complaints from local women about how my wife's continental-style bikini insufficiently concealed her ample curves). Or we took turns playing the Fireball pinball machine in the Fun House. We ate pizza, steamed clams and baked bluefish. By night we hung-out at the live music club called The Stone Pony where we danced all night (yes, it turned out I could dance after all) to the house band Southside Johnny and the Asbury Jukes – on a couple of occasions, early in the evening, mid-week, practically the only customers in the place.

This music we were dancing to was what would come to be called SOAP – the Sound Of Asbury Park. After all those years of cerebral Rock for 'Heads' but not bodies, here in the pounding, syncopated, primordial, infectious beats of Springsteen, Southside Johnny and the other exponents of SOAP, was a music you could – indeed, had to – get up and dance to. Even me.

In a decade Rock and I had both come a long way – as it happens, all the way back to Rock 'n' Roll and all the way back to the Jersey Shore (where, as Tom Waits tells us in 'Jersey Girl', 'everything's all right'). Were Lynn and I the last couple ever to honeymoon in Asbury Park? Nice to think how we had Southside Johnny and the Asbury Jukes playing our wedding reception – Steve Van Zandt on electric guitar licentiously leering (as no one else can leer licentiously) from the tiny stage of The Stone Pony as it became increasingly evident that my wife Lynn's boob tube was fighting a losing battle with her rocking and rolling bazooms. Van Zandt (who, of course, in time we will see in *The Sopranos*, occasionally on the boardwalk at Asbury Park) was born in 1950 in Boston, but moved to New Jersey when he was seven. Southside Johnny was born in 1948, just one year after me and, like me, in Neptune, New Jersey. Lynn's errant boob finally escaped its tube and the band went crazy but never missed a beat.

As his eminence Wolfman Jack pronounced in *American Graffiti*: 'Rock 'n' Roll will stand, man – if I'm lying I'm dying.'

And, for the first time, from the mid '70s on, it would be under new - Baby Boomer - management.

Chapter 8

Protest

Sunday November 24, 1963

All weekend the family has been in the living room unable to disconnect from the continuous television news coverage, which functions as our only point of focus and reassurance as a nation stunned by the assassination of President John F. Kennedy. A junior in Neptune High, I had first heard the news on Friday when the school's Principle, Mr Coleman, had suddenly made an announcement on the crackling speaker positioned above the blackboard in every room of the shiny new building.

At home, the whole family, like the nation, is in a state of shock and united in grief. Republicans and Protestants, fearful of both big government spending and a country controlled by the Pope himself, neither of my parents had voted for Kennedy, but that didn't seem to matter now. America had lost a President and was smack in the midst of a national trauma which had still fully to sink in – even for the likes of Walter Cronkite and other avuncular, normally reassuring TV stalwarts.

Then on Sunday, just at the point where what had seemed a terrible dream was finally beginning to be acknowledged as reality, even as we sat there watching this strange man Oswald brought in handcuffs through the basement of Dallas Police Headquarters, a figure intrudes, a shot rings out, Oswald's face contorts in pain – the whole thing live yet, even the contortion of Oswald's face and the almost comic wide-eyed disbelief of the policeman handcuffed to him, looking like just another B&W TV cop drama. And when Ruby's handgun fires we all, the entire family gathered in front of the flickering screen, as one, cry out in shock, fright and astonishment for what is happening to and in our country.

Wednesday, August 28, 1968

Once again the family, my family, is sitting in the living room – the same living room – watching the television news. This time it's the riots outside the Democratic National Convention in Chicago. I'm home for the summer from university in Philadelphia – living at home begrudgingly and missing my Hippy friends; my hair trailing down to my waist, aged 19 and having tasted the sex, drugs and Rock 'n' Roll lifestyle. I am here in this suburban, wallpapered, floral-carpeted living room because my parents have decided that living at home for the summer, while painting our neighbor old Mrs Northrop's house in order to earn a little money, is what will help me to 'see sense'.

I'm sat on the sofa next to my mother, my father in his rocking chair, my younger brother and sister on the floor. Once again there is chaos on the television screen. Outside the Hilton Hotel in Chicago, in what would later be described as a 'police riot', protestors – kids who might well be friends of mine; Yippies and Hippies who with their long hair and frayed, patched hipster jeans might be me – are being assaulted with batons, fists, rifle butts and teargas. Cameras point this way, that way, there is choking on tear gas and screams on what seems like a battlefield – one not in some Vietnamese jungle but in the center of downtown Chicago. The war has well and truly come home: America is attacking its own children. Although I sit no further away from my family than I did in 1963, I am now a million miles from them in spirit. And they from me. For now, instead of being united in grief, my parents and I are separated by anger, frustration, fear and loathing.

For my father, the only valid interpretation of what is appearing on the (now colour) screen is that these no good, Commie, dope-smoking, fornicating Hippies – crazy kids, like his own eldest son – are destroying America. In my father's view (which was not contradicted by my mother in this instance), an insane, ungodly madness had swept across our once-great country. My parents, in their way, loved me and I, in my own way, loved them – yes, undeniably, absolutely and this is what made it all so terribly hard – but now we were on opposite sides of a great and awful civil war. In my parents' eyes (Because of drugs? Because I'd 'fallen in with a bad crowd'? Because I no longer went to church?) I had become the dupe of those 'outside agitators' (so feared by upright Americans like Benjamin's landlord in *The Graduate*) and other anti-American forces which (like '50s sci-fi aliens) threatened the destruction of our nation. But now in the late '60s threatened it not from some exotic Out There but rather from within – threatened by those kids who had grown up with *The Howdy Doody Show*, hula-hoops and dancing cheek to cheek at the prom but who now, in the blink of an eye, had become precisely those people – those no good punks – their parents had warned them about.

In my eyes, my parents were the enemy. How could they not see that – not simply a tactical mistake, not simply a threat to young male Americans like me – Vietnam was morally wrong and an abomination against humanity? For me, still grieving for the loss of Robert Kennedy in June, sickened that the Vietnam War supporting Hubert Humphrey rather than the 'peacenik' McCarthy will clearly win the nomination of 'my' party, I can only stare in disbelief and horror at the television – suddenly aware that an unbridgeable fault line has earthquaked its way through our living room.

Our living room and millions others like it across America. It has only been five years since Kennedy's assassination – the years of my and all the other baby boomers' youth – but America and the whole world has been changed in a manner and to an extent which has never been seen before, and all in just five years. Vietnam is at the heart of this transformation, but by now Vietnam has become the semiological marker of a division which goes far beyond that one point of contention: my parents and I are now in 1968 citizens of completely distinct, separate countries. Two countries which, while sharing the same geography and DNA, are at war with each other.

Today in the 21st century, whenever we think, talk, write or make documentaries about the '60s – whether it be on the sex, drugs, Rock 'n' Roll or the 'protest movement' – our minds immediately jump-cut into the *late* '60s era of Hippies, bell-bottom jeans, LSD and Vietnam. But, as has been said here before, this is to ignore the fundamental, irreducible duality of this extraordinary double – two for the price of one – decade.

In terms of aesthetics and worldview (always two sides of the same coin), we go from the sleek, minimalist, progressive, buttoned-down, technologically enthusiastic modernism of the early '60s, to the let-it-all-hang-out, hairy, psychedelic, ultra-decorative, back to nature, traditionalist, alternative, tune-in drop-out world of the Hippies and other counterculturalists from 1966 onwards. Musically, we travel in the same short time span between the teen delight/angst of early Rock 'n' Roll, or the cool sophistication of Modern Jazz to, in the later part of the decade, a Rock which ditched the Roll in favor of something altogether more cerebral, experimental and trippy (and, given that you can't have everything, whatever we may have thought at the time, far too hot, over excited and delirious to be cool). Sexually we go from the swinging, shaken-not-stirred-martini-in-hand *Playboy* (and his carefree, your place or mine, mascara sharp, carefully coiffured, mini-skirted promiscuous 'bunny') to the make love not war, do it in the road, unisex-styled Hippy who flowered (literally) in the 1967 'Summer of Love'. Protest bubbled up above as well as below the surface of the entire Sixties but, as with sex, drugs and Rock 'n' Roll/Rock, it had radically different objectives and styles in the two contrasting eras contained within this ten-year period.

The decade which would become synonymous with anti-Vietnam War protest was also the decade which saw protest take on and (to some extent) win a separate, arguably even more significant battle against centuries of racism, discrimination and segregation. Another mistake is to presume that this battle was fought only in the American Deep South. Segregation, discrimination and racism may have been less visible and explicit in the northern states – states like New Jersey where I grew up – but the indisputable fact (perhaps, hopefully, difficult for some young Americans to comprehend today?) is that America – all of America, North as well as South – was even in the '60s as divided by race as Britain has traditionally been divided by class throughout its own history.

The suburban neighborhood where I grew up in the '50s and '60s had no black families – and this would remain the case until well into the '70s. In the days when everyone in my family would collect the quarters father lined up on the dinning room table for placing in the collection plate in Sunday School, our Hamilton Methodist Church had only whites in its congregation (probably simply a product of neighborhood demographics rather than malicious design; at least once a year the choir of a nearby Afro-American Methodist church came for a spirited performance of gospel music and were always warmly received). It was only when I got to Neptune Junior High School that I had black kids in my class – and even then both races generally kept to themselves; the idea of interracial relationships completely, utterly unthinkable in my day. I loved Jazz and Blues and so many of my heroes were what we today term 'African-Americans', but when I glance through my high school yearbook from 1965, despite the fact that at least a third of my graduating class were African-Americans, I can find only one black fellow student – the wonderfully named Tyrone D. Hasty – who had signed my yearbook: perceptively noting 'It's been a great pleasure and an honor knowing you Ted, for your personality is one that the boys and girls of N.H.S will never forget, best of luck, Ty'

And even in this instance, if I'm honest, I can't remember Ty all that clearly and I most certainly never socialized with him after school. Where, after all, would a white and a black kid have hung out in Neptune in 1965? You almost never saw 'Negroes' (as we would have labeled them then) in the same supermarket or restaurants which middle-class whites frequented. Blacks had their own neighborhoods in post-war America (as, indeed, they had been segregated by race into separate regiments during the war) and when school finished at 3pm they quickly disappeared into their own world, as we white kids did into ours.

And so things might have remained were it not for shifting trends in popular culture and the Civil Rights legislation of the '60s which, while most explicitly aimed at the belligerent extreme segregation of the Deep South, would also have seismic ramifications in the North as slowly, with great courage, Afro-Americans in states like New Jersey began to challenge the usually unspoken (yet none the less formidable) barriers which kept them 'in their place'. In John Updike's *Rabbit Redux*, even in 1969, even in Pennsylvania where Lincoln delivered his Gettysburg Address, reminding us that America's founding fathers, also in Pennsylvania, had proclaimed that 'all men are created equal', we see just how dangerous it could be for a black person to move into a house in an all-white suburb in a northern state. Believe me, no one – not a single person in all of '50s, '60s or even '70s America – could have imagined that someday America would have a black President. In the America in which I grew up as a first wave Baby Boomer the idea that 'Negroes' and whites might even enjoy themselves on the same beach was still controversial. I have a very early but distinct memory of a 'Whites Only' sign on, I think, the main beach at Asbury Park. Certainly, even if segregation wasn't an official policy, it was rare to see racially mixed beaches even in the north and even in the '60s

Interestingly, the key white instigators of this most fundamental change in the American way of life would nearly all be Southerners. It was the terrible – too terrible at times even to contemplate; always bizarre and seemingly beyond fiction – circumstances of John Kennedy's assassination which brought into office the bumptious, unsophisticated to northern eyes, Lyndon Johnson who, while more remembered today for the moral and military catastrophe of Vietnam, succeeded in twisting America's arm until (at least officially) 'One Nation Under God' would no longer be bifurcated by race. The irony is that a John Kennedy – slick, upper crust, a Massachusetts Yankee, Catholic – could never have managed it. And if he had tried, America once again – as in its long and terrible, almost terminal civil war – would have been irreconcilably divided between North and South.

But even the tough and politically astute Lyndon Johnson might not have managed to drag America kicking and screaming towards racial integration had it not been for another Southern Good Old Boy, Elvis Presley. Demographically perfect White Trash Redneck material, it was Presley and not some northern kid of exotic ethnicity and religious background who lay in bed searching his radio dial for the stations which played 'race' music, who snuck into all black Rhythm & Blues concerts, who bought his sharper than sharp clothes in a dodgy black neighborhood and who, throughout his life, never hesitated to give credit to the black sources of musical inspiration which he had fused together with a local Hillbilly sound which – like the Blues, a product of poverty and hardship – had its own hard won integrity and soulful spirit. Once this unlikely yet ultimately inevitable musical marriage had been consummated, and once Elvis himself had conquered the world, White America and Black America could never again remain completely independent of each other. And the baby boom generation, suckled on Rock 'n' Roll, grew up fully (even if subconsciously) aware of this fact.

Where Elvis and the other Good Old Boys of Memphis led in the '50s, the Texan Lyndon Johnson followed with the Civil Rights Act of 1964 which outlawed racial discrimination in public places and institutions – the President handing the pen with which he signed this historic document to the Rev. Martin Luther King. Of course it is one thing to sign a piece of paper and quite another to bring about such a fundamental shift in human relations in practice.

Throughout the early '60s, across America, in the North as well as in the South, thousands of collective and individual acts of courage would have to take place before progress – real progress, often glacially slow – could be made. In the second series of *Mad Men* – set in 1962 – we see how one of Don Draper's (all white) Sterling Cooper team (the bearded, pipe-smoking, would-be Hipster young copywriter Paul Kinsey) dates and then shacks up with a middle class black woman, Sheila White. At first his motives seem simply a lusting after the exotic, coupled with a hope to be seen as cool and avant-garde, but eventually he actually does put himself on a bus headed for the Deep South and potentially big trouble.

Like *Mad Men*'s Paul Kinsey, despite the obvious dangers involved, a significant number of northern whites did indeed head for the Deep South to help with the registration of black voters. Bob Dylan and Joan Baez sang their hearts out in protest at on-going racial inequality in America. The Rev. Martin Luther King was only the most famous of all those who were arrested and, with infinite fortitude and wisdom, turned the other cheek.

But yet again, my fellow Baby Boomers and I were just too young to be pivotal or even, in most cases, participating figures in this revolution. I would like to believe that if, for example, a black family had moved into our neighborhood I would have been conspicuous in welcoming them. However, while I shed tears hearing King's 'I Have a Dream' speech on the TV news, I fail to see how a young white suburban teenager like myself (in the age before the internet and with parents who were at best ambivalent about rocking the boat on such contentious issues) might have known about, let alone participated in, the 1963 March on Washington. Yet thankfully millions of whites *did* participate in and support events such as these – events which eventually gave the American President and Congress no choice but to bite the bullet of tackling racial discrimination and segregation. As in the later half of the '60s – but arguably much more effectively – political activism and protest in the early '60s were part of the fabric of American life and changed it and the world beyond forever.

But note that (and this is a crucial difference compared to what will come later in the decade), such early '60s protest against racism and in support of a fairer, more tolerant, open and liberated society did not by and large add up to what might be termed a 'counterculture'. This protest was about making America better rather than a direct, head-on challenge to The American Way. Copywriter Paul Kinsey doesn't lose his job at Sterling Cooper because he spends his holiday registering black voters in Mississippi. Nor does such activity seem intrinsically at odds with his commitment to advertising, capitalism, making a buck and, as we learn in another episode, a penchant for the finest brandy. As every early issue of *Playboy* demonstrated in its advertising and its 'What Kind Of Man Reads Playboy' feature, liberalism and The Good Life were seen as bedfellows rather than enemies in the first half of the '60s.

And this very much included the Cool School Hipster's Modern Jazz lifestyle which, alongside a progressive stance on racial equality, promulgated sexual liberation and perhaps the occasional inhaling of a marijuana cigarette – but saw none of this as in any way antithetical to or challenging of The American Way of capitalism and the futuristic, technological clean-machine dream of modernism. A more racially integrated and multiculturally interfaced, hipper and by all means sexier, less inhibited America was to be hoped for and, if necessary, protested about. But few hipper than thou Cool Cats in early '60s America were challenging or even wary of the seemingly unstoppable upward curve of the post-war, baby boom fueled advance of the trinity of capitalism, materialism and technology. Far from it: such advances were a core component of the prosperous and liberated Modern Age which groovy Hipsters and sci-fi and *Popular Mechanics* reading nerdy squares alike hoped was just around the corner.

Speaking for myself, in my sharp suit, button-down Ivy League shirt, thin as a line in a Mondrian tie, black loafers and carefully waxed flat-top, grooving to the beat of Modern Jazz, my allegiance throughout the first half of the '60s was to modernism and progress rather than, as later in the decade, any form of counter-cultural political radicalism. A future gleaming with sleek skyscrapers, wonder drugs to cure all ills, jet planes, Hi-Fi, robots to clean your house and groovy chicks on 'the pill' and without old-fashioned sexual hang-ups, was the future for which I and millions of other Baby Boomers (who in just a few years would be railing against materialistic, greedy and 'plastic' America) passionately yearned. This was an American Dream – a new, shiny, progressive, futuristic American Dream – which could accommodate all races, all religions (and none), all ethnic backgrounds and all sexual persuasions

– and which couldn't come quickly enough as far as I and those like me were concerned.

In short: finger popping, would-be Hipsters like me were in the early '60s anything but outsiders (even if we always made a point of carrying with us and prominently displaying a well thumbed copy of Albert Camus' novel *L'Étranger*, which at the time bore the English title *The Outsider*) .

This would all change – and change with breathtaking rapidity all across America – within just a couple of years: my Hippy self of 1967 suddenly appalled and embarrassed by what my suit and tie wearing, *Playboy* reading modernist early '60s self saw as perfectly acceptable and desirable. For example, if I'd been old enough in the early '60s, I'm sure I would have jumped at the chance to work for Don Draper at Sterling Cooper – especially if the job offered me a trendy 'pad' with sleek, sharp-edged 'Scandinavian' style furniture, the latest 'stereo' and the chance to meet 'Beat' girls (as per Don Draper's bohemian mistress), and hang out in groovy Jazz clubs. Yes please!

Although bookended by Republican Presidents Ike and Tricky Dick Nixon at the very start and finish, the '60s was the decade when Democrats – even liberals – ruled and sailed in the mainstream. The extremists, outsiders and oddballs were those on the Right rather than the Left. Accordingly, it was hardly an act of great political courage when I joined the 'Young Democrats for Johnson' group at my high school in the run up to the 1964 election. There's a photo from this time which appeared in *The Asbury Park Press* showing me and the other young Dems standing with some slick-looking lawyer guy who organized such groups in the Jersey Shore area: I've got on my less is more suit with its ultra thin lapels, my Ivy League button down white shirt, my thinner than thin tie and a flat-top crew cut of which Gerry Mulligan (and, later, any of the astronauts) would have been proud.

In 1964 Lyndon Johnson was running against Barry Goldwater, whose 'extremism in the defense of liberty is no vice' brand of conservatism was testing the loyalty of more liberal-minded Republicans like my mother (but seemed to suit my father's politics just fine). Off my own bat, bubbling with enthusiasm, I took the Neptune High School 'Young Democrats for Johnson' into territory which arguably bordered on what, thanks to Nixon and his 'plumbers', would come to be called 'dirty tricks'. For example, at the Neptune City Shopping Center I and my team lovingly affixed a 'Johnson' bumper sticker to every single car in the huge parking lot – without asking a single person if they wanted one. On a sunny Saturday at the height of the campaign, skiving off from my job teaching gymnastics at the YMCA in Asbury Park, I brilliantly masterminded my merry band of insurgents down at the majestic Convention Hall where Goldwater had flown in to give a speech. Prominently waving our 'Johnson' placards, we found Goldwater's speaking style well-suited to our heckling. He would go 'There is a cancer in our society and its name is . . .' and then pause to milk the moment of its significance, and we would all chorus 'Goldwater' before he, now off his stride, could come up with his own punch line, 'socialism'.

Outside, after the speech was over, I came up with the bright idea that we 'Young Democrats for Johnson' might position ourselves on the little lawn which was exactly on the route that Goldwater would need to take in getting from the Convention Hall to his waiting helicopter. Spotting us, a group of what I presume were Secret Service men formed a sort of flying wedge to hive us off from the Republican Senator for Arizona. Unfortunately, in the midst of the ensuing mêlée, I somehow became situated *within* the flying wedge, just a couple of feet from the Senator. For a freeze frame moment, the Republican nominee for the Presidency and I stared intently at each other. I remember thinking that he was wearing a really nice suit and that, with his perfectly cut silver hair, whatever the man's politics, he was actually quite handsome. But Goldwater's returning look at me was one of sheer terror – something I couldn't understand (I'm a nice guy, really) until I heard one of the Secret Service men yell 'Get the kid with the stick' and I realized that in the fracas my 'Johnson' sign had come off, and I was now waving a piece of timber at the man who in theory, but it was already clear not in practice, might be the next President of the United States. Amazingly, after wrestling me to the ground, piling on top of me and removing my weapon, the Secret Service simply sent me on my way. Back at the YMCA I very nearly lost my job as a gymnastics and swimming teacher but, on the plus side, clearly impressed with my daring as well as my politics, a female member of Neptune High School's 'Young Democrats for Johnson' agreed to go out with me – provided (for, in truth, I was seen in Neptune High School more as an oddball than as the groovy Hipster I was aiming to be) that I promised not to tell anyone she was doing so.

Three years later I'd switched my crew-cut for waist length hair, my suit and tie for frayed, patched jeans and a 'granddad' shirt, and my support for Lyndon Johnson, while still acknowledging his courage and achievement in civil rights and in forging 'The Great Society', had waned – ultimately, turning to contempt. The reason: Vietnam.

This astounding transformation in my life – from insider to outsider in just a couple of years – had been replicated across America. In what seemed like every household in the land there had been this grinding tectonic shift which rumbled up from deep in the substructure of our country. Imagine if you will the normal American family sitting in their normal American suburban house, watching the TV or eating dinner at the kitchen table, when suddenly these tiny, spidery fault lines start – one at first, then hundreds, thousands of them – snaking across the wallpaper, across the plasterboard of the ceiling, across the polished hardwood floorboards and even between the fibers of the shag pile rug . . . and then, in just the blinking of an eye, the whole normal American home splits into two – leaving one or perhaps two members of this once tightly-knit, loving family on one side of the rift, the rest on the other side of a bottomless chasm that has suddenly appeared out of nowhere but which, as seen through the picture window, jigs and jags across the otherwise perfectly tended lawn, across the road and, as far as the eye can see, off into the distance.

And everywhere you went – Foodtown, Pat's Dinner, Uncle Doug's gas station, Mom's Italian Restaurant, the Hamilton Methodist Church – there would be some 'nice' person with a congenial, kindly smile who, cleverly wrong footing you before you had a chance to so much as open your mouth, would explain as simply as possible (for this person fully appreciated that the fancy so-called 'education' you were getting at college would only confuse someone like you) that only commies and cowards opposed this noble conflict. And the worst of it was that this war against peasants on the other side of the planet was being waged not by a Republican but by the very Democrat, Lyndon Baines Johnson, for whom you had risked the wrath of the unknowingly bumper-stickered and even felt the weight of the Secret Service. And now this 'nice' man or woman, friend of the family, stalwart of the community, was giving you the chance of owning up to being either a Commie or a coward, or instead to see the light and get onside in defense of The Free World. The choice was all yours.

And the pain: the grinding you down, pulling you apart,

gut-wrenching pain of it, together with the guilt which festered in every cell of your body like a cancer. You loved your parents – *your* parents, the only parents you had; they who comforted you when you fell off your bike or when your cat was run over on the highway; they who had bought you presents for Christmas, who always remembered your birthday, who (you eventually realized) had dutifully played the part of the Tooth Fairy each and every time your 'baby' teeth had fallen out. Your Old Man: he'd been in The Big One, WWII; had walked half way across France, risked all for his country. And you've tried a hundred, a thousand different ways of explaining why WWII and Vietnam are morally different, incomparable, but it just doesn't equate with your Old Man who still, despite having patiently heard you out, looks at you with withering contempt and, worse, irrevocable sadness, unsure only of whether his son is a Commie, a coward or both.

And, of course, it's more than just the war in Vietnam and your opposition to it. It's the girly long hair, the raggedy jeans, the Make Love Not War, the MARIAJUANA – with the certain knowledge that one puff and you're hooked, then on to Heroin as sure as shoot'en. In just a couple of years you had become the sort of vile, degenerate, not to be trusted person your parents had warned you about when driving in the family car down Corlies Avenue, past the pool hall where leather-jacketed, tattooed, greasy-jeaned, lank-haired, goodfornothin' juvenile delinquent punks smoked cigarettes and wormed their way into the nightmares of decent, law-abiding citizens. And it wasn't just you: apparently this whole, enormous, bulging at the seams baby boom generation of kids had been lured away from the old, safe, solid, righteous, God-fearing American Way by the Pied Piper Dope Fiends, the bearded, loony Beatniks, the Sexual Degenerates or those Reds who – despite Senator McCarthy's best efforts – still lurked, like cockroaches, under each and every bed in the USofA.

And then, finally, a point was reached in hundreds, thousands, perhaps millions of families across America where the utter truth of that Thomas Wolfe novel you had read in English Lit101 finally hit you in the solar plexus: you really can't go home again. For some, not ever, literally. For many others like me: never fully in spirit, never as a place where you could trust in finding sanctuary and let your guard down – which, when you think about it, is the essence of what we hope a home will be. Now you were an outsider, not only to your country and your culture, but even within your own family.

So began, for many, a frantic search for a new family – a primordial need which one fears Charles Manson must have fully appreciated when he named his sick, murdering gang 'The Family'. Huge migrations got under way – most heading off into the sunset, out West as far as you could go before you fell into the sea. Or, dodging the draft, to Canada. Or, like me, to Britain.

And, all the time, wherever you were, you were seeking to build not only some new kind of family but, bigger than that, nothing less than a whole New Society – an alternative, mutually supportive, non-competitive, pacifist, dope-smoking, laid-back, never uptight, skinny-dipping, love the one you're with, in touch with nature, hassle-free, satisfaction guaranteed, Pagan friendly, traditional yet completely new and improved American Dream (order now to avoid disappointment).

And – here's the rub – the vast, overwhelming majority of us taking on this massive, unprecedented task of building a new American Dream didn't know shit. Our split-session, over-crowded educations having provided us with a very limited understanding of history. Our upbringings in pampered, post-war prosperity having equipped us with little if any knowledge of the harsh realities beyond our suburban ranch style doorsteps. Our persistent and unrelenting labeling as 'teens' giving us no sense of what it meant to be an adult – even though, by the late '60s, our teenage years and the bubble gum sweet promises of Rock 'n' Rock dreams now, in truth, outside our demographic. Ironically, despite our protests against American imperialism, our citizenship as Americans – at precisely the time when our country's cultural and economic dominion over the entire Free World seemed an absolute law of nature – giving us a misplaced sense of being a Chosen People destined to lead all of humanity to the promised land in the golden Age of Aquarius when even the movements of the planets and the stars would (as the musical 'Hair' explained it) be guided not by Newtonian or Einsteinian physics but by love and peace. Far - fucking - out, man.

We were so sure – as sure as sure could be - that we alone, having felt the vibes, having smoked enough weed and dropped enough acid to have achieved sufficient consciousness expansion, knew ourselves and our (and everyone else's) destiny. In short: never before or since had an entire generation been so damn cock sure of itself while, in reality, knowing so damn little about anything one actually might need to succeed in the awesome task of constructing a new and improved Alternative Society.

Just three months before the infamous August 1968 Democratic National Convention in Chicago, a strike by students – soon joined by workers – brought Paris to a halt and came very close to toppling de Gaulle's long standing, seemingly everlasting French government. I remember seeing it on the TV news and feeling confused, even dumbfounded. What I couldn't get my head around was the idea that the workers had joined in a strike initiated by the students. In America, in my experience, no such alliance seemed remotely feasible: the average worker more likely to tell the average student to get a haircut (or worse).

This opposition between intellectuals and workers appeared to me to be a natural and inevitable state of affairs. Of course a more careful commentator would have grasped that the problem was not simply our being students but that, unlike in Paris, most of us doing the protesting were also what the press had taken to calling 'Hippies' – a subculture which had as one of its most fundamental beliefs the view that getting a job and clocking on, working your butt off, an honest day's work for an honest day's pay, was to be avoided, even disparaged. Remember that most of us were middle class kids who had never worked a day in our lives at a 'real' job and who had no experience of poverty and hardship, of lying awake at night worrying if you could pay the electricity bill – money in our view offhandedly, blithely, flippantly denigrated to 'bread'. But more than simply a lack of experience of the working man's (or woman's) world, many of us hairy Hippies, while not often truthful enough to say so explicitly, actually looked down upon and felt superior to working men and women. Patronizing prats, we pitied those who refused to liberate themselves from the soul destroying – completely unnecessary in our view – 9-to-5 grind.

The sad irony of all this is that, in so far as we Hippies possessed a coherent worldview, it was one which had evolved through the left-wing 'Folk' tradition of Bob Dylan, Joan Baez, Pete Seeger and others, which had been founded upon and given sustenance by the likes of Woody Guthrie and his 'This land is your land' celebration of the common man/woman way back in the Depression.

As in France and elsewhere in Europe, there had once in America long ago been the possibility of a fragile yet natural alignment between the intellectual and creative Lefties and the workers – including all those who would gladly be workers but couldn't get jobs because of the Depression, the disaster of the Dust Bowl, etc. Hippies like me may have played at being poor or disadvantaged, at being Native Americans or ghetto-dwelling black Hipsters but, in truth, it was only a condescending game based upon cardboard cut-out stereotypes which must have been utterly offensive to those towards whom we sought to show sympathy. And then, unlike the students in Paris, in focusing our would-be revolution on sex, drugs and Rock 'n' Roll – the long hair, the scruffy clothes, the bouncy bra-less breasts, the lazing about contemplating one's navel – we made it virtually impossible to do that which had happened in Paris and bring the workers onto our side. Woody must have been rolling in his grave.

On the other hand, however, it must be said that, unlike in Europe, the dream of a really viable, sustained and powerful alliance between workers and left-wing creatives and intellectuals had been undermined if not destroyed in America long before the '60s. McCarthy had seen to that. Or, more precisely, McCarthy had cleverly exploited a fundamental, atavistic fear on the part of the American working-class for anything which smacked of socialism; a fear which ultimately derived from the (theologically bizarre) conviction that one couldn't be both a Lefty and a Good Christian. I can recall my surprise on learning some years ago that in Britain the labour movement and the Labour Party historically had their strongest roots in the Methodist and other Protestant communities of the coal mining towns and villages of Wales, England and Scotland; that Wesleyan Chapels doubled as meeting halls for early trade unionist gatherings.

A truck driver most of his life, my father saw being against the Unions and the Lefties and being in favor of unimpeded Big Business and voting Republican as part and parcel of being a good Methodist. And his father, a dirt-poor electrician and gas station attendant, felt exactly the same. Much was made of working class 'Reagan Democrats' in the '80s, but in actual fact this American equation of working class, wrong-side-of-the-tracks Christian Fundamentalism and The Right (an equation which, oddly, casts Christ as some sort of 'Greed Is Good' cheerleader for Big Business) went all the way back at least to the Depression, when so many poor whites who desperately needed the support offered by the New Deal, despite their circumstances and operating directly against their own best interests, enthusiastically concurred in casting FDR in the role of the devil.

So while we unisex, free-living and loving, dope smoking Hippies further diminished any chance of bringing the workers within the Age of Aquarius, the simple fact is that the American Left, whatever length its hair, was never going to succeed at reaching out to and connecting with the white, God-fearing working-class. The gulf between the radical, far out, alternative vision of the protesters and the bedrock of mainstream, hard working America – even, perhaps especially, those trade unionists who have always formed a core component of the Democratic Party's political base – could never have been bridged in '60s America. And after Chicago in '68 we knew it – most of the Democrats gathered in 'The Windy City' unable or unwilling even to speak out against Mayor Daley and his 'police riot' which left protesters bleeding in the street and sympathizers like me silently shedding tears in front of the TV. And then a few months later, the 'Silent Majority', eager for a return to sanity, calm and the Good Old Days, gave Tricky Dick Nixon the victory which the young, clean shaven Kennedy had denied him in 1960.

Defeated in the Real World, we Hippies turned evermore inward to contemplate our navels and dream of the New Age, which we desperately hoped was just around the corner. Sadly, however, as 'our decade' neared its end, our magical, alternative parallel universe was itself beginning to collapse under the weight of its illusions, lack of concrete foundations, child-like naivety and over-reaching promises. In her 1968 essay 'Slouching Towards Bethlehem' Joan Didion gives a terrifying account of how the Hippy community of San Francisco – once the proud prototype of the New Age – was falling apart under the weight of drugs, madness, under-aged runaway kids and impossible dreams. Further south, in LA, Charles Manson unleashed 'Helter Skelter': horrific, deranged, vile murders which, in the eyes of mainstream America, looked all too convincingly like the logical, inevitable conclusion of the path taken by *all* long-haired, drug-taking, unbelieving, un-American

Hippy types. Also in California, also in 1969, the Altamont Speedway Free Festival which featured the Rolling Stones saw a fan stabbed to death by one of the Hells Angels who, ostensibly, had been entrusted with security at the event.

Yes, over on the East Coast, Woodstock had enjoyed 'Three Days of Peace & Love' without anyone getting murdered and without half a million ill-prepared Hippies starving to death. But, while much was made (and is still being made) of this commercially motivated event as a model of how the Hippies' alternative society could successfully be put into practice, the fact is that, leaving aside the ecological implications of traffic jams stretching all the way back to New York City and mountains of empty Coke cans, three days in a field smoking dope and listening to ultra rich pop stars is hardly the same thing as a sustainable, viable, alternative way of life. Near the end of Dennis Hopper's 1969 cult film *Easy Rider*, Peter Fonda's Captain America character – resplendent in his red, white and blue helmet – concludes 'We blew it' and, forty years on, it's hard to disagree.

It is hard too to see this defeat/unraveling/collapse of the counterculture experiment as anything other than a tragedy of epic proportions. While the Hippies' vision was flawed and their methods were madness, the fact is that America's militarism and imperialistic haughtiness did indeed need to be challenged. Equally, the franchised, advertised, commoditized materialism which spread and prospered with such unprecedented success in the '60s did need to be framed within some sort of system of meaning and values which made a human being more than simply a consumer.

Nor was the Hippies' defeat in any way a triumphant victory for the Silent Majority's Old America – the nation having been fractured beyond repair, its next generation of adults all too often lost, dispirited, directionless and drugged out of their tiny minds. And then, despite Nixon's carpet bombing of Cambodia and Laos, despite tons of the deadly Agent Orange being dropped on innocent people and thousands of other horrors perpetrated in the name of freedom, mighty America was nevertheless defeated by a bunch of rag-tag Asian peasants. Finally there was Watergate – God-fearing Americans like my father horrified by Nixon's 'expletives' while remaining untroubled by his bombing thousands of innocents in Southeast Asia. The neocons love to tell us that all the world's present and future ills stem directly from the crazy, demented liberalism which flowered in the '60s. My own view is that a great many of the world's present and future ills stem directly from the failure of the crazy and demented liberalism of the '60s to flower successfully and sustainably.

But let's try and finish the story. Within just a few weeks of my graduating from Temple University (a BA in anthropology) in the spring of 1969, I had been issued with an appointment to see a medical examiner who would determine whether or not I should be drafted into the US Army to serve my country in the jungles of Vietnam (flying planes around Texas like George W. Bush not an option available to me). With great trepidation, my blonde hair flowing down to my waist and constrained only by my best, hand-knitted Native American style headband, I made my way to an office block in downtown Asbury Park in order to await my fate. I took with me a fat folder of documents from a psychiatric counselor I'd seen while at university – documents which demonstrated beyond any shadow of doubt that I was a singularly unsuitable candidate for service in the United States Army.

Or so I thought. Ushered into the medical examiner's room at the appointed time, the first thing which struck me was that the doctor there to examine me was positively, extraordinarily ancient; one entire wall of his office covered with framed, signed certificates from Presidents he had served under – so many of them that, while one couldn't read the names on the ones furthest down the wall, it had to be assumed that they stretched from Richard Nixon back at least to Abraham Lincoln.

'I don't think much of this newfangled psychology stuff', the medical examiner exclaimed after flicking through my hefty folder of psychiatric documents for just a few seconds. Then, dismissively, contemptuously sweeping it to the side: 'You look like you'll make a fine soldier - I'm sure you'll do your country proud'.

I considered pontificating on the morality of this war; even proclaiming that if forced to join the army I would do all in my power to discredit America and undermine its imperialistic adventurism – but, shattered, I just slumped defeated in my chair as newsreel footage of horrifically wounded GIs and endless rows of body-bags ran on a continuous loop through my mind.

'Come back next week for your full medical', I heard the old doctor say from what seemed like a distant country – one without the leech-infested jungles which, already in my mind's eye, were my new home. 'Oh', he added finally, 'don't urinate for several hours before you come so we can take a urine sample'.

'I can't do that', I responded quietly, matter-of-factly, in all honesty, already resigned to my sorry fate.

'You what?'

'I can't urinate with people around. At university I would always walk miles across the campus to find an empty men's room.'

'You can't piss with people around?'

'Yes sir . . . I mean no sir.'

'How the hell do you expect to be in the United States Army and serve your country if you can't piss with people around?'

'I don't know sir.'

Now the old medical examiner stared out of the window for what seemed a very long time. Finally: 'Well, I'm sorry son but it just won't do. You won't do. I'm signing you off as 4F, unfit for military service.'

And that's how it came to pass that I didn't die a horrible early death in the jungles of Vietnam and, instead, left for England to work as an archaeologist – very much hoping to meet (and more) lots of groovy, hot to trot, miniskirted 'dolly birds'. A couple of weeks before this fateful appointment with the U.S. Army's medical examiner, riding on a bus in Philadelphia, an old lady, seeing my long hair and Hippy attire, had threatened me with her umbrella and advised me in no uncertain terms: 'You Commies should get out of the country'. Now, 4F and fancy free, I resolved to do exactly that.

Chapter 9

Swinging London

In 1947, the year I and the rest of the first full wave of Baby Boomers were born, work had just begun on developing Idlewild Golf Course on Long Island into a small airport – one which it was hoped would provide extra back-up to New York's main destination, LaGuardia. There wasn't a great deal of urgency as commercial air travel remained – and seemed destined to remain in the foreseeable future – an exotic possibility available only to the seriously rich.

Yet as my generation grew up, and did so during an era of unprecedented expansion of the comfortably off middle class, Idlewild Airport would become an ever expanding, evermore frenetic, hub of activity. In time this demographic blossoming of air travel into something even the masses did as a matter of course, even necessity, would undermine any notion of glamor. But, throughout the '50s and '60s the 'jet set' and the airports they flew from retained an aura of, on the one hand, old school privilege and, on the other, sci-fi futurism; yesterday and tomorrow compressed into a magical domain where no one lived and everyone was going somewhere. Commercial air travel existed long before the Baby Boomers were born, but my generation was the first to see flying as normal and conventional rather than exotic and exceptional (with the climate change implications of this transport revolution becoming evident also within this single, transformative generation's lifecycle).

When Idlewild Airport changed its name to Kennedy International in 1963, just a month after the assassination of the President, it was still a symbol of glamor and, even more so, of modernism – the rivalry of its various carriers in the cutting-edge design of their own separate terminals ensuring that this worldview/aesthetic was constantly translated into distinctive, iconic architecture. Another kind of iconic architecture was achieved with the help of a girdle: as the 2011 TV series *Pan Am* shows, the airline stewardess of the '60s became a living and breathing (abet with difficulty given that girdle) symbol of a future which was as uninhibited as it was international.

In 1964 it was at Kennedy that The Beatles' Pan Am flight from London touched down and, the airport bulging at the seams with screaming fans, thus began that 'British Invasion' of pop music, fashion, photography, cinema, art and satire which established Britain – and most especially 'Swinging London' – as the only fully successful challenge to America's seemingly invincible post-war monopoly of global popular culture; a popular culture which, increasingly, especially under Britain's stewardship, challenged the old guards' establishment notion of Culture. When the Beatles' Pan Am Yankee Clipper Flight 101 from London landed on February 7 1964, it brought with it a notion of pop culture which, while first born in America, now possessed a cocky, cheeky disregard of elitist High Culture which could only have been nurtured in a country like Britain which had, for centuries, had its fill of the Establishment and its contempt for anything 'common'.

On the 7th of July 1969 my parents drove me from Neptune, New Jersey to JFK International where I was to become the first member of my immediate family to fly on a plane. My stated objective was Winchester, England, to work for the summer helping with some archaeological excavations at England's most ancient capital. But, more excitingly, my real objective was to travel – in a jet plane would you believe! – to the source of that earlier, previously mentioned, British Invasion; hoping to get to the beating heart of WHERE IT'S AT. I'd seen the Italian director Michelangelo Antonioni's 1966 film *Blow-Up* which features a very David Bailey-like trendy fashion photographer, lots of young English women in mini dresses with huge mascaraed and fake-eye-lashed eyes and, in one scene forever engraved on my brain, the teenage Jane Birkin not even wearing so much as a mini-dress.

Most of my Hippy friends had set out for California and the dream of a naturalistic life, perhaps on a commune in the countryside, where escape might be found from the 'plastic' hell of the modern, materialistic world. While I appreciated the ideological earnestness of that dream, after seeing *Blow-Up* I knew that, however politically incorrect, I couldn't resist the lure of the ultra artifice of geometric haircuts, pop art printed mini dresses and kinky plastic boots which the magical, mythical London of *Blow-Up* offered, in marked opposition to the Hippies' delight in all things natural (including, most visibly, the unchecked growth of head, facial and body hair and a puritanical repudiation of make-up for women as well as men).

Having never flown before or even been in an airport, the ritual of checking in, passing through (a then minimal) security, the departure lounge, boarding, etc. – the rituals of flying which we now take so much for granted – were all novel excitements. It was all very modern and, despite my Hippy appearance and values, I'd never really shaken off my delight in and desire for all things modern and futuristic. Accordingly, in anticipation of this my first experience of air travel, I'd bought myself one of those sleek, molded plastic, Samsonite suitcases which, years before, I might have seen advertised in *Playboy* (the ad designed by Don Draper with a little, unacknowledged, help from Betti) and lusted after ever since. Not futuristic enough to foresee a time when little wheels would take the lug out of luggage, such Samsonite suitcases as mine – like so much of '60s modernism – were not actually all that practical and, however sexy and aesthetically appealing, should have been replaced with a back pack.

I would be traveling with a friend from university, David, whose destination was Oxford to explore existentialist theology with a group of Dominican monks (as one does). We would travel with Air Iceland, which at that time offered the cheapest flights from Kennedy to the UK – another $20 saved if, like David and me, you flew to Glasgow and then hitch-hiked to London. Air Iceland also offered a superb prawn cocktail (very hip '60s cuisine) and a scenic, aerial view of Iceland's volcanoes. This was the first time I'd seen the world from the air – my generation the first in history to experience en masse, and even take for granted, a perspective which has only existed, even for a tiny minority, for but a fleeting nanosecond of human history.

Our first night in the United Kingdom was spent in a Glasgow youth hostel which shook to the war cries of visiting Scottish football supporters. The second was spent in 'digs' above a pub in a town somewhere in the north of England – on the advise of the kindly Welsh lorry driver who, seeing these sleep-deprived, no longer hopeful, hitching Hippies on a slip road outside Glasgow, had given us a lift south into England (all the while speaking what we assumed was Welsh as we couldn't understand a word he said). The next day, after a few more hours with our convivial but incomprehensible Welshman, he headed West and David and I found ourselves with our thumbs out yet again. This time, on the M1 into London, we got a lift with a young couple from Newcastle and, finding these

CHAPTER 9. SWINGING LONDON

'Geordies' even less comprehensible, were forced to the reasonable but worrying conclusion that no one in the UK actually spoke English.

London! Swinging London! Yes! Seeing guidebooks as far too conventional and unadventurous, David and I simply took ourselves and our cumbersome suitcases to Piccadilly Circus where, at the statue of Eros, we asked anyone with long hair if they knew of a cheap place to stay. Instead everyone wanted to sell us some drugs but eventually, darkness falling, we were directed to something called The Arts Lab on Drury Lane in Covent Garden (then a rather down at the heels, insalubrious, even dodgy part of London) on the grounds that they sometimes let alternative types sleep on their floor. Unfortunately, the groovy-looking girl on the desk at the Arts Lab (ironically, a precursor of The Institute of Contemporary Arts, where I would work for a time in the '70s) said that the police had forbidden them from letting anyone sleep there and, when we begged for an alternative suggestion, directed us to a home for alcoholic old men – who, looking wide-eyed at our shiny new luggage, refused us on the grounds that we were neither alcoholics nor old.

They did, however, suggest to us another building on Drury Lane which, a sports facility by day, for 2/6 (two shillings and six pence or half a crown in Britain's bizarre, incomprehensible 'old money') let you sleep on one of their two basketball courts – one for males the other for females. Every inch of space was already occupied by bedded-down, hairy, primarily American Hippies – all, one guessed, like me, lured to London by sexy sirens in mini dresses and kinky boots but now bedded down instead with other hairy rather smelly Hippies. I'd heard that in Britain you got bed and breakfast as a combination deal but, when I inquired at what time this would be served, the response was one of side-splitting laughter.

Neither of us slept a wink. In the morning we found somewhere to get some breakfast and, dragging and pushing our suitcases, we eventually got ourselves to the Embankment where we sat watching the historic old River Thames flow through a venerable, ancient London which, to my eyes, seemed to be completely carved from stone – and from history; the granite and chain-linked architecture of the Embankment, the Houses of Parliament and Big Ben just visible in the distance, signaling a permanence and solidity which seemed to defy time and dismiss any doubt that this was *Great* Britain. (Surprising to learn some years later that so many of these seemingly ancient buildings, Tower Bridge and the Embankment itself, were built by the Victorians – but built, no doubt deliberately, in a style which would succeed so successfully in convincing any who saw them that they had indeed been there forever. Architecture as clever PR for an Empire which wanted to convince that it itself was an unconditional and timeless component of the natural order.)

But, at least for now, encumbered with our unwieldy, wheel-less suitcases, having been without sleep for what seemed a very long time, we'd had enough and, finding a tube station, David and I parted ways: he to Oxford and I to Winchester. It would be many weeks before I would make it back up to the capital, to visit that most famous epicenter of Swinging London: Carnaby Street. I couldn't wait.

Even up to and including the 1950s, Carnaby Street was unfashionable, inexpensive and infrequently visited – strangely so, given its location in West Soho, just a few minutes walk from the dark throbbing heart of London nightlife. Architecturally undistinguished and visually unremarkable, there were in the '50s a couple of second-rate tailors who would not have made the grade in Seville Row, a tobacconist and a shop where you could get your chandeliers cleaned. Back in the 19th century, in *Nicholas Nickleby*, Charles Dickens described Carnaby Street as 'a bygone, faded, tumbledown street, with two irregular rows of tall meager houses . . . the fowls who peck about the kennels, jerking their bodies hither and thither with a gait which none but town fowls are ever seen to adopt . . . are perfectly in keeping with the habitations of their owners'.

A backwater right up until it took off in the early '60s, the only thing which had drawn people – specifically, gay men – to this part of Soho were the public baths and swimming pool on Marshall Street, two blocks to the east of Carnaby Street. Gay sex was still illegal in Britain in the '50s and the Marshall Street Baths were an important, clandestine meeting place. Bill Green, a photographer who also, as 'Vince', ran a mail order business selling Continental style briefs and swimming trunks, hit upon the idea of renting a shop on adjacent Newburgh Street and, finding early success, 'Vince's' quickly became a shop which sold a wider range of clothes in rather adventurous styles which, in time, were sought after by sartorially uninhibited straight as well as gay men. This was in 1954. Like Mary Quant's bizarre little shop 'Bazaar' which opened over on Chelsea's King's Road in 1955, 'Vince's' was an early example of a 'boutique' – a place where, breaking with past traditions and decorum, shopping was meant to be fun, with pop music blaring and attractive young sales assistants who wore the clothes on sale in the shop.

In 1959, one such young, good-looking shop assistant in Vince's decided to have a go at designing and selling clothes on his own. Ambitious but having next to no money, John Stephen (a welder's apprentice in Glasgow only a few years previously) rented a shop one street over on Carnaby Street where rents were cheaper still – £7.10s a week securing him a shop with a ground floor window. Only problem: a window isn't much good if no one walks by, and in 1959 nobody walked down Carnaby Street if they could avoid it. Yet, amazingly, by 1965 John Stephen would own some eight separate shops on Carnaby Street, sell his 'gear' to pop stars and, for a time, employ a young lad called David Robert Jones (aka Davy Jones, then, David Bowie) as a designer. And, within this same short time span, this 'bygone, faded, tumbledown street, with two irregular rows of tall meager houses' had become the symbolic heart of a city which had itself become the epicenter of the pop culture universe.

Which was entirely appropriate given that, as we have seen, Carnaby Street itself was very *pop*: one day it was nowhere and the next – in the blink of an eye – it was Where It Was At. *Pop!* And pop too in the sense that this extraordinary retailing phenomenon was rooted in a kind of alchemy whereby nothing much was turned into something amazing – an amazing something created and sustained only by an invisible, indefinable buzz, a vibe, which, in time, reverberated throughout the entire pop universe.

And went on reverberating long, long after all the things which had made Carnaby Street Where It Is At had moved on or disappeared altogether. The Carnaby Street which I saw in 1969 on a day trip up from Winchester was not that far removed from the caricature of Swinging London one sees so delightfully portrayed in the Austin Powers films – a heady psychedelic swirl of all things over the top, flamboyant, loud, unrestrained, showy, gaudy and – yea baby – shagadelic.

By 1969 Carnaby Street had become the world's first pure pop urban tourist attraction (that is to say, a tourist destination which has no *raison d'être* outside the realm of popular culture but, unlike a theme park such as Disneyland, is located within a 'real' city). Traditionally tourists had visited London to see The Tower, Buckingham Palace or Big Ben but, by the end of the '60s, a new breed of tourists like me were coming in their thousands to see what, in reality, was just a street of shops – shops that had long since stopped selling the kind of cutting-edge fashions which had originally attracted cutting-edge popstars (who now, if they came at all, did so only if they were paid to star in a publicity event).

And yet this Austin Powers style Carnaby Street which I saw in 1969 was precisely what the other pop tourists and I were looking for. Sure, I was disappointed that – would you believe it? – not a single one of the mini-skirted, kinky-booted dolly birds who worked in the shops begged me to get it on with her. But, on the plus side, joining up with a few other American tourists (one of whom had bought a psychedelic paint your face/body kit), I had a fine time with my new-found friends – all of us sitting on the pavement painting each others' faces with groovy psychedelic swirls.

I doubt that any of us would have done such a thing back in America. But thanks to Carnaby Street's pop magic, we felt free to make an exhibition of ourselves in Swinging London – a Swinging London which in 1969, if indeed it could be said to be still swinging at all, was doing so on the power generated by tourists like me and my new friends, who found what we had come looking for because, like pilgrims at a shrine, *we believed*. And this magical enchantment – this mojo – still works today: even in the 21st century you see hordes of young kids from countries like Germany or Sweden – countries which stereotypically are not known for their sartorial daring – gleefully spraying fluorescent pink crazy colour in their hair sat, as I had done in 1969, on the pavement of Carnaby Street.

To put it another way: the world's first pure pop urban tourist attraction, Carnaby Street, functioned – and to an extent still functions even today – as a sort of theme park where, uniquely, the attraction and excitement is provided by the visitors themselves. And it works: pop!

Deservedly, London has long been seen as a place where sartorial experimentation and blatant exhibitionism are tolerated, even encouraged – a live and let live approach to appearance which, in the '70s and the '80s, would give rise to the truly mind-boggling extraterrestrial possibilities of Glam, Punk and Goth. In 1969 such sartorial freedom and experimentation were key components of Swinging London and, geographically, Carnaby Street was seen as the stage upon which this freedom could be indulged with the greatest abandon. Indulged in even by a tourist who, back in his or her own country, would never in a million years have considered wearing the flamboyant 'gear' on display in the likes of 'I Was Lord Kitchener's Valet' (where one might find something reminiscent of the dazzling marching band uniforms the Beatles wore on the cover of *Sergeant Pepper's Lonely Hearts Club Band*) or at the 'Bird Cage' (offering the shortest and most eye-catching of miniskirts and where, on occasion, dolly bird models would dance and even change their clothes in a giant birdcage suspended in front of the shop).

It was all very Far Out. But the irony – purists would

say the tragedy – was that this Austin Powers Carnaby Street where nothing was restrained and all things were over the top was stylistically (and style of course was the life blood of Carnaby Street) the complete opposite of that which had kick started and empowered this fashion Mecca in the first place.

From the start, John Stephen focused on an understated, refined, less is more look which drew inspiration from American Modern Jazz and European (especially Italian and French) menswear. Always, with John Stephen, the emphasis was on subtle detail and achieving more from less – always steering clear of anything gaudy or showy. The only thing excessive about this too often neglected British designer was an obsessional attention to achieving a look which was just right and no more.

And, fortuitously, this was precisely what the original, true 'Modernists' or 'Mods' were looking for. As in the case of the Dandies before them, history misrepresents the British Mods of the late '50s and early '60s by imagining them as velvet and lace wearing Austin Powers lookalikes or psychedelically festooned, any colour as long as it isn't black inhabitants of the Beatles' Yellow Submarine.

Even as late as 1964, Carnaby Street on a Saturday was chock-a-block with the kind of perfectionist, ultra restrained, sartorially fixated, minimalist Mods who fretted about the number and length of vents in the back of their jackets and the correctness of one, two or three buttons on the front. They grooved to Modern Jazz, Soul or the Blue

Beat and Ska which the rapidly increasing number of Jamaican immigrants had brought with them from the West Indies.

They grooved but were not groovy – at least not (most certainly not) in the manner of Austin Powers and his far out psychedelic friends. And note that the authentic, original Carnaby Street was a place populated primarily by dress-obsessed young *males*. While the world often remembers '60s Swinging London for its mini skirts and dolly birds, an even more important visual revolution which it hosted was one which saw the emergence of a new kind of preening, visually experimental male – a revolution which would in time reverberate through Glam, Punk, the New Romantics and the Goths, and which would always allow Britain to punch above its weight as a world leader in the incubation of innovative streetstyle and visually creative pop music.

But whether at John Stephen's 'His Clothes' or Mary Quant's 'Bazaar', whether on Carnaby Street or the King's Road, what set London's new take on fashion and style apart was its obsessional emphasis on youth. For hundreds of years Paris had been the unchallenged capital of fashion but always with its sights set firmly on rich, curvaceous, fully-formed adult *women*. What set London apart in the '60s – and what provided its edge in knocking Paris off its perch – was that London enthusiastically accepted that, as in pop music, fashion should now be aimed specifically at teenage *girls* (and not their mothers), adolescent *boys* (and not their fathers).

And – POP! – it changed fashion forever. And more besides. The teenager may first have been pandered to in America, but Britain handed them the keys and, blowing raspberries at the Old Guard, just told them to get on with it. Strange to think that this was happening with such ferocity in an old country which had for what seemed an eternity been ruled by near geriatric 'Old Boys' like Prime minister Harold Macmillan, and an 'Old Boy' network which couldn't stomach the sight of new blood.

But that was precisely the point. The Old Boys and their Old Guard had cocked it all up and, their authority undermined by loss of Empire and then the egg on face *faux pas* of Suez, had fractured the previously unquestioned equation whereby age equals wisdom and indubitable authority. Then in 1963 Macmillan's Minister of War, John Profumo, was caught, almost literally, with his pants down when his involvement with a young showgirl/callgirl named Christine Keeler (who it turned out was also sharing her favors with a Soviet spy and a West Indian drug dealer – you couldn't make this stuff up!) sank without trace the Old Guard's claims to the moral high ground.

Age toppled from its perch, Britain in the mid-60s fell head over heels in love with all things youthful, and cheeky young Turks elbowed their elders aside to set a new pace in British fashion, cinema, theater, art, graphic design, music and even politics. Old School Parisian fashion couldn't keep up and, for the first time ever, ceased to be the definitive wellspring of all things avant-garde. Even America's Rock 'n' Roll – the soundtrack of teenage life for a decade – now found itself invaded and conquered by four cheeky lads from Liverpool. Flipping Britain's old ageism on its head, Swinging London now invited only the young to the party. And all this, with perfect timing, just as all the world's post-war Baby Boomers – Boomers like Swinging London's own definitive icon, Twiggy (born 1949) – were 'coming of age'.

With startling foresight, the British novelist Colin MacInnes saw it all coming. Set in London in 1958, MacInnes' *Absolute Beginners* tells the tale of an unnamed 18-year-old paparazzi-style photographer who fears turning 19 because, no longer an *Absolute Beginner*, he will be *past it*. As the blurb on the back of the 1992 edition puts it: '1958, the young and restless – the *Absolute Beginners* – were busy creating a new world of cool music, coffee bars and freer love, as different from Mrs Dale and traditional England's green and pleasant land as they dared to make it.' Amazingly, demonstrating yet again that it was the '50s rather than the '60s which were truly revolutionary, everything which would make Swinging London swing in the mid-60s is already in place in MacInnes' sharp-eyed account of London in 1958: the obsession with youth, the way that class barriers are (and are not) starting to fall, an emancipation from old No Sex Please We're British sexual inhibitions, the enriching of British culture with input from immigrants from Jamaica and other former colonies, the *Revolt Into Style* (to use George Melly's phrase) which sees aesthetic sensibilities become the new boundaries, the new sociology, separating between the tribes of 'Us' and 'Them'.

And, one might add, the iconic role of the cheeky, upwardly mobile photographer who, 35mm SLR always to hand, is recording the twists, turns and dead ends of London life in the way that a Boswell or Pepys scribbling away did in times gone by. It is surely no coincidence that Antonioni's 1966 film *Blow-Up*, like MacInnes' 1959 novel, takes as its anti-hero hero a photographer – and, moreover, one who comes from the lower orders but who has no hesitation in gate crashing the party.

Of course, in real life this definitive role was played by David Bailey. Born in London's East End, far outside the territory of Britain's Establishment, Bailey and a coterie of other fashion photographers from the wrong side of the tracks stormed the citadels of London's stuffy, privileged fashion world just as London was beginning to swing and, in the process, set themselves up as the definitive symbols of a Britain which had lost an Empire but had the potential to create another – one based on youth rather than age, talent rather than inherited privilege, sexual provocation rather than stiff upper-lipped uptight inhibition. A shooting star, virile, a tough, take no lip, cock-sure East Ender catapulted into the innermost sanctum of the snooty world of fashion, young, and suddenly rich . . . Bailey *was* Swinging London.

Likewise David Hemmings' Bailey-like character in *Blow-up* whose dress style, mews studio/flat, photogenic eye, sports car and ability to smoke a cigarette against the beat of Herbie Hancock's impeccable Jazz soundtrack are all *just right*. No more no less. Yet, just as David Bailey and Antonioni's fictionalization of him are all the things which made Swinging London break free of the Old Guard's moribund Britain and build a new, dazzling, constantly changing British Empire of Cool, so too they are symbolic of the ultimate failure of this *Revolt Into Style*. When blown up again and again and again – like Swinging London itself, ultimately, beyond all proportion – Hemmings' 35mm photographs become meaningless. When faced with grim reality Antonioni's photographer can't do what a man's got to do. So perhaps, even more than the cocky young photographer, the real symbol of Swinging London is the camera itself: Click. Pop!

Countries are brands and it is breathtaking to note how successfully two countries – Britain and Italy – rebranded themselves for the better in the decades after the war. Previously the single word which clung persistently, for better or for worse, to both of these national brands was 'old'. Additionally, in the aftermath of the war, both countries were also saddled with the negative PR of being losers: Italy for loosing the war, Britain for losing an empire which had once stretched around the globe and, in its time, like the Embankment which precisely contains the ancient meanderings of the River Thames in stone, seemed invincible.

Not to mention the fact that, the war over, Britain and Italy were both broke.

Yet by 1960 Federico Fellini wouldn't have to cheat cinematically or stretch our credulity in order to show us, in *La Dolce Vita*, an Italy of cutting-edge, icy cool, future confident modernity. Language limited Italian popstars' capacity to follow and imitate American Rock 'n' Roll – and ultimately made impossible any 'Italian Invasion' of the citadel of American pop. But, no matter: Italy's post-war cinema was capturing the world's attention with its ever innovative directors, its breathtakingly sexy stars and its startling B&W imagery, which revealed monochrome to be more futuristic than Kodachrome. Beyond cinema, Italy would focus its creativity on conquering the world of design: its scooters, fashion, cars, cappuccino makers, accessories, furniture, lamps, typewriters and graphics the look of tomorrow available for purchase today.

Design – youthful, cheeky, impetuous, fun, sexy, disrespectful, often cheap and cheerful – was also the key to Britain's rebranding of itself and the rise of its own new world empire. Design and music – and, crucially, the marriage of the two. As we saw in the chapter on Rock 'n' Roll, throughout the '50s and into the '60s, a small but ultra fanatical group of white British kids had been listening long and hard not only to white American popstars like Elvis and Buddy Holly but even longer and harder to the original Afro-American creators of Blues, Rhythm & Blues and, later, Soul. Having absorbed the real deal of black American music in a way that most American white kids like me had not, the British kids who formed bands like The Beatles, The Rolling Stones, The Yardbirds, The Animals, Manfred Mann, Herman's Hermits, The Kinks or The Who figured out how to reconfigure the basics of the Blues in order to make this music their own.

And while previously Hollywood had enjoyed a near total world monopoly in the creation (or at least the dissemination) of sex symbols – from Gable to Brando, Harlow to Monroe – now it was Britain, Italy and that other modernist rising star, Sweden, which gave us a new generation of idols to lust after: Michael Caine, Julie Christie, Roger Moore, Sean Connery, Twiggy, Jean Shrimpton, Marcello Mastroianni, Sophia Loren, Anita Ekberg. Once bywords for old-fashioned prudery, inhibition and rectitude, suddenly, in the '60s, the national brands of Britain, Italy and Sweden emerged as the new, anything goes, lands of sexual license and oh so casual pop sex.

And, as well as sexual freedom, experiments in the possibilities of gender – particularly of the boundaries of masculinity – were also in progress in Britain. Once known throughout the world for its particularly drab, bowler-hatted, body concealing image of masculinity, from the '60s onwards Britain would increasingly be known for its outlandish gender-bending androgyny. While 'unisex' in the USA in the later half of the '60s had seen females throw away their make-up, hairspray, stilettos and foundation garments to join their male colleagues in a celebration of all things natural, in Britain unisex had typically taken the form of a few daring young males – from mascara-eyed Mods to Mick Jagger shaking his booty in a frock – experimenting with what had previously been considered purely 'feminine' adornments. While significant, such daring androgyny was actually more the exception than the rule in '60s Britain but then, early in the '70s, what began as a trickle suddenly became a flood as the United Kingdom was invaded by gender-bending Spiders from Mars.

A baby boomer, David Bowie was born David Robert Jones in Brixton, South London in 1947. Determined to be a pop singer from an early age, Davy Jones (as he called himself for a time) went through countless musical and stylistic cha-cha-cha-changes – Mod, Hippy, Psychedelic, you name it – throughout the '60s. In 1966, to avoid confusion with Davy Jones of The Monkeys, he changed his name to 'David Bowie'. In 1969 he had something of a hit with 'A Space Oddity' which celebrated (and, as we will consider in a moment, didn't celebrate) the first moon landings. Then the flickering flame of fame seemed to be extinguished as quickly as it had ignited. But, biding his time, Bowie focused his attentions on running a folk club and then an Arts Lab in his native South London. Under the tutelage of British mime artist, dancer and choreographer Lindsey Kemp, Bowie fine-tuned his theatrical, visual and movement skills – skills which would in time make it possible for him to reinvent Rock as an equal partnership of musical and visual creativity. This new approach was evident in Bowie's 1970 album *The Man Who Sold The World* and in his 1971 *Hunky Dory*. But it was the crash landing on earth of *Ziggy Stardust and the Spiders from Mars* in 1972 which showed what could come of a true union of sound and vision.

With his shock of flaming red, backcombed hair and his glittering, unworldly Kansai Yamamoto costumes, Bowie (and the other 'Glam' musicians who would emerge in the UK in the early '70s) did much more than simply change the course of Rock. In his pioneering 1930 book *The Psychology of Clothes*, J.C. Flügel identified what he called 'The Great Masculine Renunciation' – the sudden shift away from adornment, finery, fancy dress, tight-fitting garments and peacock-like preening and posing which came as a knee-jerk, defensive response in the wake of the French Revolution, as British and some European aristocrats frantically sought to disassociate themselves visually from that luxury and idleness in which the upper class had previously rejoiced. The any colour as long as it's black, undecorated, puritanical, business-like, figure concealing and pointedly unsexy image which resulted from this 'Great Masculine Renunciation' was pushed further in the context of Britain's cerebrally-fueled Industrial Revolution and (eager to demonstrate a presumed superiority over peacock-like colonial subjects) its era of Empire. Until, in Victorian times, the respectable British male had become H.G. Wells' *The Invisible Man*.

And this practical, dull, mind over matter, body concealing, unembellished vision of masculinity became one of Britain's principle exports in the 19th and 20th centuries – the drab, soberly suited businessman and politician, the symbol of modernity and westernization the world over. In the '50s America in which I grew up it went without saying that no 'normal' man in his right mind would dare use make-up, put too much thought to his hairstyle or wear clothes which were skin-tight and revealing. Of course our heroes of Rock 'n' Roll pushed and pulled on this envelope – and, from the start, that was one of the key reasons why they were our heroes. And such peacock-like exhibitionism was also one of the key reasons why an older generation was so fearful of these Rock 'n' Roll rebels in their fancy blue suede shoes, towering quiffs and show everything you've got drainpipe trousers.

In truth, however, even the Rock 'n' Roll and Teenage revolutions of the '50s and early '60s saw little which fundamentally challenged established notions of the Real Man: women increasingly wore the trousers but even the sartorially obsessed Rockabillies and Hipsters left frocks, make-up and curlers to the girls. However, 'The Great Masculine Renunciation', as well as a rejection of anything 'feminine', was at its most fundamental and invidious a puritanical rejection of delight in the male body itself, and here the early rebels of Rock 'n' Roll did depart from tradition. Any fool could see that Elvis categorically refused to jettison or feel an iota of shame in his physicality, and so (allegedly) it was decreed that he should only be filmed from the waist up on

The Ed Sullivan Show.

Fifties America alternated between this discomfiture with masculine physicality and, on the other hand, a strident 'body fascism' (to use a contemporary feminist label) which held that if men were to have bodies and show them off – for example, at the beach or stripped to the waist while mowing the lawn – then it damn well better be the pumped up, angular, rock hard body of a 'Real Man'.

Every single American comic book (I honestly think without exception) published during the late '50s and early '60s had on its back page an ad for Charles Atlas' body building course, which featured a cartoon strip where some poor, skinny guy is sitting on the beach with his girlfriend minding his own business when, in the next frame, this hunky pumped-up bully comes along, kicks sand in his face and then, in the penultimate frame, triumphantly, arm in arm, walks off with his curvaceous bikini-clad girl. The final frame of the strip finds Mr. Skinny wrecking his bedroom in frustration and vowing to send off for Charles Atlas' free booklet. Presuming myself too skinny even to benefit from the good Mr. Atlas' exercise equipment, my course of action after entering my teen years, despite living just a few miles from the sea, was to avoid going to the beach altogether, and spend my summer holidays reading French existentialism and wasting what I was constantly told were the best years of my life. It wasn't just my love of Jazz and a yearning for bohemian cool which kept me from joining in the Beach Blanket Bingo of normal teenage life. It was Charles Atlas.

But time travel to 1972 London and behold Ziggy Stardust! Even skinnier than I was as a teen, dripping make-up and hair dye, figure-hugging Lycra showing us absolutely everything he's got. And do the girls laugh in his face and go off with some guy who has kept at the Charles Atlas body building course every minute of the day until he bulges with rock hard muscle and good-old-fashioned masculinity? They do not. Ziggy Stardust threw down the gauntlet to challenge every aspect of 'The Great Masculine Renunciation' – everything from its puritanical distaste for adornment, to its Real Man comic book vision of a male body pumped up to remove any hint of femininity or sensitivity.

And it was the old masculinity which blinked first. Before long a whole battalion of British Glam Rockers took delight in demonstrating that real men could wear whatever the hell they wanted. And shake their Lurex-clad, spray can fit, platform-boot-elevated butts. And get the birds. And not only the Rock stars: as so often in Britain, even such exotic, extreme looks started to be seen on the street – even outside London, on High Streets up and down the land where old men and women who had survived the Blitz and thought they had seen everything stopped and stared, and simply couldn't believe their eyes. The Great Masculine Renunciation had finally disappeared down the plug hole of history (or so it seemed at the time).

Ziggy and his pals challenged not only centuries old

notions of masculinity but, equally, simultaneously, the late '60s Hippy and 'Prog' (progressive) Rock devotion to all things natural, traditional, bearded and more than a bit twee. In the early '70s in Britain two fundamentally opposed aesthetic systems were locked in a battle to the death. On the one hand there were the back to nature, old worldy, hairy, scruffy, denim-clad Left Over Hippy/Prog Rock Boring Old Farts. In the other corner were the futuristic, extraterrestrial, newly emerging Glam Rockers who, deliberately provoking Mr and Ms Natural, exalted all things artificial, plastic, glittering, even tasteless and trashy.

As always with such *Style Wars* (to use Peter York's phrase) this was a seismic collision of worldviews. Here in 1972 was the '60s counterculture's final stand against the 'plastic' materialism which, as they saw it, demanded a return to nature and to the values and aesthetics of traditional cultures. And, on the other hand, here was – many thought: at long last! – an alternative to the Alternative Culture which, its glittering Lycra banner raised up defiantly, demanded that it was now time to give up on waiting for the Age of Aquarius to arrive and get on with the party.

It took what at the time seemed an eternity but slowly, inevitably, at some point between Ziggy's arrival in 1972 and Punk's birth, kicking and screaming, in 1976, the Boring Old Farts Left Over Hippies and Prog Rockers – once so ubiquitous, even in Britain – went the way of the Neanderthals (or they went to live in some commune in Devon or Wales, where they remained largely invisible until they would re-emerge in the '80s as 'New Age Travelers'). In their place arose a glittering army of sexy, pervy, postmodern futurists.

When Ziggy and his alien friends landed on Planet Earth in 1972 I was living in London, doing a graduate degree in anthropology at University College – paid for with a $5,000 inheritance from my mother's father, the right-wing Methodist Bishop who, surely, must have been looking down from heaven with seething rage. This money was to be held in trust until I turned twenty-one in October of 1969 – a time when I was in my final year at Temple University and when, as it happened, I was suddenly without funds because my father had finally succeeded in convincing my mother that my character would benefit from working my way through college. When I pointed out to my parents that, turned 21, I was now due this inheritance, my father refused on the grounds that I was irresponsible and couldn't be trusted with money. Given my excellent grades Temple offered me a full scholarship, but this was dependent upon my parents signing a form to the effect that they were no longer supporting me. They refused to do this. Eventually, with the aid of a legal advisor from Temple, a letter was sent to my parents threatening them with legal action if they continued to block the transfer of my funds. It never went to court. The money paid for my final year at Temple and then, rather economically as it turned out, my gap year travels in Britain and Europe and, finally, my graduate education.

CHAPTER 9. SWINGING LONDON

In 1972, a student once again, I had finally achieved my dream of living in London but, at least in terms of my appearance, I'd hardly changed from that day in 1969 when I'd first set eyes on the Thames. Indeed, with my flowing, near waist-length blonde hair, crudely patched, worn to threads denim jeans and my native-American hand-woven headband, I was something of a poster boy for the Left Over Hippy Neanderthals. And so I might have remained except that, like Bowie before me, I was about to go through another wave of cha-cha-cha-changes .

Since moving to London I had been in the habit of taking myself to the Portobello Road market on a Saturday. A laid back, Hippy-ish sort of place (far from the rather gentrified Portobello Market one sees in the film *Notting Hill*) this was a cozy, comfortable, pleasantly ramshackle environment for a Left Over Hippy like me. But then, for reasons I can no longer recall, one Saturday I took myself instead to Kensington Market.

A hastily converted, decrepit and in places dank and dingy old department store in an incongruously upmarket part of town, Ken Market offered three floors of often tiny shops which, rented on a £20 overdraft or perhaps the proceeds of selling a little dope, offered anyone with a bit of style (and many with none whatsoever) a chance to design and sell their vision of what the future might hold for London streetstyle. Sadly no longer with us (Kensington Market closed in the '80s), forgotten in the history books, given only a paltry couple of lines in Wikipedia, shabby old Kensington Market was a wellspring of new ideas, new styles, new designs. In the early '70s it was Kensington Market – complete with a young, totally unknown Freddy Mercury flogging old fur coats – which offered the first opportunity for real, ordinary/extraordinary people on planet Earth to dress like Ziggy Stardust and his Spiders from Mars.

Like going to a nightclub (only better as you didn't have to walk home afterwards if you had no money for a taxi), Ken Market on a Saturday afternoon buzzed with stylish, hip, outrageous, sexy, exotically dressed, occasionally undressed, often completely off their heads Glam Rockers. Music blared from every little shop and if you tired of one 'scene' you just rounded a corner and found another. No longer turned-on by the old worldy, faded denim of Portobello Road, I came to spend pretty much every Saturday afternoon – often on Acid – entranced by the delights of Glam London's dystopian (in a *Mad Max*, *Blade Runner* sort of way) futuristic equivalent of some Middle Eastern bazaar.

Inevitably, my own style began to change. I traded my battered sneakers for (excruciatingly uncomfortable, but who cared) patent gold platform boots. My ancient threadbare jeans with their statigraphy of layer upon layer of patches I switched for skin-tight, figure-hugging trousers (tights really) made of some alien, shiny, stretchy, show off/freeze your bum fabric. I got rid of my old trusty, hand-woven native-American headband and let my long golden locks waft about like those of a popstar. And, finally, I ditched the huge, over-sized, hand-woven jumper/wrap-around jacket I'd bought in a peasant market in Mexico on my trip there in 1967, and replaced it with a skimpy little jacket made of black velvet and edged all over with a metallic, gold, red, silver and blue trim which sparkled and radiated dazzling light to such a degree that one wondered if it might not be prudent to run a Geiger counter over it. This was 1972 or maybe 1973 (memories are dim indeed from this period, photos also unfortunately rare). The Hippy me was no more. Now, at least in my mind's eye, emerging at last from the chrysalis, I was the spitting image of Ziggy Stardust.

How my old Hippy friends would have hated this new me. Could there possibly have been a more perfect visual repudiation of all that the Hippies had stood for? Synthetic, trashy, tacky and glittering, my new Glam outfit – like Ziggy's – was precisely the opposite of what one was meant to wear in the Age of Aquarius. But then that was the point: the revolution had failed. Time to face facts, time to ditch the dream. For, as Ziggy told us, instead of the Age of Aquarius, we'd be lucky to have 'Five Years' before everything goes down the plughole. Rose-tinted, positive thinking, not.

Moreover, Bowie and the other Glam invaders were not just throwing cold water on the Boring Old Farts' Left Over dreams. Despite its futurist aesthetic, Glam was also mocking that '50s and early '60s modernist dream which, like the Age of Aquarius, was now clearly past its sell-by date. Bowie and his mates were dancing licentiously around modernism's death bed, wearing costumes straight out of ultra low-budget sci-fi B movies. Although kitted-out in futuristic gear, Glam never possessed an iota of modernism's energizing optimism. Instead, here was a cynical yet now undeniably realistic assertion that, let's face it, both of the great dreams of the '60s – that of shiny modernism *and* that of a return to a premodern idyll – had failed. As Ziggy, never one to pull his punches, told us: rather than bubble-gum popping, dance all night at The Hop Rock 'n' roll, our extraordinary times demanded nothing less than 'genocide'.

Back in 1969, with his first hit 'A Space Oddity', Bowie had made his position clear: even as the world celebrated what, ostensibly, was modernism's ultimate triumph – the first moon landing – Major Tom was lost, alone in the infinite cold vastness of space. Doomed. Ironically, perhaps because no one had listened carefully enough to Bowie's bleak lyrics, the BBC used 'A Space Oddity' again and again as the soundtrack to their coverage of subsequent moon landings.

Bowie wasn't alone in a nagging feeling of tragedy – or at least of Mission Not Accomplished – in the face of this technological, all-American triumph. I was in Winchester doing my bit for archeology when the Eagle landed on July 20th 1969. In Britain the landing occurred in the middle of the night. In the morning, at breakfast, someone had fixed up a TV set and we all watched the reruns of this historic event in astonishment. As a young teenager I had watched every minute of each space mission as if glued to the set, refusing to budge even for school. In 1969, watching the ultimate, final great culmination of all these earlier missions, I was excited, yes, but I also felt a detachment, an alienation from what I saw on the flickering screen as Neil Armstrong made one giant leap for mankind.

So much had changed. John Kennedy had first boldly propelled the project on its way, but now President Tricky Dick Nixon was speaking to Americans on the moon by phone from the Oval Office. And the astronauts' crew-cuts, once in my mind linked to the likes of Gerry Mulligan and other cool cats, now, Vietnam still raging, reminding me that these brave men had their roots and no doubt their hearts firmly in the military and were most definitely not left-wing peacenik Hippies like me. For, in an America festooned with billboards which pleaded 'Make America Beautiful – Get A Haircut', the length of one's hair had by 1969 graduated from an aesthetic to a political phenomenon.

But this sense of detachment and disillusion went way beyond politics. Perhaps more than any other single event in my lifetime, this successful moon landing epitomized that futuristic modernism which had held out such tantalizing promise throughout the '50s and the early '60s. A promise to which, throughout that period, I had fully and enthusiastically subscribed.

Yet now, as I ate breakfast and watched the looped repeats of 'One small step', at the very moment when this modernism had proved its worth so concretely, I found myself thinking 'So what?' What good the moon if life on earth was going to hell in a hand cart? When President Kennedy – himself so young, forward looking and hopeful – had begun this adventure in 1962 we all, every last one of us, believed that, *ipso facto*, the future would be better than the past. No question. But now, by the end of this momentous, unbelievably fast-paced and, in the end, incredibly troubling decade, a lot of us were no longer so sure.

Within another seven years the Punks would spell it out as clear as clear could be: 'No Future'. But even in 1969, even in the triumphant glow from the technological miracle of the first moon landing – seemingly the ultimate demonstration of the inevitability of progress – there was nevertheless a hesitation, an underlying doubt which kept intruding on the momentous occasion. I wouldn't have been able to put a label on this hesitation and doubt in 1969 but now, in hindsight, I can: already by the end of the '60s the world had entered a *post*-modern age.

A strange, delightful, experimental new play, a musical, 'The Rocky Horror Show', opened in London in 1973 at the tiny, 63 seat Theater Upstairs. The brainchild of Richard O'Brian, 'Rocky' was an instant success. When it transferred to a slightly larger venue in an old cinema on the King's Road, I went to see it with a girlfriend, Philippa (who, unlike me, always seemed to know what was going on in London).

Like Bowie's often disturbing but always boogie on down danceable wham bam thank you ma'am dystopian visions, 'The Rocky Horror Show' took the accoutrements of all-American, '50s futuristic science fiction and deconstructed these into pervy, deranged, sexy fun for all the family (not). Then O'Brian threw all sorts of other, seemingly random, perversely eclectic pop culture tidbits into the mix and scatter gunned it into a kind of 'Po-Mo' (Post Modern) story of our time. With dance routines. Thus, like Bowie's ever changing cast of characters, the pumped up Real Man Rocky (the product of taking Charles Atlas' 'I can make you a man!' literally), his diabolical creator the treacherous but ultimately likeable transvestite from Transsexual Transylvania Frank-N-Furter, Brad, Janet and the delectable pre/proto-Punk Punkette Columbia do their funky thing within a No Future future which offers no promise and makes no sense – and all within a rubble-strewn landscape of post-war Western pop culture.

It's only 1973 but the '60s are now far, far behind. So too the sense of direction and purpose which empowered both modernism and the Hippy's search for peace, love and understanding in the Age of Aquarius. I think the sombre-voiced narrator of 'The Rocky Horror Show' articulated this new mood perfectly: '... crawling on the planet's face, tiny insects called the human race, lost in time, and lost in space - and meaning.' It's that final nail in the coffin - 'and meaning' - which clinches it: Welcome to the post-modern age - the age which can only define itself by what it is not. Welcome too to the '70s – 'The Decade That Taste Forgot' according to *The Face*, passing judgment from that smug designer decade, the '80s. And, believe me: you ain't seen nothin' yet.

Chapter 10

No Future

'During the course of this year all the people pictured here will be 30 or over.'

This was the headline to a cover story for a January 1976 edition of the British *New Musical Express*. Pictured were virtually all of the world's top Rock musicians – with the exception of David Bowie, a baby boomer born in 1947, who was still, just about, the right side of the Big 3 0. As we have seen, in truth, Rock 'n' Roll had been founded by middle aged guys like Bill Haley who had a lot more candles on their birthday cakes than did their teenage fans. Yet, somehow, the Rock which emerged in late '60s and early '70s had managed to spin the myth that it was and always would be a product of 'youth culture'. Now, however, the sharp and influential NME (pronounced 'enemy') was pointing out that in terms of harsh demographics, the Rock Emperor was actually stark bullock naked.

In Britain one saw further proof of this Rock gerontocracy in the form of the BBC's premier alternative pop music show *The Old Grey Whistle Test*, where 'Whispering' Bob Harris – born 1946 but always coming across as positively antediluvian; with his scraggly beard and scraggly denim jeans almost a deliberate parody of the Left-Over Hippies – presented and pontificated upon the latest, most pretentious 'Prog' ('Progressive') masterpieces as performed, more often than not, by middle-aged, university educated musicians who hoped to prove, beyond any shadow of a doubt, that Rock had become a 'serious' music which even the likes of BBC2 could take seriously. The problem, however, was that 'Prog' Rock delivered the precise opposite of what it said on the tin.

So what happened to the *Absolute Beginners*? You will recall the apprehensions of Colin MacInnes' 1959 novel's narrator who, almost nineteen, fears that life is passing him by as he leaves behind the magical, golden age of youth. Certainly in the late '50s and throughout the '60s it seemed obvious to one and all that the center of pop culture gravity – where it was *at* – was moving to a younger age range each and every year. Yet by the mid '70s, as the NME headline tellingly pointed out, the trend was clearly in the opposite direction with *Absolute Beginner* teens, as in pre-war eras, expected to defer to their elders.

As has already been hinted at in previous chapters, what happened by the mid '70s was that the pre-Boomer and Boomer generations who had grown up, blossomed and thrived in the golden age of youth – the age when Rock 'n' Roll, the teenager and 'youth culture' prevailed – had little inclination themselves to hand the baton of 'youth' onto a new generation of acned upstarts.

Accordingly, my generation's precious 'Rock Music' – for many Boomers our most cherished invention – grew ever more 'adult', 'serious' and 'progressive' with seemingly never-ending guitar solos sacrificing gutsy passion for technical accomplishment. And a similar situation prevailed in fashion, style, design, cinema, marketing and throughout the media. Hypocrisy reigned supreme: having wrested control of all facets of popular culture on the basis that we were young and therefore knew what was 'happening', 'with it' and 'groovy', in the mid '70s we now, approaching if not already within the wizened grasp of middle-age, hastily pulled up the drawbridge to exclude the pimply hordes of actual adolescents who, entirely reasonably, felt it was now their turn to inherit the legacy of 'youth'. And we had more than just arrogance and hypocrisy on our side: the birth-rate having leveled off and in some instances declined in the later '50s, the Boomers were still the largest target market. And if these aging Boomers wanted desperately to hold onto the increasingly disingenuous myth that they were cutting edge 'youth' then only a deranged marketing man would point out the obvious. As throughout our lives, our demographic strength saw to it that we remained the center of attention and, if that was the way we wanted it, remained within some constantly reinvented, stretched beyond logic, banner of 'youth'.

All of which must have been doubly frustrating for those who actually *were* teenagers in the mid '70s, but who had been crossed off the guest list to the great youth culture party by a bunch of Boring Old Farts who never missed a chance to mouth the merits of youth. One such sidelined *Absolute Beginner* was a kid called John Lydon who (as his adroit 1994 autobiography helps us to appreciate) was finding it more than a bit irritating to be growing up in the shadow of an older generation who (as they saw it) had a monopoly on all things hip and happening.

Born in 1956, part of the first post-Boomer generation of teenagers, John Lydon grew up on a tatty, grim council estate in Finsbury Park in north London. His parents were recent economic immigrants from Ireland trying to cope with the 'No Irish No Blacks No Dogs' inhospitality which greeted them in their new country (even though Britain had long depended on hard-working, underpaid Irish construction workers like John Lydon's old man). Despite Christopher Lydon's long stints as a crane driver on oil rigs and such like the family were always dirt poor. Accounts of chipped enamel baths with insufficient pots and pans to heat up enough hot water, and rats breeding incessantly in a broken sewer pipe beneath the house, remind one that the post-war dream of prosperity for all had come to naught for so many. Likewise that great social myth of the '60s which saw all working class heroes like David Bailey instantly catapulted from down-and-out slums to fame and fortune.

Maybe it was the rats but, tragically, the young Lydon was struck down with spinal meningitis when only seven – emerging from more than a year in hospital with a bit of a hunch back, bulging eyes which squinted and starred as they struggled to focus properly and a feeble frame that invited bullying. So one might think the young John Lydon would play it safe and try to fade into the woodwork but instead, defiantly and with a sartorial creativity which was as innovative as it was daring, he strove to stand out from the crowd; resisting conforming to the dictates of fashion or popular subcultures like Glam and the Skinheads.

It was Lydon's unconventional appearance which got him thrown out of school and, later, from the family home when his dumbfounded father caught sight of his bright green hair, the startling colour having been achieved with the aid of clothing dye. Sampling & mixing a strange, eclectic collection of garments/rubbish into a style which was all his own, Lydon prefigured not only the Punk look with which he would forever be associated but also that creative, rule-breaking and subjective approach to personal style (making a 'statement', not being a 'fashion victim') which is now seen as normal, even mainstream, in the 21st century. Snipping off nipple-exposing holes in his jumpers and, when presented with a fancy dress suit by his hopeful parents, ripping the thing to shreds and then cobbling it back together with safety pins, the young Lydon established the process of what would come to be called 'deconstruction' when it was appropriated by chic Belgian designers in Antwerp during the '80s.

As well as experimental, eyebrow raising, jaw-dropping style, Lydon loved music – spending most of the money he made working on construction sites with his father on lovingly cared for records of everything from Captain Beefheart to Iggy Pop, Miles Davis to Reggae. And he also loved literature and film – finding inspiration in that 'gorgeous piece of nastiness' 'Macbeth', Laurence Olivier's portrayal of malformed *Richard III* in the 1955 film of Shakespeare's play, the poetry of Ted Hughes, the vile, beyond redemption yet mesmerizing character of the young, cocky yet doomed gang leader Pinkie in Graham Greene's *Brighton Rock* and in the erudite letters and thoughts of that sharp tongued, ultra quick-witted Irishman in London, Oscar Wilde.

Having been thrown out of the family home for his primitive/extraterrestrial hair color experiments, John squatted for a bit in a condemned building in upmarket Hampstead with his daft, unstable fashion victim friend John Simon Riche. The worst part of squatting for Lydon was all the old Hippies with their joss sticks. But then Riche's mum was also an old Hippy who, to John Lydon's disgust, would cook things like deviled kidneys (at which genuine working class parents like his own would have turned up their noses). As well as being an old Hippy, Riche's mum was also a drug addict and that meant more than just the cuisine got a bit weird and confused. For example, she seems never to have been entirely certain whether her son's name was John Simon Riche or John Beverly. Eventually John Lydon resolved the matter by rechristening his friend 'Sid Vicious' – after a pet family hamster in the Lydon household who had originally simply been called Sid, but who acquired the surname of Vicious after sinking its teeth into Christopher Lydon's hand.

By the mid '70s John Lydon and his friend John Grey would enjoy hanging-out and strolling up and down on the King's Road in south west London. Long and meandering, the King's Road starts out at the ultra posh Sloane Square, but way over west it eventually creeps into a poorer neighborhood known impressively as 'World's End'. Here was to be found a strange little shop called SEX – its name proclaimed in huge, candy-pink plastic letters. More affordable and at least as interesting to the two Johns, also at the World's End end of the King's Road was a second hand clothing shop called Acme Attractions, which was managed by Don Letts the hugely dreadlocked son of Jamaican immigrants (much later in this story the DJ at the first full-on Punk club, The Roxy).

The entire length of the King's Road was one enormous catwalk and John Lydon took considerable pleasure in disturbing the retail therapy of the rich, trendy shoppers with his unique mind-bogglingly eclectic, jarringly juxtaposed, Dickensian B movie Sci-fi, slashed and burned, dystopian look. Strolling down the King's Road in 1975 the sickly, dirt poor, working class kid from Finsbury Park north London was in the process of reinventing himself as a character in a novel or perhaps an epic poem which, so far, existed only in John Lydon's florescent green head. A little bit of Oliver in *Richard III*, a pinch of Pinkie, a big, juicy dollop of Oscar Wilde's wit and flamboyance, a twist of Iggy Pop's just-do-it brain-damaged brilliance and a whole lot of the 18 year old John Lydon's teenage angst and boyish charms, were fusing into one of the great dramatic characters of the 20th century: Johnny Rotten.

In the mid '70s I was finishing my graduate studies in anthropology at University College, London, had started on my first book (*Fashion & Anti-fashion*), was living with my girlfriend and future wife Lynn Procter in north London (at one point on Wilberforce Road in Finsbury Park, not all that far from John Lydon's family's home in the shadow of the Arsenal football ground) and working part time at London's Institute of Contemporary Arts. Founded in 1946 by Herbert Read and Roland Penrose, the ICA (especially during the mid '70s) excelled in outraging the conservative press while simultaneously biting the hand of the British Arts Council which provided much of its funding. The highlight of this provocation came in October 1976 when the ICA opened COUM Transmission's 'Prostitution' exhibition which featured, most famously, performance artist Cosey Fanni Tutti's used tampons. Questions were asked in Parliament about Arts Council funding for such filth and the exhibition was closed prematurely but, although rarely acknowledged as such, this exhibition had staked out the aesthetic and ideological parameters of that subcultural volcano which, although still lacking a name, was about to blow: Punk.

Some months prior to the 'Prostitution' exhibition, encouraged by the wonderful Sir Roland (who would occasionally find time to recount tales of his fellow surrealist artists Man Ray, Dali or, my own hero, Duchamp over a coffee) I began work on organizing what was perhaps the ICA's first exploration of the interface between art and fashion. 'Fashion Forum', as it came to be called, would be a series of informal discussions with established and emerging London-based fashion designers. Following on from successful evenings with the likes of Ozzie Clark and Zandra Rhodes, I was determined to turn my attentions to opening a peephole on what the future might hold for British fashion. In particular I'd noticed a strange little shop at the 'wrong' end of the King's Road called SEX and, despite its forbidding black, mysterious facade, I steeled myself to take a look inside and see if I could find someone to lure into appearing at the ICA.

The only person to be seen in SEX on the day I braved entering was a curious man called Malcolm McLaren who, in a state of considerable and mounting agitation, explained to me that unlike the ICA, which was a hopelessly bourgeois and insipid institution, he was a true 'Situationist' artist and that my bourgeois institution and I could piss off. In truth I had never heard of the Situationists (I would look it up later: Marxist revolutionary arts movement originating in Paris in the '50s; their principle UK event, in 1961, taking place, strangely, at London's Institute of Contemporary Arts) and I left SEX disappointed that I'd failed in my mission.

But I had left my ICA card with Mr McLaren and it came as a surprise when he phoned me some weeks later to propose a 'deal'. It seemed the police had raided the SEX shop and busted them for selling obscene t-shirts – in particular one which featured an illustration borrowed (licensed?) from the homoerotic artist Tom of Finland, showing two exceptionally well-endowed cowboys who had forgotten to put on their trousers. McLaren's deal was this: if I would appear as a character witness at their forthcoming trial – vouching for their importance as serious, creative British fashion designers (none of which I felt would be stretching the truth) – then his partner Vivienne Westwood and their extraordinary, often fetishistically attired shop assistant Jordan would take part in my 'Fashion Forum' programme (but not, I noticed, McLaren himself who was presumably still too committed a Situationist to appear at the bourgeois ICA).

I'd never attended a trial before and I expect this one was not exactly typical. For starters, although Britain has a long history of laws governing what one could and couldn't wear (most such sartorial laws, dating back to the middle ages, prohibiting the wearing of certain colors or fabrics deemed suitable only for the true aristocracy), it was most unusual for a British court in the 20th century to turn its attentions to such things as t-shirts. But then these were no ordinary t-shirts. At one point, if my memory is correct, the prosecution alleged that the two cowboys' penises were touching. 'No M'Lud', protested the defense counsel and after someone had found a ruler, the precise gap between the two offending sets of genitalia was duly recorded. A big bone of contention (so to speak) was whether one of the offensive t-shirts had in fact been displayed in the small window at the front of the shop, where innocent people passing by might have been shocked to discover that cowboys have something other than their horse between their legs. My memory is that when specifically questioned on this point by the defense counsel, none of the policemen who had raided the shop would swear to having actually been the one to remove the offending garment and thereby protect the public from the sight of engorged male genitals. Under oath I said my bit – not very well, jumbling my words, but it probably made no difference. McLaren, Westwood and SEX lost the case, were fined and, in the process, gained their first taste (as history records, not their last) of juicy publicity.

Some weeks before the scheduled SEX 'Fashion Forum' event I had another phone call from McLaren. As a sideline to the shop he was putting together a band called the Sex Pistols who he assured me were going to be bigger than Elvis. Would I, he wondered, like to have them play at the ICA? Sounded good to me, but when I made inquires I was told that the ICA lacked the appropriate music license – and so it came to pass that the Sex Pistols would debut elsewhere.

On the evening of the 'Fashion Forum' event we had a packed house, Malcolm and his Sex Pistols were nowhere to be seen, Vivienne and Jordan looked splendid in their skin-tight rubberwear and at one point in the evening fire alarms started going off throughout the ICA. As the host and presenter I no doubt should have made everyone leave the building, but the sound of the alarms seemed distant and so I just carried on. A little later, precisely on cue in the midst of a discussion about rubber fetishism, three firemen dressed in fetching black and yellow rubber strolled into the room and, as if on a catwalk, up to the front to tell us that it was a false alarm. Later, the rumour circulated that Malcolm McLaren had instructed some or all of the Sex Pistols to run around the ICA setting off the fire alarms. Malcolm McLaren indulging in such a childish and (if the fire services had been genuinely needed elsewhere) possibly dangerous event? Surely not.

Religiously attending all the 'Fashion Forum' events and seated prominently right at the front of the one celebrating SEX were the always visually enthralling threesome of the fashion designer Zandra Rhodes, the cult film director Derek Jarman and his partner the jewelery designer, artist and creator of the yearly 'Alternative Miss World' event, Andrew Logan. Somehow Jarman and Logan had acquired one of those huge old derelict warehouses which fronted onto the Thames just to the east of Tower Bridge.

Today this same warehouse is one of the most expensive and desirable properties in London – housing on the ground floor one of Terence Conran's swish restaurants and adjacent to the prestigious, small but perfectly formed Design Museum, but in the mid '70s anyone wanting to live in London's crumbling Docklands was completely unheard of. How times change.

When the huge but ultimately unsustainable Biba department store in Kensington closed in 1975 (hardly more than a year after it had opened with much fanfare) Logan and Jarman managed to acquire the facades of the fairyland castles which had adorned Biba's children's department. These same Disneyland style battlements, together with the remains of some sets used in Jarman's pioneering film *Sebastiane*, now served to divide up the cavern-like interior of this warehouse on the south bank of the river.

Energetic, generous hosts as well as partygoers, Jarman and Logan held a 'Valentine's Ball' in their warehouse on February 14, 1976. Jordan – bleach blonde bouffanted, racoon-eyed, curvaceously packaged in fit-to-bursting black fetish gear; always in my opinion the most potent, creative stylistic force at SEX – was said to have had her clothes ripped from her on a make-shift stage by a very out of it John Lydon aka Johnny Rotten. But, if it happened, sadly I missed it.

There was eventually a raucous, short but hardly sweet performance of sorts from the Sex Pistols – one of their first – but it was hard to distinguish what was tuning-up, brawling and the gig itself. Apparently there were some journalists from the *New Musical Express* at the event and (according to Jon Savage's superb *England's Dreaming: Sex Pistols and Punk Rock*) McLaren was determined to spark something press worthy and suitably Situationist. My own recollection is that, as poor Derek and Andrew looked on fearfully, the one certainty which emerged from the chaos was that the young upstart Rotten and the middle-aged Situationist entrepreneur McLaren loathed each other. How, one wondered, would this dysfunctional band ever get off the ground? (In Tama Janowitz's 1986 short story collection *Slaves of New York* there is an only slightly fictionalized account of me – born in Neptune, New Jersey, resembling 'a young Andy Warhol' and 'a bit creepy' – meeting the story's narrator in the Tate Gallery and then, after a meal, taking her and my wife Lynn to this famous party near the Tower of London. Strangely, while history remembers the evening for the antics of the Sex Pistols, Janowitz recalls that the party featured exotically dressed guests flipping pancakes. Or has my memory mistakenly merged two separate parties at the same exceptional location into one? By the way Tama: I loved the book but you might have pointed out that the large pile of 'various sexual devices' in our living room was there because Lynn was writing an article about sex aids for a magazine.)

Around this time my wife and I became friendly with a vivacious, enticing young woman named Max who was newly arrived in London from somewhere in the sticks.

Like the always stylistically innovative John Lydon, Max cruised charity shops and sampled and mixed and deconstructed a unique, post-apocalyptic, post-modern style which was all her own. Always in the know about such things and determined to position herself right at the center of the coming subcultural storm, Max (and Jordan who was also a friend at this time) kept Lynn and I up-to-date on the latest adventures of the Sex Pistols. One day Max phoned to tell me excitedly that the Pistols were that very night playing at a tiny and little known club on the Finchley Road, which was just a few blocks from where Lynn and I lived in north London.

It's little surprise that this gig, one of the Sex Pistols' very first, is so little written about – even in Jon Savage's remarkably comprehensive (but for lack of an interview with myself) *England's Dreaming*. Hardly surprising because, aside from Max, myself and perhaps fifteen other fans of the group, there was no one else present except for the dozen or so regulars at the club, who incongruously appeared to be comprised of bright-eyed European au pair girls and heavily tanned Mediterranean guys with big-collared, well-ironed shirts opened down their chests, to reveal a lot of gold jewelery nestled amongst the hair.

The Sex Pistols were in good form. The minute dance floor in the shabby club felt enormous due to the lack of people. Up on the little stage the extraordinary persona of Johnny Rotten took form right before our eyes: scary, bent in what seemed like every sense of the term, leering, angry, utterly compelling. Here were Richard III, Pinkie, Wilde and the young John Lydon all rolled into one amazing character from whom you simply couldn't take your eyes. At one point in the short set, between songs, a pretty Swiss or maybe French au pair girl ventured hopefully across the empty room and with a sweet smile and in a charming accent asked Mr Rotten if they might turn down the volume just a little. Hunched, coiled above her, the demented smile which spread slowly across Johnny's face like a plague was a wonder to behold – something which even Olivier, Richard Attenborough (who plays Pinkie in the 1947 film adaptation of *Brighton Rock*) or Wilde at his most petulant would have struggled to equal. Obligingly the band cranked up the volume still further, until the uproar blotted out even the rumbling of the underground trains below us. The au pairs fled and only a dozen or so of us remained. No one knew it – there were no press present, no cameras – but the world had changed.

Not just a new music, but an entire, wall-to-wall new subculture was beginning to coalesce in London: flotsam bobbing and clumping together swept up by a surging tide of a new, long over-shadowed generation's teen angst. But even throughout most of 1976 this was still a far cry from a coherent, easily identified subculture like, for example, the Mods and Rockers of '60s Britain. You did see some of this new crowd wearing the ripped-up and safety-pinned back together style which John Lydon had experimented with even in the days before his reincarnation as the iconic Johnny Rotten – the style which would soon become the cartoonists' stereotype. But there were lots of other completely unrelated, often contradictory stylistic experiments going on at the same time and within the same loosely bounded group of a few hundred or so adventurous/demented souls. This was a come as you really are party – a celebration of diversity which, at least early on, deliberately and determinedly strove to avoid the conformity of any or all subcultural 'uniforms'.

The only stylistic feature shared by most members of this emerging subculture was a passionate eclecticism – rooting through countless charity and second-hand shops like Acme Attractions on the King's Road (or, more cheaply, the Oxfam shop in your own unfashionable part of town or suburban backwater) to find the most unlikely combination of garments and accessories, and then whacking these together in the most startling and disconcerting of ways.

For example, down on the King's Road on a Saturday afternoon you might see a group of teenage girls wearing the traditional British schoolgirl uniform of blazer, white shirt and tie, but put together with, say, an itsy bitsy shiny black PVC or leather mini skirt, which showed off more than it concealed of slutty, ripped-up fishnet stockings and a cheap garter belt from a sex shop, worn up high on the thigh. But this was only the start: hair might be in any and all primitive/futuristic florescent shades, and either backcombed to buggery or glooped up with Vaseline (it is said that some experimented with semen) into a gravity defying 'Mohican' which formed a thin strip of hair from back to front across an otherwise razored scalp. And on the girls' feet you might find a chunky pair of classic Dr. Marten's work boots, manly and proletarian footwear which would have been right at home on any of Christopher Lydon's construction sites. Around the neck – to REALLY freak everyone out – a chunky black leather collar and lead as available from your local pet shop.

This car crash of semiological oppositions – innocent schoolgirl/cheap whore, ancient primitive/futuristic extraterrestrial, macho/feminine, classy/down and out tramp – was often to be seen amongst this emerging subculture of what Peter York would later classify as 'Them'. But nothing, not even this penchant for what we would today term 'postmodern' sampling & mixing, was 100%. For nothing was taboo – with the single exception of rigorously and religiously avoiding anything reminiscent of the denim flairs worn by the hirsute Left over Hippies and other Boring Old Farts who still prowled the streets and still (despite being well past their use-by-date) saw themselves as the epitome of 'youth culture'.

Throughout the exceptionally hot, long summer of 1976 this ill-defined but powerful, newly emerging London subculture had no name for itself and had still to spark the sort of widespread moral panic which would come later. But it did have a geographic focus at the 'wrong' end of the King's Road by day and, in the dead of night, a strange tiny club called 'Louise's' on Poland Street near the top of Soho. Long one of London's few lesbian hangouts, throughout the summer and then the fall of '76, Louise's cheek-to-cheek dancing dykes and their pretty girly partners began to find themselves rubbing shoulders with this bizarre new subculture which would soon be labeled 'Punk'.

Near the door on the ground floor as you entered you might spot the always elegant Frenchwoman, Louise herself, sat at a little round table sipping champagne with her friend the artist Francis Bacon. Downstairs, from November of '76 when the Sex Pistols had released their first single 'Anarchy in the U.K.', you would find the unfortunate girl who was the DJ struggling to satisfy the demands of, on the one hand, her regular lesbian clientele's requests for slow, schmaltzy dance classics and, on the other, the riotous 'Them' crowd's requests for the Sex Pistols' solitary recording to be played repeatedly until worn down to nothing.

Then on the 1st of December EMI's big, chart-topping mega group Queen dropped out of an interview on Thames Television's live *Today* show, and EMI decided to sling their new signing the Sex Pistols into the slot. Clearly rattled by the appearance style and up yours attitude of the Pistols and their little coterie of friends, the (some said tipsy) presenter Bill Grundy encouraged them in swearing and, as soon as the programme went off the air, the telephones were ringing non-stop with complaints – one man phoning in to say that it had all been so upsetting he had smashed his TV set to smithereens. So finally the Sex Pistols broke out of obscurity and a tsunami of publicity now broke over this newly christened bunch of no good, dirty 'Punks'.

A few days later I passed John Lydon on the stairs of Louise's. Always feeling a bit of a Boring Old Fart Boomer interloper in this world of antsy '70s youth culture and not wanting to be seen as someone latching-on to this sudden media buzz, I gave John a little nod and was continuing on my way when he backed me against the railing of the stairway and demanded to know 'What? Now I'm famous you don't speak to me any more?' How very like John Lydon to need to cloak a friendly (and, for my part, much welcomed) gesture within an atmosphere of belligerence.

Just as 'Swinging London' came to symbolize Britain in the mid '60s, now in 1977 'Punk' became the iconic shorthand for a new, disturbing vision of Britain present and future. As fate would have it, 1977 was also the year of Queen Elizabeth II's 'Silver Jubilee' – the youthful Elizabeth having ascended to the throne twenty-five years earlier on her father's death in 1953. Throughout the land bonfire beacons were lit, street parties featuring 'Coronation Chicken' were held, buses painted silver and commemorative stamps licked. But, in truth, jubilation came hard to a Britain still reeling from a succession of oil crises, recession and a Labour government caught in a seemingly irresolvable deadlock with the very unions which supported it politically and economically.

Of course it wasn't only Britain that was mired in recession and a sense of promises of the good life unfilled. For decades now – since the end of the war and the start of the Boomers' story – the West had floated buoyantly on an ever upward optimism born of prosperity and technological progress. But the oil crisis of 1973 which saw petrol pumps run dry, the crash of Wall Street in 1973/4 and then waves of unemployment everywhere, shattered that equation of change equals progress which had always been at the heart of modernism and its rose-tinted hopes for the future.

Britain's emergence as a world pop culture superpower with the Lads From Liverpool, cheeky miniskirts and Swinging London had provided the ultimate symbolic manifestation of modernism's always upward and onward historic arc; a post-war world where every year, every month, every day brought change for the better. More so even than America, the Britain of '60s Swinging London had epitomized the shiny triumph of modernism because, unlike America, Britain had such a tough time of it in the '50s – rationing even more severe than that during the war, coupled with the hangover which came and for so long refused to go away when the realization finally sank in that Britain had won the war but lost its Empire. And so when prosperity finally did arrive in the '60s it tasted doubly sweet and cocky optimism seemed simply irresistible.

Now in 1977 the pulling of the rug from under that optimism gave the Silver Jubilee an air of strained celebration at best. Especially for a new post-Boomer generation which, unlike its mollycoddled predecessor, faced the prospect of a life on the dole. Accordingly, the emerging Punk subculture's Up Yours two fingered salute and No Future mantra seemed more in keeping with the spirit of the times. When in 1977 the Sex Pistols gave their own take on the Silver Jubilee in the form of their single 'God Save the Queen' it was probably only a small minority, even amongst the young, who literally agreed with John Lydon's lyrics which labeled the Queen as a 'moron' and her government as a 'fascist regime', but the vast majority shared in a sense that this was not a time for jubilation.

Throughout 1977 the aforementioned party giver and cult filmmaker Derek Jarman was devising and filming his own cinematic articulation of this new mood of cynicism and despair, which had settled like dirty, slushy snow over England's once green and pleasant land. Scooping together many of the most intriguing, larger-than-life emerging personalities of the now widespread Punk subculture, Jarman situated them within a story which time travels from the distant past into a decidedly dystopian future. Made like all his films on a tiny budget, *Jubilee* (1978) features Jenny Runacre as a Queen Elizabeth I who, with the assistance of her occultist John Dee (Richard O'Brian), sees into the future to a time when her ill-fated successor and namesake Elizabeth II gets unceremoniously and arbitrarily mugged in a car park; a time when Britannia is ruled by gangs of feral, dysfunctional (or, perfectly functional in a dysfunctional time) punky teens and an insane pop media mogul (part Malcolm McLaren perhaps; as with so much of this film's perceptive predictions of the future, part Simon Cowell).

Jordan (of SEX, etc.) stars in *Jubilee* as a sort of prim history teacher come kinky/kitsch pop phenomenon Amyl Nitrate, who finds her fifteen minutes of fame singing an operatic 'Rule Britannia' in the guise of a barely dressed, see-through knickered, stocking and suspendered Boudica, the Warrior Queen of the Iceni who led an ill-fated revolt against the Romans. Toyah Willcox as Mad plays with fire. Adam Ant, The Slits and Siouxsie and the Banshees shine. Murder, mayhem, dingy cafes, anarchy in the UK and bingo are the order of the day. Tellingly, in one scene of smoldering street desolation we spot a graffiti scrawled across the ruins of a wall: 'Post-Modern'.

A scrappy but underrated film, *Jubilee*, like *Blade Runner*, envisions a time when the once smoothly efficient machine of modernism – of fashion, 'direction', rationality, form-follows-function design and a technology which solves all problems – clatters crashing to a halt and the center no longer holds. Like Punk, *Jubilee* itemizes all the essential features of a post-modernism which has previously only been sketched out in the form of esoteric theory. The perception of time as a straight, single line of perpetual progress is replaced by a quantum NOW within which, segueing back upon itself in endless fractal layers, are to be found semiotic traces, stains – or maybe just the shadows – of other lands, mythologized subcultures, primitive peoples, B movies, historical eras, wet dreams and future fantasies. Then *Jubilee* – and, more broadly, Punk – playfully sampled and mixed all these eclectic parallel universes into unlikely, deliberately contradictory and unstable combinations – in the end, prophetically, giving us a pretty damn good vision of post-modern life in the 21st century.

The other point about the blossoming new post-Boomer Punk era which *Jubilee* grasped so well was its deliberate, determined, drooling childishness. Sick to death of the grown-up maturity, technical skill and slick professionalism which characterized the Boring Old Farts' pompous 'Prog' Rock, these new upstarts were determined to regain the crude but enthusiastically sketched teen dreams and nightmares of the original Rock 'n' Roll. Musically, famously, the Punk route was 'learn three chords and start a band'. Stylistically, we saw exactly the same process in the way that most Punks expressed themselves visually – not by becoming professional designers but instead by rummaging through charity shops and jumble sales and then, like children playing at dressing-up, parading around in the most unlikely of garments, accessories and make-up in a parody of adult appearance. Or, regressing in age, we saw teenage girls posing as prepubescent schoolgirls gone really, really bad in their deconstructed traditional school uniforms. And, for both sexes, there were infantile 'bum flaps' which mimicked nappies. In *Jubilee* we see a *Lord of the Flies* type world in which unchaperoned, disturbed (mostly female) children run amuck and trash their once glorious now not so United Kingdom.

The crass childishness which is depicted in *Jubilee* (and which is at the heart of Punk) is the exact, deliberate and carefully deliberated opposite of the beard stroking, educated, technically accomplished, grown-up world where the Boring Old Farts had reduced the old anything goes spirit of Rock 'n' Roll to a limp, aging shadow of its former self. The undisciplined, bratty little monsters of Punk positioned themselves in precise, exact opposition to the Leftover Hippies. Instead of slick, mature, educated but vapid professionalism, deliberately childish and amateur but gutsy and heartfelt Rock 'n' Roll for one and all. Instead of Love & Peace, 'bovver boots' and Up Yours. Instead of gently flowing naturalistic locks adorned with flowers, the eyeball jarring, glow in the dark artifice of Crazy Colour fluorescents. Instead of the Age of Aquarius, 'No Future'.

Not just another, yet another, read all about it amusing post-war youth (sub) culture, Punk was in point of fact a precisely articulated response to two unique, by chance intertwined, historical events: the overdue, long overshadowed and therefore pent-up dam-bursting emergence of the first post-Boomer teenage generation and, as fate would have it, this taking place within the setting of the first significant, dole-queue lengthening, optimism shattering, cynicism inducing post-war recession.

Or, the way Malcolm McLaren and Vivienne Westwood told it, Punk was simply the creation of two extraordinarily creative Renaissance people – Situationist artists, revolutionary designers, patient nurturers of musical talent, far-sighted visionaries – namely themselves. Indeed, if filmed on his own, McLaren was inclined to brush aside even his former-wife's contribution to claim (as he did in a 2009 BBC documentary) that Punk was born 'in my little shop'. This view presumes that history is shaped not by great economic, demographic, cultural or political forces but simply by the actions of a few all-important individuals – in this case Malcolm McLaren single-handedly firing the shot which did for Archduke Ferdinand and thereby started the First World War.

Not only is this view a reductionist distortion of how history happens – and actually did happen in 1976 – but it also fails to give credit where credit is surely due to the startling, unprecedented creativity of hundreds and then thousands of teenagers like John Lydon, my friend Max, the always extraordinary Jordan, Siouxsie Sioux and so very many others whose contribution was great but whose names were never known to us; kids who reinvented themselves and then had the balls to ride home on the bus. But all this aside, the most telling, straightforward and indisputable rebuttal to McLaren's 'my little shop' thesis, is the fact that Punk was actually born not in London in 1976 but rather in New York City at least a year or two before. Punk and, as we will see, much else besides.

New York New York – so good they named it twice. The ultimate symbol of modernity and of capitalism. Yet by the mid '70s The Big Apple was a bad apple, more rotten than Johnny's teeth. Teetering on the brink of bankruptcy it was touch and go whether the police, teachers, garbage collectors and other municipal workers would be paid. Heroin was rampant and zombie junkies prowled the streets – not only in Harlem and the war zone resembling South Bronx but even in the shadow of the sleek skyscrapers in parts of Manhattan like the East Village.

And everywhere, even in the most salubrious parts of town, as was all too clearly demonstrated by a string of highly publicized incidents, if danger loomed your fellow citizens turned away and left you to the wolves. The film *Escape from New York* – in which all of Manhattan has become one huge no go area cum Alcatraz – would not come out until 1981, but its dystopian inspiration was already playing out for real in mid '70s NYC. Yet amazingly it was from this decaying, rotten environment that three of the most influential subcultures and musical genres of the 20th century would take root and flourish: Punk, Hip Hop and Disco. Or perhaps, not amazing at all. Punk in London was also born in a time of severe economic decline and, while the boom years of Japan's economic miracle produced only millions of kids shopping in Paul Smith, when the 'bubble' burst in the early '90s there followed wave upon wave of evermore exotic subcultures which would position Japan as the new capital of streetstyle and youth culture by the end of the century.

In 1973 Hilly Kristal, a musician and promoter, opened

a dingy little club called CBGB in the bleeding heart of Skid Row on the infamous Bowery in Manhattan. The name derived from Kristal's intention to showcase live Country, Blue Grass and Blues, but by the middle of the decade CBGB became the place to hear a new, rough and ready Rock 'n' Roll which had its roots in 'Garage' and bands like Iggy Pop's Stooges. As would happen soon in London, this new Rock 'n' Roll deliberately favored a childlike, untutored, brash amateurishness over the slick and sophisticated. Like Mr Pop himself (born 1947), most of those musicians who played at CBGB in the mid '70s were Boomers or even pre-Boomers – Richard Hell (born 1949), Debbie Harry (born 1945), Tom Verlaine (born 1949), Patti Smith (born 1946) – all determined to challenge the airy-fairy, love-and-peace-man-wear-flowers-in-your-hair worldview-aesthetic which, refusing to accept the demise of the '60s, still pervaded the '70s like the smell of patchouli oil.

Especially in New York – so often sidelined in the rush to San Francisco in the late '60s – there had long been this belligerently urban, gritty, trashy rebuttal to the saccharine back to nature naivety of those who flocked to California to await the dawning of the Age of Aquarius. It had been there in NYC with Andy Warhol and his Factory – and in Warhol's musical experiment, The Velvet Underground. Going solo, the Velvet's Lou Reed crystallized this mood in his 1972 album *Transformer*, which celebrated those 'Vicious' urban degenerates who would 'Walk on the Wild Side'. This mood hung heavy in the foetid air at CBGB in the mid '70s – but, eschewing Reed's slick production (courtesy of David Bowie and Mick Ronson), these new bands sought something rougher, more immediate, more childlike even childish.

Childlike and childish yet, in contrast to what would happen in London in 1976, almost all these new kick-ass musicians who performed at CBGB in its initial, golden age were not themselves teens. Even The Ramones – who always contrived to look like definitive juvenile delinquents – were actually well into their twenties when they first took the stage at CBGB in August of 1974. Joey Ramone was born Jeffery Ross Hyman in 1951. Dee Dee Ramone was born Douglas Glenn Colvin also in 1951. While Johnny Ramone – John William Cummings – was born in 1948. But whatever their actual ages, The Ramones in their battered Perfecto black leather jackets, skin-tight, ripped drainpipe jeans and cheap sneakers came across as petulant, attention deficit disordered children, playing fast and furious songs like 'Blitzkrieg Bop' and 'I Wanna Be Sedated' which were over almost before they had begun. As journalist Legs McNeil described it: 'They were all wearing these black leather jackets. And they counted off this song ... and it was just this wall of noise.... They looked so striking. These guys were not hippies. This was something completely new.'

Completely new yet at the same time completely retro. The Ramones seem to have taken some early childhood sighting of juvenile delinquents hanging out on the street corner of the Forest Hill, Queens neighborhood where they had all grown up, and then reformulated this ancient '50s memory into a 'Rocky Horror Show' type '70s pastiche – a cartoon – of definitive '50s bad boys where everything was served up within quotation marks and with a knowing wink.

Indeed, such post-modern retro recycling was to be found amongst most if not all of those gathered in CBGB in its early days – the city which had so long been the ultimate, definitive symbol of futuristic modernism now kicking its time machine into reverse. Neatly ignoring the '60s, the plan was to (de)construct the ultimate '50s B movie – with The Ramones as the degenerate delinquents from central casting and Debbie Harry providing the love interest (her peroxide and permed hair harking back to the '50s glamor of Monroe or Mansfield, while making perfectly clear that here was no nature loving Hippy). As would happen in London, instead of a straight replaying of the past, this new Rock 'n' Roll retro pastiche sampled weird little moldy leftovers of the past and then whizzed them up in a cosmic crazy blender until, while steeped in nostalgia, as Legs McNeil puts it in the quote above, 'This was something completely new'.

But what to call this new thing? In 1975, together with cartoonist John Holmstrom and publisher Ged Dunn, Legs McNeil started work on a deliberately scrappy, amateurishly put together magazine (what would come to be known as a 'fanzine') which would feature all the creatures of the night who braved the Bowery to gather together in the heady atmosphere of CBGB. Featuring cartoons and photo stories complete with old-fashioned speech bubbles, here was yet another reformulation of the Boomers' collective, distant memory of their '50s childhood. The name of this strange fanzine? *Punk*.

When I was a kid growing up in Neptune in the '50s, if the family were driving down Corlies Avenue past the town's pool hall, and father caught us eying the cigarette hanging off the lip, black leather jacketed, drain-pipe jean wearing juvenile delinquent guys and a few girls who sat on their motorcycles outside, warningly, he would admonish us that these were 'no good punks'. Likewise, in films such as *The Wild One* and *Rebel Without a Cause*, this was the label which would be hurled abusively at the likes of Brando or Dean. It's what the sheriff spits at the hoodlum he's collared as he locks him in the cell and throws away the key.

Going back centuries, the word 'punk' originally referred to dried, decayed wood used in lighting a fire. Gradually the term also acquired a secondary meaning as something (and then someone) of inferior quality, worthless, good for nothing. What was striking about these new good for nothing 'Punks' of mid '70s Manhattan, was that they enthusiastically and proudly appropriated a term of abuse which had for decades been hurled at degenerate losers like themselves and lobbed it back like a grenade at the upright citizens who would henceforth be robbed of a favored put down. Yes they were Punks and, unlike their '50s B movie predecessors who flinched just a little (even the tough guys) when this harsh label was stuck on them by the jabbing finger of respectable society, these '70s Punks wore their label with pride.

While the Punks were spawning in their underground lairs in Manhattan, up in the South Bronx another very different subcultural revolution was brewing. Different but, in its own way, just like Punk, precisely positioned as a rebuttal to that lingering whiff of patchouli oil Hippy sweetness which, even if increasingly more in myth than reality, remained as the late '60s paradigm which – from all different sides – had to be challenged in the '70s.

Especially in the grim reality of what had happened to New York's South Bronx, a community literally ripped apart when a monstrous expressway was hacked through it, ground down by recession, poverty and drugs. The middle class Hippies' anti-materialistic vision had never carried much appeal for the struggling Afro-Americans of the ghetto (or poor whites for that matter) who could not reject on ideological grounds a prosperity which they had never known and were, in reality, exceedingly unlikely ever to know. Accordingly, when the rapping, the Hip Hop and the breakdancing which first emerged in the hot, sweaty street parties in the rubble of the South Bronx found a wider audience in the '80s, its musicians adorned themselves in the most expensive designer sportswear brands and lashings of gold bling – a celebration of success and excess which middle class, economically secure '60s Hippies like me would have found repugnant.

In time becoming the world's most successful musical genre, at the heart of the Hip Hop which slowly but steadily spread from mid-'70s NYC was the DJ. Increasingly a musician in his or her own right, it was pioneers like the Jamaican born DJ Kool Herc who brought to the Bronx street parties huge portable sound systems equipped with two separate turntables, on which vinyl records could be 'scratched' to extend the rhythmic instrumental 'breaks' during which the 'B-Boys' (the 'B' signifying these all important 'breaks') could show off their athletic dance moves. DJ Kool Herc himself was nearing the end of his teens when he got the South Bronx firmly in the groove but the Hip Hop stars who followed, as the term 'B-*Boys*' suggests, were full-on youth, *Absolute Beginners*. Young, Hip not Hippy, the stars of this new musical genre and subculture were ready and able to take on the world – and win. But they would have to be patient: although already laying down a soundtrack for the desolate Bronx in the mid '70s it would take until the early '80s before DJ Run Love (born 1964), Jam-Master J (born 1965) and Darryl 'D.M.C.' McDaniels (born 1964) would see *Run-D.M.C.* go to gold.

Another musical genre and subculture which would have at its heart the use of the turntable as an instrument – also elevating the role of the DJ and that of dance – was Disco. And, yet again, its evolution begins in the unpromising conditions of near bankrupt '70s New York.

But we need a little back-story to set the scene. In the early hours of June 28th 1969 the NYPD was raiding yet another homosexual hangout. On this occasion it was the dingy little Stonewall Inn down in The Village but this time the police were in for a surprise: when they emerged from the Stonewall Inn with their arrested drag queens the handful of officers found themselves hugely outnumbered by a large angry crowd which had gathered on the street chanting 'Gay Pride'. In time this incident prompted a strategic shift on the part of New York's mayor who, aware that the city's huge and growing Gay population constituted a not to be ignored voting block, restrained the police from raiding any and all Gay establishments and clubs.

The result was a mushrooming of small Gay clubs where an anything goes atmosphere prevailed – knowing that a police raid was now extremely unlikely. Reportedly there was wall to wall sex fueled by amyl nitrate 'poppers' and cocaine. And there was non-stop high energy music played, as with Hip Hop, off a duel set of turntables to ensure that there were no awkward gaps between one record and the next. 'Disco' music as such didn't exist in the mid '70s, but the unrelenting percussion of the lush 'Philly Sound' coupled with Jazz fusion influences, like the bop till you drop cool heat of Cameroonian saxophonist Manu Dibango's irresistible 'Soul Makossa' (1972), set the stage for Disco's unsyncopated 'four on the floor' sound and packed out the sweaty dance floors of NYC's thriving Gay clubs and parties.

But by 1977 'Disco' was seen by the wider world as straight as John Travolta's greased back hair and as white as his three-piece *Saturday Night Fever* suit. Travolta's 19 year old Tony Manero works in a hardware store in Brooklyn by day, and only glimpses the good life in the glittering light of the mirror ball of the 2001 Space Odyssey Disco on a Saturday night.

If *Saturday Night Fever* recast Disco as part of a gritty, working-class lifestyle, the opening of Studio 54 in the heart of Manhattan – also in 1977 – made it synonymous with the rich and famous. To the blinding glare of paparazzi flashbulbs, Bianca Jagger celebrated her thirty-second birthday by making an entrance on the back of a white horse. As was evident in Studio 54's emblem, depicting a glittering 'Man in the Moon' with a silver spoon positioned under his nose, the drug of choice in the hedonistic world of uptown, upmarket Disco was cocaine.

Providing an instant (but short-lived) hit of sexy, confident, on top of the world energy, cocaine was far removed from the contemplate your navel Hippy drugs of the late '60s. Dazzlingly expensive, best enjoyed when snorted up in a tightly rolled $100 bill, cocaine was the most telling sign of all that the anti-materialism (arguably naive, often embarrassing but heartfelt and some of us thought timely) which the Hippies had promoted in the late '60s was now officially out of fashion.

So too that decade's idealism and principled concern

for the well-being of others. Disco's hedonism heralded a brave new world focused on the individual self and founded on the principle that, in the words of L'Oréal's famous punch line, I (simply because I can afford it) am 'worth it'. While as Hippies we had the decency at least to feel a bit of puritanical guilt about our middle class, economically privileged status, the party on, if you've got it flaunt it world of Studio 54 floated on a silver cloud of never-ending guilt free indulgence.

Tom Wolfe famously called the '70s 'The Me Decade' and, especially when we enter the time machine and set the controls to transport us to Studio 54 in the late '70s, we see that (as is so often the case with Wolfe's social commentaries) he is spot on. Certainly in comparison with the idealism of the '60s – which, while rarely shunning sex, drugs and Rock 'n' Roll, did also pause to consider the world beyond the individual self – the '70s stand out as the moment of transition away from 'Us' and towards 'I'.

But, as Jay McInerney's *Bright Lights Big City* (1984), Tom Wolfe's *Bonfires of the Vanities* (1987) or Oliver Stone's *Wall Street* (1987) make more than clear, this self-centered 'Greed Is Good' worldview which took root in the '70s then went on to become the mainstream creed and driving force of the '80s. Elected President in 1981, Ronald Reagan and his 'neocon' chums saw the liberal '60s as the time when everything started to go to hell in a handcart and they explicitly set out to shape the '80s into a mirror opposite antidote to the sharing, caring, commie loving, give away your possessions and reawaken your spiritual self Hippy nonsense of the '60s.

To accomplish this Reagan would cut taxes and 'get the government off people's backs'. Well, at least the backs of the rich people. Across the pond, Britain's first female Prime Minister Margaret Thatcher wholeheartedly agreed: pointing out that there is 'no such thing as society, only individuals and their families'. What was needed was simply to unleash individual enterprise and thereby liberate capitalism to its full potential. First off, obviously, was to undo all those unnecessary, fuddy-duddy government restrictions which needlessly tied the hands of the clever 'Masters of the Universe', who would then push down on the accelerator and show what the souped-up hot rod of capitalism could really do. Wealth would be unbounded – and it would 'trickle down' into even the pockets of the poor who would themselves become home owners, Wall Street speculators and credit card flashing consumers. What could possibly go wrong?

Chapter 11

2022

It's the late '80s and we're having a picnic in a never completed, derelict suburban housing development on the outskirts of Palm Springs, California. As you do. To amuse ourselves and each other we take turns telling stories – stories about being in a supermarket checkout when the atom bombs start going off, or about being a lesbian trapped in a man's body, stories about the planet 'Texlahoma' where 'kids do drugs and practice the latest dance crazes at the local lake', and 'where the year is permanently 1974, the year after the oil shock and the one from which real wages in the US never grew ever again'. And, yes, stories seeping 'Boomer Envy' on the part of a new, post-Boomer generation – the first since at least the war to realize that 'our parents had more'. Born in the '60s, part of the 'Baby Bust' generation which came as the pill and a feeling that there were other things to do than have kids and raise a family took hold, we're characters in Douglas Coupland's cult 1991 novel *Generation X: Tales from an Accelerated Culture*.

Coupland (born 1961) initially, erroneously attributed the label 'Generation X' to the British Punk musician Billy Idol (born William Michael Albert Broad in 1955), who was lead singer in the band he formed in 1976 with Tony James and John Towe which they called 'Generation X'. In fact, Idol (once a neighbor of mine and to whom I still owe several taxi fares) had nicked the title from a 1965 sociology book in his mother's library written by Jane Deverson and Charles Hamblett which lambasted '60s teens – Baby Boomers – as adolescent degenerates who had sex before marriage, didn't believe in God, respected neither their parents nor even, heaven forbid, the Queen.

The young Canadian Coupland recycled the Generation X label to refer to those who, like him, had been born *after* the great baby boom, who felt themselves to be a distinct, culturally differentiated generation and who – like Generation Punk in London in the late '70s – were fed up with being forever bracketed together with and living in the shadow of the Boomers. An amusing, strangely disturbing novel, *Generation X: Tales from an Accelerated Culture*, depicts young adult Americans in the late '80s who, while highly (arguably even overly) educated and from comfortable, affluent family backgrounds, find themselves mired in going nowhere 'McJobs' and increasingly aware that modernism's great dream of perpetually onwards and upwards economic advancement is now kaput and that their generation in all likelihood faces a future which is *less* rather than more affluent, and *less* rather than more promising than that of their parents.

These are young Americans stuck up some strange yet strangely familiar cul-de-sac, in a broken down Chevy which is unfortunately beyond repair. Bummer. Yet in Coupland's telling, unlike Generation Punk in the '70s, America's '80s Generation X for the most part deflected or sublimated any obvious seething anger at their unenviable situation – only occasionally letting-off steam in the form of senseless but for the most part insignificant vandalism. These are not irate Punks screaming, gobbing and kicking furiously at life's limitations, irritations and existential futility. Here instead is an overly affected yet strangely affectless post-modern lifestyle in which everything is recycled from the past – especially from that much treasured golden idyll of the '50s – but always given an ironic, shoulder shrugging, 'time cannibalizing' (in Coupland's perceptive phrase) twist.

Determined never, ever to be caught out in that heartfelt, fully-committed but (seen retrospectively) somewhat foolish purposefulness of the late '60s Hippies, Coupland's Generation X heroes (of sorts, but neither are they anti-heroes) are like extraterrestrial anthropologists observing yet never fully participating in '80s America. They collect odd, seemingly (but never actually) random objects which might find pride of place in some museum back on their home planet – Viva Las Vegas booties, a black rotary dial phone, '60s PVC floral appliqué earrings, a jar of souvenir matchbooks, a Venetian gondolier's shirt or a bottle of Honolulu Choo-Choo Pink nail polish – and they talk, 24/7, in the manner of characters in a perfectly scripted TV situation comedy.

One is tempted to think that the likes of Andy, Claire and Dag are simply the product of a clever writer's imagination, but as marketing men and women begged Coupland to translate *Generation X* into a fully-articulated blueprint for maximizing sales to this newly defined target market (and were by all accounts spurned) it became clear that this glimpse of a post-Boomer, post-modern present-future was more fact than fiction. Films like the shoestring budgeted, plotless, aimless yet, like, totally spot-on *Slacker* (set in Austin, Texas, also appearing in 1991, directed by and featuring 1960 born Gen Xer Richard Linklater) and an endless sequence of cinematic imitators further confirmed that Coupland had identified rather than simply imagined a significant sociological phenomenon.

Perhaps in the greater scheme of things what is most significant about *Generation X* is not the particular ethnographic peculiarities by which this group of late 20th century young adults might be identified, but rather the fact that the notion of generation remains a – *the* – key feature which binds together an 'Us' in an age of ever-increasing individualism. To Baby Boomers like me the significance of generation as the crucial tie which binds more cohesively than any other socio-cultural glue seems a natural, inevitable phenomenon. But just as historians are (rightly, as we have seen throughout this book) dubious about the idea that history is neatly bundled into discreet decades, so too we need to recognize that the stream of history is not inevitably broken-up by fixed, definitive points which neatly mark the end of one generation and the beginning of another. In the normal flow of history it is difficult if not impossible to meaningfully bracket off a generational unit of which those born between specific years can and will feel a part. Only real, particular and exceptional demographic or profound historical events make such a generational identity something more than journalistic whim or advertising-speak lingo.

The 20th century provided two such unarguable and obvious generational markers – both a product of war. The tragic 'Lost Generation' came out of the horror of the First World War with far fewer young men than women; begetting spinsters like my own Aunt Charlotte and, on my mother's side of the family, Aunt Agnes whose failure to marry seemed such a mystery until, years later, one appreciated the sad demographics of their situation. Of course the other obvious generation produced by 20th century demographics was the Baby Boomers: so it comes as little surprise that, on top of everything else, the Boomers bestowed upon the world the presumption that the division of history into discreet generational bundles is a natural and inevitable reality.

But although less statistically dramatic, Douglas Coupland's Generation Xers do themselves have a shared demographic reality. In the US and elsewhere in the developed West there was a marked *downturn* in the birthrate from the late '50s until the late '70s, when the birthrate once again began to rise (but nowhere near as spectacularly as it did in the years immediately following the war). Whether the shift downward was simply generated by the advent of 'The Pill' or, as seems more likely, a heightened desire to remain footloose and fancy free (with the aid of 'The Pill' as it became more generally available in the early '60s), isn't so important to our story as the fact that anyone born from about 1957 onwards will typically start to have fewer siblings and will increasingly inhabit a world that (unlike early '50s America, which crammed plenty of kids and babies into every ad for station wagons or for soft drinks consumed around the family barbecue) was less focused on the family and on the joys of procreation. Insofar as the future will be dominated by China rather than America, it will be 'The After-Eighty Generation' born after the introduction of the one-child policy who will become the new generational force in shaping the perception and the reality of history – these cosseted, economically better off 'Little Emperors', like the 'Baby Bust' members of Generation X a product of sudden demographic *shrinkage* rather than expansion.

The other interesting point about post-Boomer generations is the extraordinary extent to which they are speeding up. Perhaps this is what Coupland is referring to in his subtitle *'Notes for an Accelerated Culture'*. Neither London's teenage Punks nor America's Generation X were a generation on from the Boomers in biological terms. It would only be 'Generation Y' – born in the late '60s and early '70s to Boomer parents – who could once again lay claim to a biological rather than purely cultural notion of 'generation'.

Generation Y? Yes, and hold onto your hats because intrepid market researchers have already got Generation Z (born in the '90s and '00s, on-line and plugged into the World Wide Web from birth) cross-haired within their rifle sites. But what then? Never fear, help is at hand: in 2009, ahead of the pack once again, Douglas Coupland brought out his thirteenth novel *Generation A*. Generous as usual, Coupland gives us the true source of this new title in an epigraph:

'Now you young twerps want a new name for your generation? Probably not, you just want jobs, right? Well, the media do us all such tremendous favors when they call you Generation X, right? Two clicks from the very end of the alphabet. I hereby declare you Generation A, as much at the beginning of a series of astonishing triumphs and failures as Adam and Eve were so long ago.' This wonderful insight is from a commencement address at Syracuse University given by Kurt Vonnegut way back in 1994.

Coupland's *Generation A* is set some time in the future (no specific dates are given) when life really is entirely dominated by the internet and when bees have become extinct. While thinking that Coupland is all too likely to be correct about the god-like omnipotence of the internet and the disappearance of bees, I wonder if he has got it right about the seemingly endless need for new generational labels. China's 'Little Emperors' aside, could it not be that when the demographic blips which marked the starting points of both the Boomers and Generation X have been smoothed over by history there will be no obvious or significant markers to set apart specific generations and that, moreover, there will be other cohesives to bind collective identities together?

Or, perhaps, no binding cohesives whatsoever to counter that jet rocketed propulsion of individualism which began in 'The Me Decade' (Tom Wolfe) of the '70s. For beyond the marketing men/women's dream of a whole world which can be labeled and targeted, beyond too that part of the population which really does feel comfortable within the cozy duvet of 'Gen X' or 'Gen Y', one senses a present-future populated by evermore atomized individuals and a vast, impenetrable, red-shift expanse of cosmos between each and every human being. Could it be that, at least in the West (insofar as the notion of 'The West' will itself exist in the future) the final dying off of the Boomers will mark the end not only of a particular generation but of the importance of the notion of generation itself?

In my studies of streetstyle I am continually urged to take note of new 'cults', 'subcultures' or 'tribes' which, if you believe the journalists, marketing researchers and 'cool hunters' (?!) are perpetually pouring out of the woodwork like battalions of cockroaches. And if one looks to places like Japan or South America one sees that, indeed, there are new, exciting subcultures to investigate – ones which ultimately challenge the neo-colonial cultural view that streetstyle is a uniquely American and British phenomenon. But nine times out of ten, especially when looking closer to home, it appears that these highly-hyped new subcultures are in fact simply the imaginative creation of journalists and marketing people desperate to track down and nail with a name some previously unidentified emerging 'tribe'. For me a key tool in distinguishing between the imagined and the real is to consider how many people are in fact actually happy to put their hands up and say 'I am a Chav', 'I am a Grebo', 'I am an Emo', 'I am a Hipster', 'I am a New Raver', 'I am an Indie Boho', or whatever new subculture has been recently identified on the horizon.

Likewise, when it comes to the question of whether and to what extent post-Boomers have and will see their generational peers (their 'birth cohorts') as their 'tribe', I think it unlikely that the sort of full-on 'I Am A Boomer And Proud Of It' group identity will survive – or at least survive with the same enthusiasm – in a post-Boomer world. Identifiable as they are as a specific generation at a specific point in history, I even wonder if Coupland's Andy, Claire and Dag would see it as a very Generation X thing to do to enthusiastically proclaim to all and sundry 'I Am A Generation Xer And Proud Of It' (the enthusiastic proclaiming of anything, one would have thought, a most unlikely Gen X characteristic). And, however much marketing and advertising people might wish it were true, I find it equally hard to believe that there really are real people out there in the real world who embrace the label 'Generation Y' – and now 'Generation Z' and 'Generation A' – as enthusiastically as my generation proudly proclaimed and carrying on proclaiming (to our dying breathes one expects) our shared group identity as 'Boomers'.

Nor do we have to hypothesize about the future in order to find examples of people whose sense of identity is not primarily bracketed within parameters of 'generation'. My sister Nancy was born in 1959, and when asked if she sees herself as either a Boomer or an Xer replies 'neither, we're sort of in-between all that'. So too the latest addition to the pantheon of great American fictional characters, Patty and Walter Berglund – the focal point of Jonathan Franzen's 2010 novel *Freedom*.

Like Nancy – and as far as one can tell, give or take a year or two, Patty and Walter Berglund – Jonathan Franzen was born in 1959. Traditionally the baby boom has been seen to stretch from 1946 to 1960 – or even 1964. Yet the birth rate in the US was decreasing from about 1957 and, especially with the late 20th century's sense of an ever accelerating pace of history, it seems quite a stretch to lump together those initial Boomers like me born in the late '40s with those born more than a decade later. Compare our cultural reference points: from Rock 'n' Roll to

Punk, from lineal modernist 'direction' and 'progress' to chaotic post-modern fragmentation, diversity and throttle back to retro mode. That is to say, from the sexy all-in-one jumpsuits and gleaming futuristic machinery of '50s sci-fi to the bleak dystopian rubble of *Jubilee* and *Blade Runner* (or, with a cheeky, playful, post-modern twist, 'The Rocky Horror Show'). From *I Love Lucy* to *The Addams Family*. From ever-upward economic expansion to the oil crises and world-wide recession of the '70s. From racial segregation, the Cold War, Vietnam and Flower Power to ongoing problems of racial integration, feminism, Gay & Lesbian rights and the ever-darkening shadow of ecological catastrophe. In 1965 when I graduated from high school and went off to university, the music charts were topped by The Righteous Brothers ('Unchained Melody'), The Rolling Stones ('Cant Get No Satisfaction') and The Beatles ('Help', 'Yesterday' and 'Ticket to Ride'). In 1977 when I'm guessing Patty Berglund (nee Emerson) graduated from high school and went off to Macalester College in Minnesota, the US music charts were dominated by The Eagles ('Hotel California'), Donna Summer ('I Feel Love'), Boney M ('Ma Baker') with The Beatles transformed into Wings ('Mull of Kintyre').

Nor does it seem a fluke or simple coincidence that the first 21st century equivalent of Gatsby, Rabbit or Tony Soprano turns out to be (in my sister's phrase) a generational 'in-betweener': Patty Emerson-Berglund (university basketball star with a brain, liberal pit-bull with lipstick soccer mum, cookie-baking, tire-slashing MILF) shines so brightly at least in part because she isn't constrained or overshadowed by generational stereotypes. For better or worse Patty is on her own trying to hack a path through the tangled undergrowth of life at the end of the 20th and beginning of the 21st centuries. And my guess is, China's 'Little Emperors' aside, the generationally uncategorized and uncategorizable in-betweener Patty, rather than the neatly boxed inhabitants of Generations X, Y, Z or A, is the more likely prototype for the future – both the absence of clear demographic markers of generational distinction and the ever-growing addiction to unchained individualism pointing to a Patty or a Walter making their own DIY way in the world.

And what a strange, brave new world it is in which Patty and Walter Berglund (and, the third point of their relationship triangle and contemporary, Richard Katz) are trying to make their way in in the late '80s/ early '90s. The '60s (Don Draper and Hugh Hefner at least as much as Abbie Hoffman and Jim Morrison) and the '70s and early '80s (Ronald Reagan and Margaret Thatcher at least as much as Punk and Disco) had torn up the old, once sacrosanct rulebook of how life should be lived, and then failed spectacularly to find any helpful, coherent guidelines to put in its place. Whether they want to or not, Dag, Claire, Andy, Walter, Patty and Richard have to start from scratch in the process of reinventing themselves and the world they hope to inhabit – lacking even that obvious, knee-jerk direction of rebellion which shaped the 'alternative' lifestyles of Beats, Hippies and Punks. Indeed, in an age when even the extraterrestrial style and up yours attitude of the Punks had been New Waved into the mainstream, how to define and how to credit even the possibility of rebellion?

As is perfectly in keeping with this era of diversity and infinite alternative alternatives, Patty and Walter Berglund plot a very different course than that of the seemingly endlessly singletons and perpetually rootless migrants of Generation X: restoring a ramshackle Victorian property in a suburban flighted downtown neighborhood of St. Paul, Minnesota and, within this rooted context, trying to figure out how one goes about marriage, parenting, being 'good neighbors' and caring about the planet in an age when, on the one hand, their parents' presumptions and hopes had been discredited and, on the other, no clear signposting of the way ahead is discernible. While I question the extent to which Patty, Walter, Richard, Claire, Dag and Andy might identify themselves as a coherent generation the way the Boomers did and do, they do clearly share a unique historical context and challenge – one which, to a degree never experienced previously throughout all of human history, comes with no owner's manual to explain how life should be lived; no unquestionable dos and don'ts, only the freedom to choose . . . whatever.

And at least in the case of *Freedom*'s birth cohorts, no sense of any form of shared, meaningful group identity whatsoever. Patty, Walter and Richard are post-generational and post-subcultural – neither Boomers, Xers, Hippies nor Punks. Neither, unlike their ancestors, are they safely cosseted within the collective embrace of a particular religion, political party, ethnicity, class, race, region or nationality. We can of course tick off their proper place on a census form – born late '50s, college educated, middle class, white, non-believers, left-wing, Americans – but none of these facts of their lives give them a shared, sustaining collectivity which encloses them in a meaningful 'Us', 'People Like Us'. And it is this refusal or inability to see themselves as part of and to conform to some generational or subcultural 'tribe' which gives them that same *Freedom* which is both their liberation and their nemesis.

Margaret Thatcher famously proclaimed 'there is no such thing as society, only individuals and their families'. Terrifyingly, this may have been the one thing she got right and, arguably for many, this was but the start of a downward spiral. For even before the 20th century was finished, even before middle-age had them fully in its clutches, Walter and Patty Berglund, having invested so much of their lives and energy in the creation of The New Improved American Family, begin to doubt even the comforting existence of the family in Thatcher's bleak prognosis.

Which leaves just lone, solitary, atomized individuals – *Atomised* being the title of a novel by the French writer Michel Houellebecq which comes at our age from a very different, European, cosmopolitan perspective than does Franzen's Freedom, but also raises the spectre of a world where every man and woman is indeed an island. The '60s had seen the loss – or at least the diminishing – of so many traditional foci of shared, communal identity (for example, the shift from ethnic urban neighborhoods to homogenous middle class suburbs) but strove to put the 'Us' of generation – 'My Generation'; 'Never Trust Anyone Over 35' – in their place. Now, judging by the characters of *Freedom*, *Atomised* and so much of 21st century fiction and film, even the 'Us' of 'My Generation' has gone, leaving only the infinite freedom and utter isolation of 'My Way'.

As with the significance of generation as a focus for shared identity, I suspect that the significance of 'youth culture' will want to be revised – downwards – when the last of the Boomers who claim to have been at Woodstock finally passes on to the great Rock festival in the sky. 'Youth Culture' and its unique place as the wellspring of all that is hip and happening has been such a fundamental tenet of belief – a law of nature beyond dispute – since the mid '50s that it often comes as a shock to realize that throughout the vast expanse of human history such a view would have been seen as laughable.

Do you remember, way back at the start of our story in 1947, when the Parisian designer Christian Dior unveiled his 'New Look'? Specifically, do you recall that both Dior's models and his prospective customers were grown *women* rather than adolescent *girls*? Indeed, in 1947 the fact that fashion was for adults would have seemed a very odd thing to comment upon or question. Throughout its history fashion had always concerned itself with adults.

So too every other facet of culture. For pop music, as we have already seen, the big change came in America in the mid '50s when the birth of Rock 'n' Roll coincided – collided – with Madison Avenue's new fixation on the 'teenager' as the ultimate target market. At this point the Boomers were themselves still pre-adolescent children but, when in the early '60s their lifecycle brought them to this magical age, the equation of adolescence and pop music became axiomatic and, seemingly, a marriage made in heaven.

Fashion took a little while longer to throw overboard its traditional focus on adults but when it happened – most obviously in the heady swirl of Swinging London which climaxed in the mid '60s – it set in motion a pursuit of ever-younger models and customers which is with us still today (most worryingly, with catwalk models who are barely even into their teenage years and an ideal of size 0 beauty which, devoid of womanly curves, keeps fashion firmly within the timeframe of adolescence).

Throughout the sixty-plus years since Dior re-established Paris (for a time) as the undisputed world capital of fashion, a kaleidoscope of different 'looks' has come and gone and, in recent years, the nature, reference points and function of fashion have changed so radically that one wonders if fashion in any meaningful sense of the term has not itself gone out of fashion – its present self now arguably better characterized as 'style'. Yet throughout all this time, not once in my memory, has the question been seriously raised as to whether at some point it might make sense to recalibrate the fashion/style system so that it is once again catering to the needs of adults rather than teenagers. After all: while the '60s saw swelling, bulging numbers of teens, we are now in a demographic situation where, compared to the number of adults, adolescents are an increasingly insignificant target market.

Again, the same point could be made with regard to any and all facets of our culture – from product design to cuisine, television to computer games, cinema to art. In the late '50s and early '60s, especially in America (a young country flexing its post-war biceps) or Britain (an old country enjoying the spectacle of its Old Guard finally outflanked) it would have seemed absurd and irrational to question the vibrant energy and creative/demographic power of youth and its dance around the clock 'youth culture'. But is this still the case today in the 21st century? Those within the establishments of marketing, advertising, fashion, design, popular music, the media and so forth will likely give a knee-jerk dismissive response to such a question, but is it really all that wise or productive – or even logical – to presume that the creative pursuits of any civilization are best, always, placed in the hands of those who, by definition, have little if any experience of adult life to draw upon?

Interestingly, I suspect that those who would scoff the loudest at such a questioning of the intrinsic and eternal value of 'youth culture', are not themselves young. From what I see and hear there is nothing which puts off and irritates today's adolescents more than when they are specifically targeted as 'youth' – when products and advertisements are all too cack-handedly directed at some magic kingdom/ghetto fenced in by age. No, here again what seems to be the case is that presumptions written in conceptual concrete during the Golden Age of Youth in the '50s and '60s, have been placed beyond doubt by Oldies who themselves cannot conceive of life defined by any parameters other than age.

The evidence of this inability to move beyond the presumed glories of youth and to grow-up litters the landscape of life at the end of the 20th century and start of the 21st. Media pundits and market researchers have identified the 'Kidult' as a (if not the) decade defining figure of the Noughties: middle-aged-plus grown men and women who pounce on any and all innovations favored by the young and, like those who would steal candy from babies, make them their own. Oldies who ought to know better on skateboards, wearing back to front baseball caps, wolfing down tabs of Ecstasy, their iPods blaring the latest Grime or Lady Gaga. And it's hard to find an ad for pensions or life assurance which doesn't feature leather-clad Boomers roaring past on Harley Davidsons or bungee jumping grannies wearing Hip Hop approved upmarket label tracksuits. In the 21st century youth culture is everywhere – except perhaps amongst those who are actually not yet old enough to be Kidults (but then, as they always used to say, youth is too good to be wasted on the young).

Jonathan Franzen's *Freedom* also offers a telling example of life lived in an era when the definition of 'youth' has become so plastic as to lose all boundaries and meaning. Walter Berglund's lifelong friend Richard Katz is a pop/Indie/post-punk/alt country musician (note the po mo refusal to be bracketed within a single genre) who only finds big-time success in his forties. Unmarried, perpetually on the make, drawn periodically to drugs and chaos, Richard perfected his teen rebel lifestyle when he actually was a teen but saw absolutely no reason to grow-up and out of this lifestyle, even when fully in the grip of middle-age. Nor does his age put off even his teenage fans: the point being that, by the end of the 20th century and the start of the 21st, one need have no fear of passing some *Absolute Beginners* age-graded cut off point. Now age *has* lost its sting. Or, perhaps more realistically, 'age' and 'youth culture' (like that which can be described as 'awesome') have now simply floated free of any moorings in reality.

And so, even as the population tilts into an unprecedented level of aging, the cry of 'youth' – or 'Yooof' as we say in Britain – grows ever louder. But make no mistake: our population *is* aging and to an extent never seen before. Opinion seems divided (at least in 2011 when I am writing this) on exactly *how* catastrophic it will be when the first army of Boomers start retiring in just a few years time, but it doesn't take a genius to see that, at best and with a great deal of luck, the next fifteen years or so will be challenging to individuals and governments. On top of the baby boom itself, improved life expectancy means that a mind-boggling number of Oldies will live in a world sustained economically by a proportionately smaller young and middle-aged workforce. And so, as if Richard, Patty, Walter, Dag, Claire and Andy didn't have enough problems (existential sat nav malfunction, decline of the American Empire, recession, dwindling oil and mineral resources, global warming, etc.) they are also navigating middle-age with the weight of an unprecedented population of Boomer Oldies resting heavily upon their and their children's shoulders.

Obviously, as the number of Oldies increases so too will pension, social security and health care costs. And this during a period when 'developed' countries like America, Britain and those in Western Europe will find their economies increasingly challenged (if not threatened) by the 'emerging' economies of China, India, Brazil and Russia. All of it, as fate would have it, against the continuing if not growing mountain of government (and personal) debt, built-up throughout the boom years and then batted out of the ballpark by the collapse of the banks and the ensuing recession of 2008/9/10/11(12?). I find myself wondering what the world – and, in particular, that suburban American world I grew-up in – will look like in, say, 2022 when a Boomer like myself born in 1947 would be 75 –

a date when, presumably at long last, just about enough Boomers will have switched off their Xboxs for good finally to have reduced our generation's extraordinary and history-shaping demographic blip to something approaching the norm.

I haven't been back to Neptune New Jersey since the mid '90s when, both parents now gone, my brother, sister and I got together to clear-out the family home before it was sold. A telling and difficult moment: my brother, sister and I had all moved far away from Neptune and now, the last relics of our family's past divided up, taken to charity shops or dumped, we would no longer have an on-going link with the suburban town in which we had all grown up. This was a hard time for all three of us but it was also a shocking time for me. Living in London for so many years, my visits back to Neptune had been increasingly rare and fleeting. More perhaps than my brother and sister, who continued to live in north-eastern America, I had come to see Neptune exclusively in terms of my memories of growing up there in the '50s and '60s.

In the '90s, looked at with adult, foreign eyes, Neptune seemed so alien and, in contrast to that optimistic modernism and comparative prosperity from the era of my youth, so shabby. Houses in the neighborhood where I'd grown up (houses which had been built in the '50s and '60s) now in the '90s – at least to my eyes – seemed tatty and, if not falling apart, at least poorly maintained. The futuristic stainless steel architectural marvel which had once been Carvel ice cream was now deserted except that, driving by, you could see that it had become storage for a mismatched collection of cardboard boxes. More than this, whole shopping centers – once greeted with wide-eyed wonder as harbingers of a shiny, sci-fi, futuristic future – now lay deserted (as can be seen across America in the startling www.deadmalls.com). And neighboring Asbury Park, once one of America's premier seaside resorts, had become a place of danger and despair – its huge boardwalk (where on an Easter Sunday in the '50s hundreds if not thousands of well-heeled women would proudly promenade to show off their Easter bonnets) now in the '90s empty, decaying and foreboding.

From a British or European perspective one presumed that America's wealth and prosperity was on an ever-upward trajectory but, seeing Neptune in the '90s, I was struck by the extent that, at least here on the Northeast Coast, this prosperity seemed thin on the ground. Or, more to the point, very unevenly distributed. And, to pick up on one of the points Douglas Coupland drives home in *Generation X*, in marked contrast to its strong upward arc in the '50s, the real income of Middle America had been in decline since the mid '70s. Returning to suburban America now in the '90s after a long period of absence, I was bowled over by the gap between the reality of what had become of my home town and my own memories and childhood expectations of what its future would hold.

But enough of the past, hang-on to your seats as we

kick the time machine into warp drive and set the controls for Neptune New Jersey USA in 2022 . . .

Isn't it fantastic to see all these Boomers peddling away on their bicycles? Good for the heart. Not that they have much choice of course – certainly not the ones who failed to put enough into their pensions, or saw their savings virtually wiped out in the '00s recession or by the stagflation of the '10s. Even as someone familiar with the price of petrol in Britain and Europe in the good old days, it comes as a shock to see what the combination of dwindling oil reserves, rising demand from the newly developed economies and the declining value of the dollar against the Yuan have done to the price of filling up your tank. Sure there are plenty of hybrids and little cars running on electricity, bio-fuels or heaven only knows what, but the bottom line is it's now expensive to get from A to B and increasingly in 2022 the citizens of sprawling American suburbs like Neptune are thinking that maybe it wasn't such a great idea back in the '50s, '60s and '70s to design a world where A and B were located as far apart as possible.

On the plus side there are now neighborhoods in Neptune where trips to the supermarket are pooled and coordinated. You even see where a couple in one suburban home, whether out of kindness or the need to make a few spare bucks, have set up a delivery service for their neighbors; their home a kind of corner shop. Buses and other forms of public transport are inefficient and expensive in such a low population density environment – especially so where there is no single town center to and from which the majority of journeys are to be made. Not that the government has the money or the will to invest in public transport anyway.

The biggest problem for Neptune as a whole, however, is that those who bring money into the community by commuting up to New York are finding it hard to finance such long journeys. The Garden State Parkway no longer sees rush hour traffic like in the old days. Yes, you can bicycle to the train station in Asbury Park and an increasing number do just that but, given that the government is so strapped for cash and that the politicians don't dare cut back on Medicare for fear of putting off their Boomer voters, there has just never been anything like the kind of investment needed to get America back on the rails.

Isn't it ironic that, after all those decades of 'urban flight', we now have 'suburban flight' where especially the upwardly mobile young are pouring back into the cities? No expensive commute and, let's face it, suburbs like Neptune are increasingly just full of boring Old Boomers – most of whom can't afford to get out of the suburbs which, in many areas, have become low-density slums.

So the urban environment is choc-a-bloc with hip young things (who are increasingly pissed off at paying ever-increasing taxes for the sake of keeping the Old Boomers alive) while suburbs like Neptune which seemed so futuristic and with it in the '50s and '60s are now full of the old, the poor and those who are both old and poor – their ancient gas guzzling cars rusting in the driveway, the garage converted to storage for stuff they desperately hope to sell for parts or whatever might make a few precious bucks. For those that can afford one, the garage has found a new function as the place where you charge-up your electric 'mobility scooter' (complete with that now mandatory 'Baby Boomer on Board' sticker). For those who can't, the place where you keep your bicycle and shopping cart to pull along behind.

Perhaps most startling of all is the way that so many of these suburban lawns (front as well as back) are now being used to grow vegetables – and/or that always valuable cash crop, marijuana. Some folks have converted their garages into chicken coops. Thanks to the internet and to neighbors swapping information between themselves everyone is now an expert on gardening and compost. Again, for millions there was simply no choice: when the price of oil started going up so did the price of food (doubly so as evermore agricultural land was used in the production of biofuels) and, for a heck of a lot of Boomers, the pension and the savings just wouldn't stretch far enough.

Of course everyone had thought they would supplement their pensions with some part-time work but the problem is that, as has been the Boomers' plight at each and every stage of their lives, there are so many other Boomers trying to do the same thing at exactly the same time. So the Walmarts and such like know full well that, even for the minimum wage, there will always be plenty of Boomers lined-up begging for their jobs.

Of course loads of the Boomers figured that, especially when the cost of transport became prohibitive, they would make money by doing something clever on the internet from their homes. Once again, the numerical odds were against them: millions and millions of Boomers sat staring at their computer screens or smart phones all trying to come up with that big, new killer idea or app which eluded all the others. Naturally a few Boomers did make money from home – some a lot of it – but as people had begun to realize even back in the '00s, it's easy to do stuff on the internet but a tricky and exceptional thing actually to make money from it (as even the likes of Facebook – remember them? – discovered in the late '10s).

And suburban property prices are going through the floor. All those Old Boomers figured how when the time came that they needed to go into a home they would just sell-up the early '60s 'Ranch' and it would provide the funds for the final part of life's long journey. No way! As has already been said, the new trend is to city life, the suburbs being so last century. But the real nail in the coffin, if you'll excuse the expression, was simply the fact that there were so many Old Boomers trying to sell-up at precisely the same time. Housing prices in places like Neptune were bound to fall. And to make matters worse, so many of these houses which sprang up overnight in the '60s – what had once been a farm suddenly sporting 'Split-level', 'Ranch' and 'Cape Cod' model homes; then hundreds more materializing within just months – were never built to last.

And most certainly never built for fuel-efficiency, so you see a lot of these Boomers just holed-up in one heated room throughout the winter. Or you occasionally see a bunch of Boomers all shacked up in one house. More sadly, you see whole neighborhoods where buildings are just falling apart and plastic sheets cover leaking roofs which no one can afford to fix. Neighborhoods which back in the '60s were seen as modern and solidly middle class are now, a lifetime later, ghettos of the poor. There's even talk of knocking down some of these developments and converting them back into farmland – making New Jersey once again 'The Garden State' (a continuation of the conversion back to farmland which started happening in the city of Detroit way back in the '00s).

This grim situation isn't made any better by the fact that, unlike their own parents, the Boomers typically didn't have many children. And what children that there were, this being America the land of perpetual geographic mobility, have long since moved half way across the country. Once upon a time, getting back to see the old folks for the occasional holiday or to help out in a period of illness was just a matter of getting on a plane. Now, however, the price of aviation fuel being what it is, such long distance travel has become exceptional rather than commonplace. No, today the Boomers have to fend for themselves – and each other. Out of necessity a new community spirit is being kindled but, however necessary and encouraging, this too is an uphill struggle in a landscape and infrastructure designed around cheap gas and the fundamental desire to see as much lawn as possible between yourself and your neighbors.

Did no one see this coming? Of course they did, but back in the '90s, '00s and even for most of the '10s it was just so inconceivable to Americans – for decades their default position being denial – that 'The American Way Of Life' might be separable from 'The Suburban Way of Life'. Two important articles in *The Atlantic Monthly* – 'No Country for Young Men' by Megan McArdle and 'The Next Slum?' by Christopher B. Leinberger – should have raised the alarm. And it's hard to see how the problem could be put more forcefully than the writer James Howard Kunstler does in the 2004 Canadian documentary *The End of Suburbia: Oil Depletion and the Collapse of The American Dream*: 'The whole suburban project I think can be summarized pretty succinctly as the greatest misallocation of resources in the history of the world. America took all of its post-war wealth and invested it in a living arrangement that has no future.'

But, hey, let's look on the bright side. It's a lovely summer day and already the roads and even one lane of Highway 33 are swarming with Oldies on bikes, trikes, mobility scooters and all manner of slow moving vehicles (some of which are very slow moving indeed). We've got us a convoy and everyone's headed for the beach.

Not the beach at Asbury Park: too upmarket for strapped for cash Oldies like us. And you never know when some yuppie will let pent-up anger at crippling taxes bubble up into outright aggression and a bit of 'Boomer Bashing' will kick-off. Ditto Ocean Grove which was headed upmarket even back in the '90s. No, it's Bradley Beach for us – known around these parts nowadays as 'Boomer Beach'. And the place is indeed booming in more ways than one. As if a soundtrack in a film, the moment we arrive the Beach Boys' 'Good Vibrations' is blaring from the sound system at 'Sid's CDs' – carrying over the whole beach, the police having given up on trying to get Sid to turn down the volume even before they gave up on trying to eject seniors without a beach badge.

On the beach a few old dears shake their booties to 'Good Vibrations' – enjoying themselves while they still can and if any of the now sadly dwindling number of men take any notice so much the better. Especially if he can be induced to haul his old ass up a ladder and fix the leaking roof in exchange for a bit of whoopee and maybe a big slice of home made lemon meringue pie.

All along the beach, spread out up and down the road, there are market stalls (some make-shift, some permanent) with Boomers selling anything from reconditioned computers to home-grown tomatoes. You name it – bike parts, dodgy meds, seeds, Viagra, fresh water to refill your vacuum flask, antique iPods, second-hand Zimmer Frames for next to nothing – somebody is selling it down here in the Do-It-Yourself retail experience which has increasingly replaced the supermarkets and shopping malls. And there are all manner of services on offer: legal or financial advice, repairmen touting their trade, some gigolos and hookers pretending to be something other than gigolos and hookers, a hairdresser, a tattooist, spiritual advisors, Born-Again Buddhists, rickshaws for hire, dance teachers, a body piercer, a never-say-die Hippy who will read your palm for a buck. Looks like one of those crowd scenes in *Blade Runner*. You could say that this market and the packed, noisy beach in front of it has become the town center which Neptune and all the other local suburban communities lacked for all these years – since the '50s when the great push into the farms and wide open spaces began; since these Boomers were small kids (the Boomers' lifecycle and the rise *and fall* of suburbia precisely coinciding).

Back in the '50s who would have thought that it might turn out like this? An organic, let's put the show on right here, do your own thing, grassroots development, this often chaotic, anarchic market and the sometimes unruly, eyebrow raising goings on down on the often crowded, no longer policed beach might be categorized as 'Third World'. Then again, if you've had a bit of weed or are just inclined towards seeing the glass half full rather than half empty, you might cast your eye over this strange state of affairs resulting from a perfect storm of demographics, economics and technological short-sightedness, and see it as nothing less than, at long last, the dawning of the Age of Aquarius.

Part I

Sources & Inspirations

Music

Late 40s

Live at the Hollywood Bowl - Duke Ellington [1947, US]
'Snatch and Grab It' - Julia Lee [1947, US]
'Good Rockin' Tonight' – Roy Brown [1947, US]
'Nature Boy' – Nat King Cole [1948, US]
'The Fat Man' – Fats Domino [1949, US]
Birdland jazz club opens December 15, 1949, NYC

50s

'Straight, No Chaser' – Thelonious Monk [1951, US]
Billie Holiday Sings - Billie Holiday [1952, US]
'That's All Right' – Elvis Presley [1954, US]
'Tutti Frutti' – Little Richard [1955, US]
Concorde - The Modern Jazz Quartet [1955, US]
'Rock Around the Clock' - Bill Haley and His Comets [1955, US]
Very Truly Yours - Jimmy Scott [1955, US]

Thelonious Monk Plays Duke Ellington - Thelonious Monk [1955, US]

'Heartbreak Hotel' – Elvis Presley [1956, US]

Songs for Swingin' Lovers – Frank Sinatra [1956, US]

'Why Do Fools Fall in Love?' – Frankie Lymon & The Teenagers [1956, US]

Birth of the Cool – Miles Davis [1957, US]

Blue Train - John Coltrane [1957, US]

The Beat of My Heart - Tony Bennett [1957, US]

Little Girl Blue - Nina Simone [1958, US]

Time Out - Dave Brubeck [1959, US]

'What'd I say' – Ray Charles [1959, US]

Chet - Chet Baker [1959, US]

The Original Blind Boys - Blind Boys of Alabama [1959, US]

Kind of Blue – Miles Davis [1959, US]

60s

Joan Baez - Joan Baez [1960, US]

'Will You Still Love Me Tomorrow' – The Shirelles [1960, US]

'Where Have All the Flowers Gone?' – Pete Seeger [1961, US]

'Please Mr Postman' - The Marvelettes [1961, US]

'The Loco-Motion' – Little Eva [1962, US]

'Telstar' - The Tornados [1962, UK]

'Green Onions' - Booker T & the MGs [1962, US]

The Freewheelin' Bob Dylan – Bob Dylan [1963, US]
'Wipe Out' - The Surfaris [1963, US]
'Variations for a Door and a Sigh' – Pierre Henry [1963, France]
'Leader of the Pack' - The Shangri-Las [1964, US]
'House of the Rising Sun' - The Animals [1964, UK]
'My Boy Lollipop' - Millie [1964, UK]
'The Girl from Ipanema' - Astrud Gilberto/Stan Getz [1964, Brazil]
'5-4-3-2-1' - Manfred Mann [1964, UK]
'(I Can't Get No) Satisfaction' – The Rolling Stones [1965, UK]
Bringing It All Back Home – Bob Dylan [1965, US]
My Generation – The Who [1965, US]
Revolver – The Beatles [1966, UK]
'Good Vibrations' – The Beach Boys [1966, US]
'Respect' – Aretha Franklin [1967, US]
'Waterloo Sunset' - The Kinks [1967, UK]
Cheap Thrills - Janis Joplin [1967, US]
The Grateful Dead – The Grateful Dead [1967, US]
Songs of Leonard Cohen - Leonard Cohen [1967, US]
Are You Experienced – Jimi Hendrix [1967, US]
'White Rabbit' – Jefferson Airplane [1967, US]
Sgt. Pepper's Lonely Hearts Club Band – The Beatles [1967, UK]
Strange Days - The Doors [1967, US]
Gris-Gris - Dr. John [1968, US]
Os Mutantes - Os Mutantes [1968, Brazil]

Hot Rats – Frank Zappa [1969, US]
Clouds - Joni Mitchell [1969, US]
Abbey Road – The Beatles [1969, UK]

70s

'Get Up (I Feel Like Being a) Sex Machine' – James Brown [1970, US]
Fun House - Iggy Pop & The Stooges [1970, US]
'Get It On' - T. Rex [1971, UK]
Imagine - John Lennon [1971, UK]
'What's Going On' - Marvin Gaye [1971, US]
Exile on Main Street - The Rolling Stones [1972, UK]
'Sail Away' - Randy Newman [1972, US]
Ziggy Stardust and the Spiders from Mars – David Bowie [1972, UK]
Transformer – Lou Reed [1972, US]
'Soul Makossa' - Manu Dibango [1972, France]
Greetings from Asbury Park – Bruce Springsteen [1973, US]
The Wild, the Innocent & the E Street Shuffle – Bruce Springsteen [1973, US]
Jolene - Dolly Parton [1974, US]
Autobahn - Kraftwerk [1974, West Germany]
Nighthawks at the Diner – Tom Waits [1975, US]
Horses – Patti Smith [1975, US]
'Bohemian Rhapsody' - Queen [1975, UK]
Love to Love You Baby – Donna Summer [1975, US]

'Chocolate City' - Parliament [1975, US]
'Anarchy in the UK' – The Sex Pistols [1976, UK]
Ramones – The Ramones [1976, US]
I Don't Want to Go Home - Southside Johnny and the Asbury Jukes [1976, US]
Blank Generation - Richard Hell & the Voidoids [1977, US]
My Aim Is True - Elvis Costello [1977, UK]
'God Save the Queen' – The Sex Pistols [1977, UK]
New Boots and Panties!! - Ian Dury [1977, UK]
Parallel Lines - Blondie [1978, US]
'YMCA' - Village People [1978, US]
Blue Valentine - Tom Waits [1978, US]
'Hong Kong Garden' - Siouxsie and the Banshees [1978, UK]
Cut - The Slits [1979, UK]
Fool Around - Rachel Sweet [1979, UK]

80s

'Baggy Trousers' - Madness [1980, UK]
'Ghost Town' - The Specials [1981, UK]
'Tainted Love' - Soft Cell [1981, UK]
Thriller - Michael Jackson [1982, US]
Kissing to Be Clever - Culture Club [1982, UK]
Swordfishtrombones – Tom Waits [1983, US]
Run-D.M.C. – Run-D.M.C. [1984, US]
Purple Rain - Prince [1984, US]
Like A Virgin - Madonna [1984, US]

Stop Making Sense - Talking Heads [1984, US]

90s

Nevermind - Nirvana [1991, US]
Stepping Out - Diana Krall [1993, US]
Dummy - Portishead [1994, UK]
Buena Vista Social Club - Buena Vista Social Club [1997, Cuba]
Soul of the Tango - Yo Yo Ma [1997, Argentina]
Exile on Coldharbour Lane - Alabama 3 [1997, UK]
All That Jazz: The Best of Ute Lemper - Ute Lemper [1998, US]
Live in Texas - Lyle Lovett [1999, US]

00s

Good Morning Susie Soho - Esbjörn Svensson Trio [2000, Sweden]
La Revancha del Tango - Gotan Project [2001, France]
O - Damien Rice [2002, Ireland]
Come Away With Me - Norah Jones [2002, US]
Fado em mim - Mariza [2002, Portugal]
Calcutta Slide-Guitar - Debashish Bhattacharya [2005, India]
Back to Black - Amy Winehouse [2006, UK]
I Started Out With Nothing and I Still Got Most of It Left - Seasick Steve [2008, UK]

'Bad Romance' - Lady Ga Ga [2009, US]
Lungs - Florence and The Machine [2009, UK]

10s

'California Gurls' - Kate Perry featuring Snoop Dogg [2010, US]
Duets II - Tony Bennett & friends [2011, US]
Let England Shake - PJ Harvey [2011, UK]
Born This Way - Lady Gaga [2011, US]
Birdy - Birdy [2011, UK]

Film

Late 40s

My Darling Clementine [John Ford, 1946, US]
Brighton Rock [John Boulting, 1947, UK]
Bicycle Thieves [Vittorio De Sica, 1948, Italy]
She Wore a Yellow Ribbon [John Ford, 1949, US]

50s

Sunset Boulevard [Billy Wilder, 1950, US]
The Asphalt Jungle [John Huston, 1950, US]
High Noon [Fred Zinnemann, 1952, US]
Shane [George Stevens, 1952, US]
The Wild One [László Benedek, 1953, US]
Roman Holiday [William Wyler, 1953, US]
On the Waterfront [Elia Kazan, 1954, US]
Oklahoma! [Fred Zinnemann, 1955, US]
Rebel Without a Cause [Nicholas Ray, 1955, US]
Rock Around the Clock [Fred F. Sears, 1956, US]

The Sweet Smell of Success [Alexander Mackendrick, 1957, US]
I Was A Teenage Werewolf [Gene Fowler Jr., 1957, US]
South Pacific [Joshua Logan, 1958, US]
Gidget [Paul Wendkos, 1959, US]
Some Like It Hot [Billy Wilder, 1959, US]
North By Northwest [Alfred Hitchcock, 1959, US]

60s

La Dolce Vita [Federico Fellini, 1960, Italy]
Breathless [Jean-Luc Godard, 1960, France]
Shoot the Piano Player [Francois Truffaut, 1960, France]
Breakfast at Tiffany's [Blake Edwards, 1961, US]
From Russia With Love [Terence Young, 1963, UK]
8½ [Federico Fellini, 1963, Italy]
A Hard Day's Night [Richard Lester, 1964, UK]
What's New Pussycat? [Clive Donner, 1965, France/US]
Faster, Pussycat! Kill! Kill! [Russ Meyer, 1965, US]
Pierrot le fou [Jean-Luc Godard, 1965, France]
Alfie [Lewis Gilbert, 1966, UK]
Blow-Up [Michelangelo Antonioni, 1966, UK]
The Graduate [Mike Nichols, 1967, US]
Barbarella [Roger Vadim, 1968, France]
On Her Majesty's Secret Service [Peter R. Hunt, 1969, UK]
Easy Rider [Dennis Hopper, 1969, US]

70s

MASH [Robert Altman, 1970, US]
Clockwork Orange [Stanley Kubrick, 1971, UK]
Carnal Knowledge [Mike Nichols, 1971, US]
Roma [Federico Fellini, 1972, Italy]
Mean Streets [Martin Scorsese, 1973, US]
Amarcord [Federico Fellini, 1973, Italy]
American Graffiti [George Lucas, 1973, US]
Nashville [Robert Altman, 1975, US]
The Passenger [Michelangelo Antonioni, 1975, US]
Jubilee [Derek Jarman, 1977, UK]
Saturday Night Fever [John Badham, 1977, US]
Mad Max [George Miller, 1979, Australia]
Quadrophenia [Franc Roddam, 1979, UK]
All That Jazz [Bob Fosse, 1979, US]

80s

Airplane! [David Zucker, 1980, US]
The Blues Brothers [John Landis, 1980, US]
An American Werewolf in London [John Landis, 1981, UK]
Escape from New York [John Carpenter, 1981, US]
Blade Runner [Ridley Scott, 1982, US]
One From the Heart [Francis Ford Coppola, 1982, US]
Diner [Barry Levinson, 1982, US]
Café Flesh [Stephen Sayadian, 1982, US]
Rumble Fish [Francis Ford Coppola, 1983, UK]
Trading Places [John Landis, 1983, US]

Local Hero [Bill Forsyth, 1983, UK]
The King of Comedy [Martin Scorsese, 1983, US]
Paris, Texas [Wim Wenders, 1984, US]
Stranger Than Paradise [Jim Jarmusch, 1984, US]
After Hours [Martin Scorsese, 1985, US]
Letter To Brezhnev [Chris Bernard, 1985, UK]
Blue Velvet [David Lynch, 1986, US]
Down By Law [Jim Jarmusch, 1986, US]
Something Wild [Jonathan Demme, 1986, US]
Ruthless People [David Zucker, 1986, US]
The Big Easy [Jim McBride, 1987, US]
Wall Street [Oliver Stone, 1987, US]
Bird [Clint Eastwood, 1988, US]
High Hopes [Mike Leigh, 1988, UK]
Women on the Verge of a Nervous Breakdown [Pedro Almodóvar, 1988, Spain]
Mystery Train [Jim Jarmusch, 1989, US]

90s

Thelma And Louise [Ridley Scott, 1991, US]
Slacker [Richard Linklater, 1991, US]
Jamón Jamón [Bigas Luna, 1992, Spain]
Tokyo Decadence [Ryū Murakami, 1992, Japan]
Groundhog Day [Harold Ramis, 1993, US]
Casino [Martin Scorsese, 1995, US]
Trainspotting [Danny Boyle, 1996, UK]

Austin Powers: International Man of Mystery [Jay Roach, 1997, US]
The Ice Storm [Ang Lee, 1997, US]
L.A. Confidential [Curtis Hanson, 1997, US]
The Big Lebowski [Joel Coen & Ethan Coen, 1998, US]
Saving Private Ryan [Steven Spielberg, 1998, US]
Buffalo 66 [Vincent Gallo, 1998, US]
Tango [Carlos Saura, 1998, Argentina]
American Beauty [Sam Mendes, 1999, US]
The Matrix [Larry & Andy Wachowski, 1999, US]

00s

In the Mood for Love [Wong Kar-Wai, 2000, Hong Kong]
The Filth and the Fury [Julien Temple, 2000, UK]
Memento [Christopher Nolan, 2000, US]
Mulholland Drive [David Lynch, 2001, US]
Last Orders [Fred Schepisi, 2001, UK/Germany]
Flags of Our Fathers [Clint Eastwood, 2001, US]
City by the Sea [Michael Caton-Jones, 2002, US]
Secretary [Steven Shainberg, 2002, US]
About Schmidt [Alexander Payne, 2002, US]
Lost In Translation [Sofia Coppola, 2003, US]
Shaun of the Dead [Edgar Wright, 2004, UK]
Kamikaze Girls [Tetsuya Nakashima, 2004, Japan]
The Notorious Betty Page [Mary Harron, 2005, US]
Casino Royale [Martin Campbell, 2006, UK]
Jar City [Baltasar Kormákur, 2006, Iceland]

The Devil Wears Prada [David Frankel, 2006, US]
No Country For Old Men [Joel Coen & Ethan Coen, 2007, US]
Burn After Reading [Joel Coen & Ethan Coen, 2008, US]
The Girl Who Kicked the Hornets' Nest [Daniel Alfredson, 2009, Sweden]
The Girl With the Dragon Tattoo [Niels Arden Oplev, 2009, Sweden]

10s

The Social Network [David Fincher, 2010, US]
Tinker, Tailor, Soldier, Spy [Tomas Alfredson, 2011, UK/France]

TV

Late 40s

Howdy Doody [1947-1960, US]
Kraft Television Theater [1947-1958, US]
The Ed Sullivan Show [1948-1971, US]
The Lone Ranger [1949-1957, US]
Come Dancing [1949-1998, UK]
1949: The Sears & Roebuck Catalog includes TVs for the first time

50s

The Jack Benny Show [1950-1965, US]
I Love Lucy [1951-1960, US]
Dragnet [1951-1959, US]
The Roy Rodgers Show [1951-1957, US]
The Adventures of Ozzie and Harriet [1952-1966, US]
American Bandstand [1952-1989, US]
The Phil Silvers Show [1955-1959, US]
Gunsmoke [1955-1975, US]

The Mickey Mouse Club [1955-1959, US]
The Steve Allen Show [1956-1960, US]
1956: Elvis Presley appears on *The Ed Sullivan Show*
Leave It To Beaver [1957-1963, US]
77 Sunset Strip [1958-1964, US]
Blue Peter [1958-present, UK]
The Twilight Zone [1959-1964, US]
Bonanza [1959-1973, US]

60s

1960: John F. Kennedy and Richard M. Nixon debate live on TV
Coronation Street [1960-present, UK]
The Avengers [1961-1969, UK]
That Was The Week That Was [1962-1963, UK]
1963: Kennedy assassination interrupts *As The World Turns* soap. Jack Ruby murders Lee Harvey Oswald live on TV
Ready Steady Go! [1963-1966, UK]
Doctor Who [1963-1989, 1996, 2005-present, UK]
The Man from U.N.C.L.E. [1964-1968, US]
1964: Beatles on *The Ed Sullivan Show*
Top of the Pops [1964-2006, UK]
Peyton Place [1964-1969, US]
The Addams Family [1964-1966, US]
The Munsters [1964-1966, US]
Till Death Us Do Part [1965-1968, 70, 1972-1975, UK]
Batman [1966-1968, US]

Star Trek [1966-1969, US]

The Prisoner [1967-1968, UK]

1968: UK hosts the first color broadcast of *The Eurovision Song Contest*

Columbo [1968-2003, US]

Hawaii Five-O [1968-1980, US]

Sesame Street [1969-present, US]

Monty Python's Flying Circus [1969-1974, UK]

70s

The Old Grey Whistle Test [1971-1987, UK]

All in the Family [1971-1979, US]

The Bob Newhart Show [1972-1978, US]

Kojak [1973-1978, US]

Happy Days [1974-1984, US]

Fawlty Towers [1975, 1979, UK]

The Sweeney [1975-1978, UK]

Saturday Night Live [1975-present, US]

1976: VHS home video cassette -v- Betamax recording system

Abigail's Party [1977, UK]

Soap [1977-1981, US]

Dallas [1978-1991, US]

Pennies From Heaven [1978, UK]

Tinker, Tailor, Soldier, Spy [1979, UK]

80s

1980: J.R. shot in *Dallas*
1981: launch of MTV
Hill Street Blues [1981-1987, US]
Only Fools and Horses [1981-1983, UK]
Brideshead Revisited [1981, UK]
The Hitchhikers Guide to the Galaxy [1981, UK]
Cheers [1982-1993, US]
Boys From the Black Stuff [1982, UK]
The Young Ones [1982-1984, UK]
Brookside [1982-2003, UK]
Miami Vice [1984-1989, US]
The Living Planet [1984, UK]
Spitting Image [1984-1996, UK]
The Bill [1984-2010, UK]
EastEnders [1985-present, UK]
Blind Date [1985-2003, UK]
Neighbours [1985-present, Australia]
1986: Bobby Ewing is alive and having a shower in Dallas (it was all a dream)
The Oprah Winfrey Show [1986-2011, US]
The Singing Detective [1986, UK]
Roseanne [1988-1997, US]
The Simpsons [1989-present, US]
Seinfeld [1989-1998, US]
Baywatch [1989-1999, US]
Desmond's [1989-1994, UK]

90s

Twin Peaks [1990-1991, US]
Beverly Hills 90210 [1990-2000, US]
Aeon Flux [1990-1995, US]
Later . . . with Jools Holland [1992-present, UK]
Absolutely Fabulous [1992-1996, UK]
Men Behaving Badly [1992-1998, UK]
NYPD Blue [1993-2005, US]
Homicide: Life on the Street [1993-1999, US]
Beavis and Butt-head [1993-1997, 2011-present, US]
Frasier [1993-2004, US]
ER [1994-2009, US]
Friends [1994-2004, US]
Wallander [1994-2006, Sweden]
Father Ted [1995-1998, UK]
Hollyoaks [1995-present, UK]
Never Mind the Buzzcocks [1996-present, UK]
South Park [1997-present, US]
Buffy the Vampire Slayer [1997-2003, US]
Sex and the City [1998-2004, US]
The Sopranos [1999-2007, US]
Queer as Folk [1999-2000, UK]
Big Brother [1999-present, Netherlands]

00s

Curb Your Enthusiasm [2000-present, US]
Pop Idol [2001-2003, UK]

The Office [2001-2003, UK]
Band of Brothers [2001, US]
Pop Idol [2001-2004, UK]
Walk on By: The Story of Popular Song [2002 (BBC doc series), UK]
The Wire [2002-2008, US]
I'm a Celebrity . . . Get Me Out of Here! [2002-present, UK]
QI [2003-present, UK]
Little Britain [2003-2006, UK]
The End of Suburbia: Oil Depletion and the Collapse of The American Dream [2004, (doc), Canada]
Pimp My Ride [2004-present, US]
Desperate Housewives [2004-present, US]
Strictly Come Dancing [2004-present, UK]
The X Factor [2004-present, UK]
America's Got Talent [2006-present, US]
Ugly Betty [2006-2010, US]
Life On Mars [2006-2007, UK]
Torchwood [2006-present, UK]
Mad Men [2007-present, US]
Ice Road Truckers [2007-present, US]
Skins [2007-present, UK]
The Killing [2007-2008, Denmark]

10s

Requiem for Detroit [2010 (BBC doc), UK]

American Dream [2010 (BBC doc series), UK]
British Style Genius: A Fashion Democracy [2010 (BBC doc series), UK]
The Pacific [2010, US]
The Hour [2011, UK]
Pan Am [2011-present, US]

Fiction

Late 40s

Tennessee Williams, 'A Streetcar Named Desire', 1947, US
Albert Camus, *The Plague* (originally Paris, 1947)
George Orwell, *Nineteen Eighty-Four*, 1949, UK
Henry Miller, *Sexus*, 1949, US
Arthur Miller, 'Death of a Salesman', 1949, US

50s

J. D. Salinger, *The Catcher in the Rye*, 1951, US
Ernest Hemingway, *The Old Man and the Sea*, 1952, US
John Steinbeck, *East of Eden*, 1952, US
Ian Fleming, *Casino Royale*, 1953, UK
Samuel Beckett, 'Waiting for Godot', 1953, Ireland
Raymond Chandler, *The Long Goodbye*, 1953, US
Tennessee Williams, 'Cat on a Hot Tin Roof', 1955, US
Allen Ginsberg, *Howl and Other Poems*, 1956, US
David Goodis, *Down There*, 1956, US

Jack Kerouac, *On the Road*, 1957, US
Chester Himes, *A Rage in Harlem*, 1957, US
Jack Kerouac, *The Subterraneans*, 1958, US
Lawrence Ferlinghetti, *A Coney Island of the Mind*, 1958, US
Colin MacInnes, *Absolute Beginners*, 1959, UK
William S. Burroughs, *Naked Lunch*, 1959, US

60s

John Updike, *Rabbit, Run*, 1960, US
Harper Lee, *To Kill a Mockingbird*, 1960, US
Joseph Heller, *Catch-22*, 1961, US
Ken Kesey, *One Flew Over the Cuckoo's Nest*, 1962, US
Kurt Vonnegut, *Cat's Cradle*, 1963, US
Ken Kesey, *Sometimes a Great Notion*, 1964, US
Thomas Pynchon, *The Crying of Lot 49*, 1966, US
Leonard Cohen, *Beautiful Losers*, 1966, Canada
Richard Brautigan, *Trout Fishing in America*, 1967, US
Philip K. Dick, *Do Androids Dream of Electric Sheep?*, 1968, US
Philip Roth, *Portnoy's Complaint*, 1969, US
J. G. Ballard, *The Atrocity Exhibition*, 1969, UK

70s

John Updike, *Rabbit Redux*, 1971, US
Jenny Fabian, *A Chemical Romance*, 1971, UK

Charles Bukowski, *Post Office*, 1971, US

Hunter S. Thompson, *Fear and Loathing in Las Vegas: A Savage Journey to the Heart of the American Dream*, 1972, US

J.G. Ballard, *Crash*, 1973, UK

Thomas Pynchon, *Gravity's Rainbow*, 1973, US

Richard O'Brian, 'The Rocky Horror Show', 1973, UK

Kurt Vonnegut, *Breakfast of Champions*, 1973, US

Philip Larkin, *High Windows*, 1974, UK

J. G. Ballard, *High-Rise*, 1975, UK

Tom Robbins, *Even Cowgirls Get the Blues*, 1976, US

Richard Brautigan, *Dreaming of Babylon: A Private Eye Novel 1942*, 1977, US

Charles Bukowski, *Women*, 1978, US

Peter Jenkins, *A Walk Across America*, 1979, US

John Le Carré, *Smiley's People*, 1979, UK

80s

John Kennedy Toole, *A Confederacy of Dunces*, 1980, US

Raymond Carver, *What We Talk About When We Talk About Love*, 1981, US

Charles Bukowski, *Ham on Rye*, 1982, US

Haruki Murakami, *A Wild Sheep Chase*, (originally Tokyo, 1982)

Jay McInerney, *Bright Lights Big City*, 1984, US

Martin Amis, *Money*, 1984, UK

William Gibson, *Neuromancer*, 1984, US

Tom Robbins, *Jitterbug Perfume*, 1984, US
Milan Kundera, *The Unbearable Lightness of Being*, (originally Paris, 1984)
Bret Easton Ellis, *Less Than Zero*, 1985, US
Jeanette Winterson, *Oranges Are Not the Only Fruit*, 1985, UK
Tama Janowitz, *Slaves of New York*, 1986, US
Carl Hiaasen, *Tourist Season*, 1986, US
Wolfe, Tom, *Bonfires of the Vanities*, 1987, US
Raymond Carver, *Elephant and other stories*, 1988, US
Banana Yoshimoto, *Kitchen*, (originally Tokyo, 1988)

90s

John Updike, *Rabbit At Rest*, 1990, US
Hanif Kureishi, *The Buddha of Suburbia*, 1990, UK
Douglas Coupland, *Generation X: Tales from an Accelerated Culture*, 1991, US
James Ellroy, *White Jazz*, 1992, US
Toni Morrison, *Jazz*, 1992, US
Walter Mosley, *White Butterfly*, 1992, US
George P. Pelecanos, *A Firing Offense*, 1992, US
Irvine Welsh, *Trainspotting*, 1993, UK
John Berendt, *Midnight in the Garden of Good and Evil*, 1994, US
Nicholson Baker, *The Fermata*, 1994, US
Haruki Murakami, *The Wind-up Bird Chronicle*, (originally Tokyo, 1994/5)

Philip Roth, *Sabbath's Theater*, 1995, US
William Gibson, *Idoru*, 1996, US
Philip Roth, *American Pastoral*, 1997, US
Ryū Murakami, *In the Miso Soup*, (originally Tokyo, 1997)
Geoff Nicholson, *Bleeding London*, 1997, UK
Michel Houellebecq, *Atomised*, (originally Paris, 1998)
Pedro Juan Gutiérrez, *Dirty Havana Trilogy*, (originally Madrid, 1998)

00s

J. T. Leroy, *Sarah*, 2000, US
Zadie Smith, *White Teeth*, 2000, UK
J.G. Ballard, *Super-Cannes*, 2000, UK
Dave Eggers, *A Heartbreaking Work of Staggering Genius*, 2000, US
Michel Houellebecq, *Platform*, (originally Paris, 2001)
Philip Roth, *The Dying Animal*, 2001, US
Elmore Leonard, *Tishomingo Blues*, 2002, US
William Gibson, *Pattern Recognition*, 2003, US
Stieg Larsson, *The Girl With the Dragon Tattoo*, 2005, Sweden
2007: Amazon Kindle
Coupland, Douglas, *Generation A*, Toronto, 2009

10s

2010: launch of Apple iPad

Jonathan Franzen, *Freedom*, NY, 2010
Haruki Murakami, *1Q84*, (originally Tokyo, 2011)

Non-fiction

Berger, Peter L. & Thomas Luckmann, *The Social Construction of Reality*, 1966, NY.

Brockman, Helen L., *The Theory of Fashion Design*, John Wiley & Sons, New York, 1967.

Carr, Roy & Brian Case & Fred Dellar, *The Hip: Hipsters, Jazz and the Beat Generation*, London, 1986.

Carter, Ernestine, *The Changing World of Fashion*, Weidenfeld and Nicolson, London, 1977.

Chambers, Iain, *Border Dialogues: Journeys in Postmodernity*, London, 1990.

– *Urban Rhythms: Pop Music and Popular Culture*, London, 1985.

Chenoune, Farid, *A History of Men's Fashion*, Paris, 1993.

Clifford, Mike (ed.), *The Illustrated Rock Handbook*, London, 1983.

Cohn, Nik, 'Today There Are No Gentlemen', in *Ball the Wall*, London, 1989.

Colmer, Michael, *Pinball: An Illustrated History*, New York, 1976.

Cosgrove, Stuart, 'The Zoot Suit and Style Warfare', in Angela McRobbie (ed.), *Zoot Suits and Second-hand Dresses: An Anthology of Fashion and Music*, London, 1989.

Daly, Steven & Nathaniel Wice, *alt.culture: an a-z guide to 90s america*, London, 1995.

DeMello, Margo, *Bodies of Inscription: A Cultural History of the Modern Tattoo Community*, Durham, USA, 2000.

Deverson, Jane & Charles Hamblett, *Generation X,* 1965, London.

Didion, Joan, *Slouching Towards Bethlehem*, London, 2001.

Farren, Mick, *The Black Leather Jacket*, London, 1985.

Flügel, J. C., *The Psychology of Clothes*, Hogarth Press & The Institute of Psycho-analysis, London, 1930.

Frost, David & Antony Jay, *The English*, London, 1967.

Gillett, Charlie, *The Sound of the City: The Rise of Rock and Roll*, London, 1970.

Goldberg, Joe, 'The Birth of Cool', in Gene Sculatti (ed.), *A Catalog of Cool*, New York, 1982.

Gottwald, Laura and Janusz (eds.), *Frederick's of Hollywood 1947-73: 26 Years of Mail Order Seduction*, Strawberry Hill, New York, 1973.

Gray, Spalding, *Swimming To Cambodia*, New York, 1985.

Gutman, Richard J. S. & Elliott Kaufman, *American Diner*, NY, 1979.

Hebdige, *Subculture: The Meaning of Style*, London, 1979.

Hofmann, Albert, *LSD: My Problem Child*, 1980, NY.

Horn, Richard, *Fifties Style: Then and Now*, New York, 1985.

Howell, Georgina, *In Vogue: Six Decades of Fashion*, Allen

Lane, London, 1975.

Huxley, Aldous, *The Doors of Perception*, 1954, London.

i-D Magazine (eds.), *a decade of i-Deas: the encyclopaedia of the '80s*, London, 1990.

Jameson, Frederic, *Postmodernism or the Cultural Logic of Late Capitalism*, London, 1991.

König, René, *The Restless Image: A Sociology of Fashion*, George Allen & Unwin, London, 1973.

Lautman, Victoria, *The New Tattoo*, New York, 1994.

Leinberger, Christopher B. 'The Next Slum?' *Atlantic Monthly* http://www.theatlantic.com/magazine/archive/2008/03/the-next-slum/6653/

Levy, Shawn, *Ready, Steady, GO!: The Smashing Rise and Giddy Fall of Swinging London*, New York, 2002.

Lydon, John, *Rotten: No Irish, No Blacks, No Dogs*, London, 1994.

Lobenthal, Joel, *Radical Rags: Fashions of the Sixties*, New York, 1990.

Macias, Patrick & Izumi Evers, *Japanese Schoolgirl Inferno: Tokyo Teen Fashion Subculture Handbook*, San Francisco, 2007.

McArdle, Megan, 'No Country for Young Men' *Atlantic Monthly* http://www.theatlantic.com/magazine/archive/2008/01/no-country-for-young-men/6578/

Melly, George, *Revolt into Style*, Oxford, 1989.

Merleau-Ponty, Maurice, *The Phenomenology of Perception* (original French edition, 1945, Paris).

Nicholson, Geoff, *The Lost Art of Walking*, New York, 2008.

Olian, JoAnne, *Everyday Fashion of the Forties: As Pictured in Sears Catalogs*, New York, 1992.

Pearce, Christopher, *Fifties Source Book: A Visual Guide to the Style of a Decade*, London, 1990.

Peellaert, Guy & Nik Cohn, *Rock Dreams*, London, 1973.

Perry, Paul, *On The Bus: The Complete Guide to the Legendary Trip of Ken Kesey and the Merry Pranksters and the Birth of the Counterculture*, 1990, London.

Perutz, Kathrin, *Beyond the Looking Glass: Life in the Beauty Culture*, Penguin, Harmondsworth, 1972.

Polhemus, Ted, *Bodystyles*, Luton, England, 1988.

– *Diesel: World Wide Wear*, London, 1998.

– *Fashion & Anti-fashion: Exploring adornment and dress from an anthropological perspective*, Hastings, UK, 2011 [originally Ted Polhemus & Lynn Procter, *Fashion & Anti-fashion: An Anthropology of Clothing and Adornment*, London, 1978]

– *Hot Bodies Cool Styles: New Techniques in Self-Adornment*, London, 2004.

– *Streetstyle*, London, 1994 (Thames & Hudson); new edition, London, 2010 (PYMCA).

– *Style Surfing: what to wear in the 3rd millennium*, London, 1996.

Polhemus, Ted & Pierfrancesco Pacoda, *La Rivolta Dello Stile*, Padova, Italy, 2008.

Polhemus, Ted & Lynn Procter, *Pop Styles*, London, 1984.

Powell, Polly & Lucy Peel, *'50s & '60s Style*, London, 1988.

PYMCA (with Ted Polhemus and others), *Unordinary Peo-*

ple, London, 2009.

Quant, Mary, *Quant by Quant*, 1966, London.

Redhead, Steve, *The End-of-the-Century Party*, Manchester, 1990.

Sartre, Jean-Paul, *Being and Nothingness: An Essay on Phenomenological Ontology* (original French edition, 1943, Paris)

Savage, Jon, *England's Dreaming: Sex Pistols and Punk Rock*, London, 1991.

– *Teenage: the creation of youth 1875-1945*, London, 2007.

Seymour-Jones, Carole, *A Dangerous Liaison: A Revelatory New Biography of Simone de Beauvoir and Jean-Paul Sartre*, London, 2008.

Sculatti, Gene (ed.), *The Catalog of Cool*, New York, 1982.

Shore, Michael (with Dick Clark), *The History of American Bandstand*, New York, 1985.

Smith, Bradley, *The American Way of Sex*, New York, 1978.

Stewart, Tony, *Cool Cats: 25 Years of Rock 'N' Roll*, London, 1981.

Talese, Gay, *Thy Neighbor's Wife: Sex in the World Today*, New York, 1975.

Tambini, Michael, *The Look of the Century*, London, 1996.

Thorne, Tony, *Fads, Fashions & Cults: From Acid House to Zoot Suit*, London, 1993.

Tulloch, Carol, 'Rebel without a Pause: Black Streetstyle & Black Designers', in Julia Ash and Elizabeth Wilson, (eds.), *Chic Thrills*, London, 1992.

Veblen, Thorstein, *The Theory of the Leisure Class*, New

York, 1899.

Warhol, Andy, *From A To B And Back Again*, New York, 1975.

Wheen, Francis, *Strange Days Indeed, The Golden Age of Paranoia*, London, 2009.

Wolfe, Tom, 'Funky Chic', in *Mauve Gloves & Madmen, Clutter & Vine*, Farrar, Strauss & Giroux, New York, 1976.

– 'Radical chic' in *Radical Chic and Mau-mauing the Flak Catchers*, Farrar, Strauss & Giroux, New York, 1970.

– *The Electric Kool-Aid Acid Test*, Farrar, Strauss & Giroux, New York, 1968.

– *The Pump House Gang*, Farrar, Strauss & Giroux, New York, 1968.

Wolff, Daniel, *4th of July, Asbury Park: A History of the Promised Land*, New York, 2005.

York, Peter, *Modern Times*, London, 1984.

Part II

Timeline

1945

- WWII ends.
- United Nations founded.
- Labour Party victory in GB.
- 1st ballpoint pens go on sale at $12.50.

1946

- Post-war baby boom begins.
- 1st mobile phone call from a car.
- US Army Signal Corps scientists at Fort Monmouth, New Jersey bounce radio signals off moon.
- 1st Tupperware goes on sale.

1947

- Baby boom booms.
- India becomes world's largest democracy.
- Biker gangs invade Hollister, California, inspiring *The Wild One*.
- Jack Kerouac meets Neal Cassady in NYC; *On the Road* will see Sal Paradise and Dean Moriarty set out across America in this same year.
- Thelonious Monk, Roy Eldridge and other Hipsters explore the roots of modern jazz at Minton's Playhouse, New York City.
- Roy Brown's 'Good Rockin' Tonight' gets to #13 in a *Billboard Magazine* 'Rhythm & Blues' chart – a redneck

named Elvis Presley likes what he hears.
- French designer Christian Dior launches the 'New Look' in Paris.
- Levitt & Sons begin work on constructing 2000 homes – the first 'Levittown' – on what had previously been a potato farm in Long Island.

1948

- Marshall Plan brings massive American aid to Europe.
- Mahatma Gandhi assassinated.
- Miles Davis begins recording *Birth of the Cool*.

1949

- Astronomer Fred Hoyle coins the phrase 'Big Bang'.
- People's Republic of China founded.

1950

- The first commercially successful solid body electric guitar, the Fender 'Broadcaster' (later, the 'Telecaster') is launched.
- Korean War intensifies - nuclear weapons threatened.
- 'Peanuts' comic appears.
- 1st TV remote on sale.

1951

- UN headquarters opens in NYC.

- UK Labour government ousted by Conservatives.

1952

- Gary Cooper does what a man's got to do in *High Noon* and millions of Americans yearn for their own 'ranch' style suburban home.

1953

- War hero Dwight D. Eisenhower becomes 34th American President.
- The British *Daily Express* newspaper introduces the label 'Teddy Boys' and moral panic kicks off.
- 1st issue of *Playboy* magazine.

1954

- US conducts hydrogen bomb test in Pacific Bikini Atoll - France counters with 'Bikini' swimsuit.
- Boeing 707 introduced.
- Food rationing ends in GB.
- 1st *Godzilla* movie premiers in Tokyo.

1955

- Disneyland opens in California.

- *Blackboard Jungle* film featuring Bill Haley and the Comets' 'Rock Around the Clock' causes 'teenagers' to go crazy dancing in cinemas.

1956

- More moral panics: Elvis on the *Ed Sullivan Show*. This Rock 'n' Roll has got to go . . . but it doesn't.
- Marriage of Marilyn Monroe and Arthur Miller.
- *And God Created Woman* makes Brigitte Bardot an international star.

1957

- *American Bandstand* goes national with Dick Clark as its host and advertisement for American dentistry.
- Cavern Club and the Jodrell Bank Radio Telescope open in the UK.

1958

- Colin MacInnes' novel *Absolute Beginners* is set in 1958 and shines a light on 'youth culture' and the 'race riots' which took place in Notting Hill, London in that year.
- World goes crazy for hula-hoops and Rio's Bossa nova beat.

1959

- Dave Brubeck calls *Time Out* and we all 'Take Five'.
- *The Twilight Zone* airs on US TV and its cosmically co-pacetic presenter Rod Serling shows Don Draper how to wear a suit.
- Motown Records founded.
- Revolutionaries win out in Cuba.
- Barbie doll goes on sale.
- Australopithecus skull found in Olduvai Gorge.
- Publication of Erving Goffman's *The Presentation of Self in Everyday Life*.

1960

- John Kennedy elected President of USA.
- The US Federal Drug Administration approves oral contraceptive pill.
- Federico Fellini's *La Dolce Vita* demonstrates that Italy is the new center of modernism and design.
- 1st wave of Baby Boomers become 'teenagers'.
- Chubby Checker (and then the world) does 'The Twist'.

1961

- Satirical mag *Private Eye* launched in UK.
- Marvel creates *Fantastic Four* - and then *The Hulk* in '62.
- US sends thousands of military advisors to South Vietnam.

- Soviet cosmonaut Yuri Gagarin first man in space.

1962

- Cuban Missile Crisis brings world to the brink of Armageddon.
- American John Glenn orbits the earth.
- 1st Wal-Mart opens.
- Andy Warhol exhibits *Campbell's Soup Cans* in LA.

1963

- Sex begins (according to Philip Larkin's poem 'Annus Mirabilis').
- *From Russia With Love* establishes the template for decades of Bond films – it was probably the last film President Kennedy saw before he was shot in Dallas on Friday, November 22, 1963.
- British TV programme *Ready Steady Go!* brings British Mod 'faces' together with their American Soul heroes.
- Rev. Martin Luther King Jr. delivers his 'I have a dream' speech at the 'March On Washington'.

1964

- Ken Kesey, Neal Cassady and their band of 'Merry Pranksters' set out from La Honda, California in their psychedelically painted International Harvester school bus 'Furthur' intent on discovering America.

- Lyndon Johnson's Civil Rights Act outlaws racial discrimination in public places and institutions.
- The Beatles are mobbed at JFK airport and the 'British Invasion' of America kicks off.
- America officially begins a ground war in Vietnam as 3,500 U.S. Marines are dispatched.

1965

- Nicking the limelight from both Paris and NYC, 'Swinging London' becomes Where It's At – the capital of global popular culture.
- President Lyndon Johnson describes his vision of a 'Great Society'.
- Draft card burnings at University of California, Berkeley - then at the Pentagon.
- 1st skateboard championships.
- Bob Dylan goes electric.

1966

- Michelangelo Antonioni's film *Blow-up* spotlights 'Swinging London' and its definitive icon, the photographer.
- Indira Gandhi elected Prime Minister of India.
- John Lennon declares Beatles 'more popular than Jesus'; Beatles release *Revolver*.
- Haile Selassie - revered by Rastafarians - visits Jamaica.
- Cultural Revolution begins in China.

- LSD made illegal in US.

1967

- At the 'Human Be-in' at Golden Gate Park in San Francisco ex-Harvard professor Dr Timothy Leary advises 'Turn on, tune in, drop out'.
- The Beatles' *Sgt. Pepper's Lonely Hearts Club Band* uses $33\frac{1}{3}$ stereo technology to create a 'concept album'.

1968

- North Vietnam's 'Têt' (Lunar New Year) attack on some 100 cities – while repulsed – raises fresh doubts about mighty America's ability to succeed in a 'gorilla' war.
- 'Police riot' at the Democratic National Convention in Chicago but it will be the pro-war Hubert Humphrey who will run again Nixon.
- Riots in a host of American cities following the assassination of the Rev. Martin Luther King Jr. but in a concert in Boston James Brown urges calm combined with 'Say It Loud – I'm Black and I'm Proud'.
- 1st interracial kiss on US television - in *Star Trek*.

1969

- Richard Nixon becomes US President.
- '3 Days of Peace & Music' (and traffic jams and mountains of garbage) at Woodstock in New York State.

- Captain America concludes 'We blew it' in *Easy Rider* and many dispirited Hippies agree.
- America lands men on the moon – but Major Tom is lost in space and meaning.
- New York cops conduct a routine raid on a homosexual bar – The Stonewall Inn – in The Village but when they emerge with their arrests are confronted by a huge 'Gay Pride' demonstration. Relaxation of police action against Gay hangouts will spur on Disco.

1970

- The Beatles break up.
- Pan Am begins first commercial flights of the huge 747 - between Kennedy International and London Heathrow.
- Heavy metal kicks off with *Black Sabbath*.
- At 1,368 feet, the North Tower of the World Trade Center in NYC is the tallest building in the world.

1971

- President Richard Nixon declares 'War On Drugs' and the increasingly not so 'Silent Majority' thinks this (unlike Vietnam) will be an easy war to win.
- UK switches to decimal currency.
- Jim Morrison of The Doors dead in Paris.

1972

- 1st hand-held calculator on sale.
- Extraterrestrials take over London when *Ziggy Stardust and his Spiders* from Mars go Glam. But Apollo 17 ends missions to the moon.
- 'Bloody Sunday' - British troops kill 14 unarmed marchers in Northern Ireland.
- Marlon Brando mumbles in *Godfather*.
- Nixon wins huge landslide for 2nd term as US President. But what about those 5 caught in a burglary of the Democratic Party's office in the Watergate building? And who disappeared the physical evidence found by the police?

1973

- *American Graffiti* gives a nostalgic take on 1962 USA.
- New Jersey Baby Boomer Bruce Springsteen sends the world *Greetings from Asbury Park*.
- President Nixon: 'I'm not a crook'. But as impeachment looms he resigns in disgrace (expletives deleted).
- Gerald Ford becomes President – pardons Nixon.

1974

- 1st barcode scanned.
- ABBA win Eurovision Song Contest.

1975

- On April 29, 1975, in what was arguably the largest helicopter evacuation ever, the US frantically pulls its personnel from Saigon as the capital city falls to North Vietnamese soldiers.
- Recession has hit the world hard. This is especially so in NYC and yet, despite or because of this, this city spawns 3 hugely influential music genres and subcultures: Punk, Disco and Hip Hop.
- Margaret Thatcher becomes leader of UK Conservative Party.

1976

- The Sex Pistols' 'Anarchy in the UK' is the first British Punk record – the band and some friends swear on Thames TV's 'Today' programme and someone is so incensed that he destroys his TV.
- Britain celebrates Queen Elizabeth II's 'Silver Jubilee' with street parties and The Sex Pistols' contribution 'God Save the Queen'.

1977

- Health authorities caught off guard as entire world catches *Saturday Night Fever*.
- Peanut farmer Democrat Jimmy Carter becomes 39th US President.

- 1st 'all in one' computer - the Commodore PET - launched.
- Elvis dies.

1978

- Britain enters its 'Winter of Discontent' as Prime Minister James Callaghan struggles with strikes, inflation and the unions which support his own Labour party. Opposition leader Margaret Thatcher waits to pounce.

1979

- Margaret Thatcher becomes first female British Prime Minister.
- It's 'Happy Meal' time at McDonald's.
- Star Trek: The Motion Picture released and US Pioneer 11 spacecraft passes within 21,000km of Saturn.

1980

- John Lennon shot dead in Manhattan.
- Former actor Ronald Reagan elected 40th US President determined to 'Get the government off the back of the people'. As with Prime Minister Thatcher's Britain, America shifts to the Right.

1981

- Launch of 1st reusable 'Space Shuttle'.

- 'Video Killed the Radio Stars' kicks off launch of MTV.
- The US Center for Disease Control reports a still unnamed disease cluster in five homosexual men in Los Angeles – in 1982 this becomes known as A.I.D.S. and promiscuity is once again, as throughout history, a potentially deadly affair.
- Hosni Mubarak elected President of Egypt.
- Picasso's *Guernica* moved to post-Franco Madrid.

1982

- Britain's 'Iron Lady' Thatcher victorious over Argentina in battle for the remote Falkland Islands.
- Michael Jackson shows off his dance moves in *Thriller*.
- Introduction of compact discs - CDs.
- *Time* magazines 'Man of the Year' is . . . the computer.

1983

- Global Positioning System (GPS) made available for civilian use.
- Democratic elections in Argentina.
- Tokyo Disneyland opens.

1984

- Not exactly what George Orwell predicted (even if 'Big Brother' will find a new meaning in the '90s).

- Worst industrial accident in history occurs at Union Carbide's chemical plant in Bhopal, India.
- Apple 'Mac' introduced.

1985

- Brixton race riots rock London.
- Nintendo Entertainment System introduced with the Super Mario Bros.
- Windows 1.0 released.

1986

- Space Shuttle Challenger explodes soon after launch.
- Chernobyl nuclear disaster.

1987

- Margaret Thatcher decrees 'No such thing as society'.
- Dow Jones Industrial Average goes over 2,000 for the first time - clearly *Wall Street*'s Gordon Gekko is right that 'Greed is good'.

1988

- Now you need Windows 2.1 and Super Mario Bros. 3.
- 1st computer 'worm' distributed by means of internet.

1989

- Berlin Wall comes down – Soviet Union shatters.
- George H. W. Bush becomes 41st US President.
- Students protest and later are killed in Tiananmen Square, China.
- Motorola MicroTAC phone has 'flip' design and weighs only 12.3 ounces.
- Golden Toad classified as extinct.
- Carbon dioxide in earth's atmosphere reaches 350 parts per million.
- Tim Berners-Lee proposes a hypertext system to help scientists at CERN communicate with each other - this becomes the World Wide Web.

1990

- Nelson Mandela released from prison.
- Gulf War - 'Operation Desert Storm' - begins.
- 3.5 billion miles from home, Voyager 1 photographs earth as a single 'Pale Blue Dot'.

1991

- Douglas Coupland's *Generation X: Tales from an Accelerated Culture* identifies the post-Boomers who were born in the 'Baby Bust' 60s when population growth declined.
- Italian clothing brand Benetton courts controversy and pioneers 'lifestyle' marketing with billboard ads which link

brand with social issues while showing no garments.

1992

- Freddie Mercury Tribute Concert raises millions for A.I.D.S. research.
- Prince Charles and Princess Diana to separate.

1993

- Democrat Bill Clinton moves into White House.
- And chips? P5 Pentium introduced.
- Maastricht Treaty establishes European Union.
- Now you need Window NT 3.1.
- Stephen Hawking's *A Brief History of Time* a huge best-seller.

1994

- 'The Scream' stolen (then recovered) in Oslo.
- Kurt Cobain dead.
- Channel Tunnel opens.
- Conference in San Francisco considers commercial potential of World Wide Web.
- *Friends* hang out in NYC. First televised lesbian kiss in UK Liverpool soap *Brookside*.
- World's first major exhibition on 'Streetstyle' opens at Victoria & Albert Museum, London.

- Nokia's 2100 has a ringtone which will soon be heard around the world.
- Amazon.com founded.

1995

- Space Shuttle docks with Russian Mir space station.
- DVD format announced.
- Now you need Windows 95.

1996

- Computer beats chess champion Garry Kasparov.
- Bill Clinton wins second term - US stock market climbs ever upward.

1997

- UK Labour Party wins and Tony Blair becomes PM.
- With some 2.5 billion viewers, the broadcast of the funeral of Diana, Princess of Wales is the biggest ever TV audience for a live broadcast.
- Gianni Versace shot dead in Miami.
- Steve Jobs returns to Apple.
- First hybrid car the Toyota Prius goes on sale in Japan.
- Internet porn giant Kink.com founded in San Francisco.

1998

- The first Baby Boomer President, Bill Clinton, assures the nation: 'I did not have sex with that woman'.
- Work begins on International Space Station.
- Google founded.
- US budget in surplus.

1999

- Euro kicks off.
- Bill Gates worth $100 Billion - now you need Windows 98.
- Music downloading at Napster makes music industry nervous.
- Apple's 'clamshell' iBook introduced.
- Tony Soprano exits the Lincoln Tunnel for the first time.

2000

- Phew: 'Millennium Bug' doesn't destroy the world.
- 'Dot-com' bubble pushes Dow Jones Industrial Average to dizzy heights.
- Vladimir Putin elected President of Russia.
- US Presidential election on knife edge as ballots recounted in Florida but US Supreme Court steps in to hand victory to Republican George W. Bush.

2001

- September 11, 2001 attacks leave nearly 3,000 dead - President George W. Bush declares 'War On Terror'.
- US energy giant Enron files for bankruptcy.

2002

- 'Operation Anaconda' kicks off US led invasion of Afghanistan.
- Dot-com bubble bursts.

2003

- Despite global protests, 'Shock and awe' launches invasion of Iraq. President Bush announces 'Mission Accomplished'.
- Space Shuttle Columbia disintegrates over Texas.
- Human Genome Project completed.

2004

- Final episodes of *Friends* and *Sex and the City* - Facebook launched.
- Massive earthquake and tsunami in Southeast Asia.

2005

- George W. Bush wins 2nd term as US President.
- 1st flight of superjumbo Airbus A380.

- 1st human face transplant.

2006

- Car bombs and mortar attacks kill hundreds in Baghdad.

2007

- Final Harry Potter book published.
- Archeologists in Japan discover a 2,100 year-old melon.

2008

- 'Sub-prime' mortgage collapse in the US and other factors triggers a worldwide 'Credit Crunch' and recession. Banks deemed 'too big to fail' are rescued at taxpayers' expense.
- Barack Obama elected President of the USA.

2009

- Iceland's banking system and government collapse. McDonald's pulls out.
- Astronomers discover the 1st planet outside the solar system on which water could occur.

2010

- Earthquake in Haiti destroys the capital and leaves 230,000 dead.
- Neanderthal genome project gives evidence that humans and neanderthals interbred.
- CERN scientists trap anti-matter for 1/6 of a second.
- 'New Labour' out but no clear winner in UK election.
- Lady Gaga wears a dress made of raw meat to MTV Music Awards.

2011

- 9.1. magnitude earthquake and tsunami kills tens of thousands and triggers nuclear emergency in Japan.
- 'Arab Spring' offers prospect of democracy.
- Osama bin Laden killed.
- World population reaches 7 billion.

2012

- 1st wave of Baby Boomers begin to retire.

Index

00s, 291, 302, 307, 310–312
10s, 294, 307, 310, 312
20s, 304, 307
21st century, 82, 84, 221, 251, 296, 299, 301, 302, 304
30s, 159, 174
35mm SLR, 227
40s, 1, 6, 12, 16, 31, 52, 159, 164, 211, 294, 299
45s, 167
50s, 17, 18, 42, 52, 57, 58, 61, 63, 65, 75, 82, 84, 91, 93, 96, 135, 156, 158–164, 166, 177, 218, 223, 226, 233, 234, 240, 242, 248, 250, 276–278, 287, 290, 295, 298, 299, 301, 302, 306, 308, 314
60s, 18, 21, 23, 25, 27, 42, 61, 63, 78, 82, 84, 91, 93, 94, 96–99, 106, 107, 110, 112, 113, 120–122, 125, 132, 138, 142, 152, 155–157, 159, 160, 166, 179, 183, 184, 186, 188, 192, 204–206, 214, 220, 221, 223–225, 230, 240–242, 244, 267, 278, 281, 282, 285, 287, 291, 295, 299–302, 308
70s, 21, 22, 25, 69, 70, 106, 112, 152, 174, 222, 231, 232, 236, 239, 243, 245, 247, 248, 250, 253, 254, 259, 262, 264, 266–268, 273, 274, 276–279, 281, 282, 285–287,

INDEX

291, 292, 296, 306
80s, 222, 245, 279, 282, 286, 287, 296
90s, 286, 291, 296, 305, 306, 312, 313

Absolute Beginners, 20, 226, 248, 279, 303
Acme Attractions, 253, 263
Adam Ant, 269
African-Americans, 60, 79, 185, 278
Age of Aquarius, 21, 23, 112, 153, 199, 240, 244, 271, 274, 315
Alan Freed, 161
Albert Camus, 192
Albert Hofmann, 133
Aldous Huxley, 138, 143
Alfie, 108
Allen Ginsberg, 136
Altamont Free Festival, 205
American Bandstand, 157, 171
American Graffiti, 170, 174, 176, 178
American Pastoral, 50
amyl nitrate, 280
Anarchy in the U.K., 265
Andre (not real name), 125

Andrew Logan, 258–260
androgyny, 230, 233
Andy Warhol, 274
Aretha Franklin, 156
Asbury Park, New Jersey, 69–71, 77, 78, 174, 176, 187, 193, 207, 306, 308, 313
Atomised, 298
atomized individuals, 292
Austin Powers, 220, 223, 224

B-Boys/Hip Hop, 273, 278, 279, 302
baby boom, 16, 40, 56, 61, 97, 294, 304
Baby Boomers, 16, 17, 21–23, 28, 29, 49, 61, 82–85, 104, 106, 110, 116, 131, 134, 146, 152, 153, 161, 167, 175, 178, 182, 189, 191, 212, 248, 249, 266, 274, 288, 289, 292–294, 298, 299, 302, 303, 305, 307, 310, 311
Baby Bust generation, 285, 290

Barack Obama, 28, 61
Barry Goldwater, 193
Beats, 3, 10, 128, 130, 170, 192, 198, 297
Belmar, New Jersey, 50
Bianca Jagger, 281
Biba, 259
Bikers, 2
Bill Clinton, 120, 152
Bill Grundy, 265
Bill Haley, 161
Billy Idol, 286
birth control, 98, 118, 191, 290
Birth of the Cool, 6
Blade Runner, 239, 269, 295, 314
Blow-Up, 98, 213, 227, 228
Blue Beat, 224
Blue Velvet, 131
Blues, 229
Bob Dylan, 189, 201
Bob Harris, 248
Booker T & the M.G.'s, 173
Boomer Envy, 285
Boring Old Farts, 23, 29, 236, 250, 264, 266, 270, 271

boutiques, 219
Bradley Beach, New Jersey, 33, 46, 50, 313
brands, 228, 230
Brighton Rock, 252, 262
British Invasion, 160, 171, 212
Broad Street, Philadelphia, 114, 125, 155
Bruce Springsteen, 9, 70, 175

Cape Cod style (house), 52, 58, 310
car design, 82
Carl Perkins, 165
Carnaby Street, 218, 220, 222–224
Carvel ice cream, 85, 88, 306
casual sex, 103, 114
CBGB, 274, 276, 277
Charles Atlas, 234
Charles Manson, 198, 204
Charles Polhemus, 31, 35, 76, 78, 81, 97, 166, 168, 181, 203
Charlie Parker, 6
Charlotte Polhemus, 36, 43, 289
Cheerios, 152
cocaine, 280, 281

INDEX

Colin MacInnes, 19, 226, 248
colonial style (house), 58
comics, 163, 234, 235
consumer choice, 91
cool, 75–77, 80, 110–112, 114, 168, 171, 176, 183, 190, 228, 229, 242
cool hunters, 293
Cosey Fanni Tutti, 254
COUM Transmission, 254
counterculture, 110, 130, 174, 236
crew-cut, 191, 195, 242

dance, 166–168, 173, 177, 278, 279, 281
Danny DeVito, 42
Dave Brubeck, 66
David (not real name), 215
David Bailey, 213, 227, 250
David Bowie, 219, 231, 235, 240, 247
David Lynch, 131
Debbie Harry, 274, 276
deconstruction (style), 252, 261, 270, 276
denim, 5, 41, 239
department stores, 69, 77, 79, 92
Derek Jarman, 258–260, 268
design, 93, 229, 301
Detroit, 311
Dick Clark, 157
diners, 85
Dior - New Look, 12, 13, 15, 299
Disco, 273, 279–282, 296
DIY, 90
DJ Kool Herc, 279
Don Letts, 253
Doug Polhemus, 37, 166
Douglas Coupland, 285–287, 290, 291, 306
Dr Richard Alpert, 134
Dr Timothy Leary, 134, 136
dry wells, 56

E Street Band, 70
Easy Rider, 2, 120, 205
Elvis Presley, 9, 158, 165, 187, 233

Fab Freddy (not real name), 138, 142
fashion, 11, 14, 15, 18, 224, 299, 300
fashion -v- style, 300

Fashion Forum (ICA), 255–258
Federico Fellini, 94, 108, 229
Finchley Road, London, 261
Finsbury Park, London, 250, 253, 254
Fireball (pinball), 174, 177
Flower Power, 295
Formica, 59, 90, 91
franchising, 87, 89
Francis Bacon, 265
Frankie Lymon, 163
Freddy Mercury, 239
Free Love, 111
Freedom, 294, 296–298, 303
Funk, 173

Garage (music genre), 274
Garden State Parkway, 308
Gays, 218, 280, 295
Generation A, 291, 294
generation gap, 163, 180, 183
Generation X, 286–288, 290–293, 297, 306
Generation Y, 291, 294
Generation Z, 291, 294
generational model of history, 16, 288, 289, 291, 292, 294, 296

George Lucas, 170
George Melly, 227
George W. Bush, 26, 27, 207
Gidget, 162
Gil Evans, 6
Glam, 222, 224, 232, 235, 236, 239, 240, 251
God Save the Queen, 268
Goths, 222, 224
Graham Greene, 252
graphics, 85, 229
Greetings From Asbury Park, 175
Grey Power, 29
Grime (music genre), 302

Hair (musical), 199
Hamilton Methodist Church, 14, 60, 196
Hells Angels, 10, 137
Highway 33, New Jersey, 54, 312
Hippies, 21, 23, 106, 111–114, 126, 130, 132, 136–138, 146, 148, 150, 156, 170, 171, 173, 180, 183, 201, 205, 213, 217, 239, 242, 244, 248, 252,

INDEX

271, 275, 278, 281–283, 287, 297
Hipsters, 3, 10, 114, 190, 233
Hollister, California, 1
Honolulu Choo-Choo Pink nail polish, 288
Hot Rats, 170
Howard Kunstler, 312
Howdy Doody, 131, 182
Hugh Hefner, 100, 103, 105, 106, 296
hula-hoops, 182
human consciousness, 101, 130, 144
human sexual desire, 101

I Love Lucy, 131, 133, 153, 295
Ian Fleming, 111
ICA (London), 216, 254, 255, 258
Iggy Pop, 252, 274
In-betweeners, 295
International Kline Blue, 7
internet, 292, 310

Jack Kerouac, 3, 136
Jack Nicholson, 42
James Bond, 109
Japanese streetstyle, 273
Jazz, 6, 7, 66, 75, 94, 110, 114, 127, 130, 165, 168, 171, 183, 185, 190, 192, 223, 228, 280
Jean-Paul Sartre, 107
jeans, 5, 128, 181, 195, 238, 239
Jenny Runacre, 268
Jerry Lee Lewis, 165
Jersey Shore, 32, 177
jet travel, 110, 211, 213, 215
Jimmy Hendrix, 172
Joan Baez, 189, 201
Joan Didion, 25, 204
Joe Polhemus, 305
John Kennedy, 19, 75, 132, 179, 187, 242, 243
John Lydon, 250–254, 259, 261, 262, 266, 272
John Simon Riche (Sid Vicious), 252
John Stephen, 219, 223, 224
John Travolta, 281
John Updike, 109, 186
Johnny Rotten, 254, 259, 261
Jon Savage, 260, 261

Jonathan Franzen, 294, 303
Jordan, 256, 258, 259, 261, 269, 272
Jubilee, 268–270, 295
jukeboxes, 87, 176
juvenile delinquents, 3, 10, 163, 197, 275

Ken Kesey, 135–137, 146
Kennedy International, 212
Kensington Market, 238, 239
Kensington, London, 259
Kidults, 302, 303
Kind of Blue, 7
Kings Road, 219, 224, 253, 263
kinky, 214, 217
Kurt Vonnegut, 291

La Dolce Vita, 108, 229
La Honda, California, 136
Lady Ga Ga, 302
Levittown, 51
liberals, 190, 192, 206, 282
Life magazine, 14, 99
Lindy (not real name), 138, 140, 146, 147, 149
Little Emperors, 290
Little Eva, 157
Little Richard, 159
London, 18, 97, 164, 175, 212, 216, 217, 221, 222, 224, 226, 227, 235, 237, 238, 244, 250, 254, 260, 264, 266, 267, 272, 300
Lost Generation, 289
Lou Reed, 274
Louises (club), 264
LSD/acid, 123, 132–134, 136, 138, 142, 145, 147, 150, 151, 239
Lyndon Johnson, 187, 193, 195
Lynn Procter, 176, 254, 261

Mad Max, 239
Mad Men, 7, 51, 75, 81, 93, 100, 103, 111, 188, 192, 296
Main Street USA, 37, 62
Major Tom, 241
Make Love Not War, 112, 114, 115, 197
Malcolm McLaren, 255–258, 260, 269, 271, 272
Manhattan, New York, 274, 277

INDEX

Marcello Mastroianni, 95, 108, 230
Margaret Thatcher, 122, 283, 296, 298
marijuana, 125, 127–129, 197
Marlon Brando, 2
Mary Quant, 18, 219, 224
Maurice Merleau-Ponty, 141
Max (Dorthy Prior), 260, 272
McJobs, 286
Merry Pranksters, 136, 138
Methodist, 31, 34, 67, 98, 100, 102, 202, 203
Michael Caine, 108
Michel Houellebecq, 298
Michelangelo Antonioni, 98
Mick Jagger, 231
Miles Davis, 6, 252
mini, 214, 217, 224, 267
minimalism, 82, 93
modern sexuality, 105, 107
modernism, 7, 65, 75, 82, 83, 86, 89, 96, 103, 183, 191, 212, 214, 240, 244, 267, 269, 272, 276, 286, 295, 305
Mods, 76, 171, 223, 231
Monica Lewinsky, 120
Monmouth Mall, 66, 68
Monty Python, 146
moon landing, 231, 241, 243
moral panics, 163, 164
Mothers of Invention, 170
Motown, 160

Nabisco Shredded Wheat, 45
Nancy (Polhemus) Savoth, 294, 305
narrowcasting, 171
natural (look), 102, 214, 236
Neal Cassady, 4, 136, 137
neocons, 26, 27, 206, 282
Neptune City, New Jersey, 32, 35–38, 42, 43, 64
Neptune High School, 60, 61, 169, 179, 193
Neptune Junior High School, 42, 166, 185
Neptune, New Jersey, 14, 53, 56, 58–60, 62, 63, 75, 76, 85, 87, 137, 178, 179, 185, 277, 305, 307, 308, 310, 311, 314
New Jersey State Parkway, 58, 85

New Musical Express, 247, 260
New Orleans, 8
New Romantics, 224
New York City, 5, 136, 170, 211, 272, 274, 279, 280
Newark, New Jersey, 50
No Future, 23, 243, 244, 268, 271
nuclear family, 131

Ocean Grove, New Jersey, 313
Oklahoma (musical), 41
Old World -v- New World, 14, 15, 18
On the Road, 3, 136, 137
one-child policy (China), 290
open relationships, 106, 120
Oscar Wilde, 252, 262
Oxford, England, 146, 150, 152

Paris, 10–12, 15, 200, 202, 224, 300
Patti Smith, 274
Patty Emerson-Berglund, 295

Peggy (Chasey) Polhemus, 14, 34, 98, 181
People Like Us, 20, 298
Pete Seeger, 201
Peter York, 236, 264
Philadelphia, 114, 123, 125, 138, 142, 157, 170
Philip Larkin, 97
Philip Roth, 33, 46, 49, 108
Pierre Henry, 148
Pink Flamingo Motel, 176
platform boots, 239
Playboy, 7, 97, 99, 103, 105, 111–113, 184, 190
Poland Street, London, 264
pop culture, 15, 166, 213, 220, 248, 249
Portnoys Complaint, 108
Portobello Road, London, 238, 239
post-Boomer generations, 268, 271, 285, 287, 290, 293
post-generational, 298
post-modernism, 82, 243, 244, 261, 264, 269, 276, 295, 297, 303
post-subcultural, 298

prawn cocktail, 215
pre-Boomers, 274
progress, 82, 83, 267, 269, 287, 295
Prostitution (exhibition, ICA), 255
protest movement, 183, 190, 200
psychedelia, 221, 224
Psychedelic Revolution, 137
Punk (magazine), 277
Punks, 23, 222, 224, 243, 251, 253, 255, 263, 265, 270–273, 275, 277, 286, 287, 291, 295, 296

Rabbit Redux, 186
Rabbit, Run, 109
race riots, 175
racial segregation, 60, 78, 157, 166, 184, 186, 187, 295
radio, 158, 171, 187
ranch style (house), 51, 52, 58, 310
Ray Charles, 97, 155, 156, 158
Ready Steady Go, 172

Real Men, 233–235
Rebecca (not real name), 116
Rebel Without a Cause, 162, 277
recession, 267, 271, 304, 307
Reggae, 252
retro, 104, 176, 276, 287
Rev. Joseph Chasey, 34, 67, 237
Rev. Martin Luther King, 188, 189
Revolt Into Style, 227, 228
Rhythm & Blues, 8, 156, 158–160, 187, 229
Richard Hell, 274
Richard III, 252, 254, 262
Richard Linklater, 288
Richard Nixon, 19, 25, 75, 134, 153, 192, 204, 206, 242
Rock, 23, 170–174, 177, 183, 231, 248, 249, 270
Rock & Roll, 10, 157–161, 165, 167, 172, 175, 178, 183, 233, 270, 274, 276, 294
Rock Around the Clock, 161
Rockabillies, 165, 233

Ronald Reagan, 122, 282, 296
Route 33, New Jersey, 37, 53
Roy Brown, 8
Run-D.M.C., 279
Russell Polhemus, 43, 44, 46, 203

Sabbaths Theater, 33, 46
sampling & mixing (style), 251, 261, 263, 271
San Francisco, 25, 134, 204, 274
sartorial laws, 256
Saturday Night Fever, 281
Scott Holderer, 167, 168
Sears Roebuck Catalog, 34, 41, 52, 53
Sergeant Pepper, 172, 222
SEX, 253, 255–259
Sex Pistols, 257, 259, 261, 265, 266, 268
Sexual Revolution, 110, 112, 116, 117, 120, 122, 138
shit happens, 57
shopping centers, 63, 66, 68, 306
shopping malls, 314
shopping trolley, 65
short -v- long hair, 107, 195, 242
Silent Majority, 153, 204, 206
Silver Jubilee, 266, 267
Simone de Beauvoir, 107
single -v- double-breasted (suits), 76, 80
Siouxsie Sioux, 269, 272
Sir Roland Penrose, 254, 255
Situationists, 255, 260, 272
Ska, 171, 224
Skinheads, 251
Slacker, 288
Slaves of New York, 260
Sly and the Family Stone, 173
SOAP, 70, 177
Soho, 265
Soul, 171, 173, 223, 229
South Bronx, New York, 278, 279
South Street, Philadelphia, 157
Southside Johnny and the Asbury Jukes, 177
split-level style (house), 58, 310
split-sessions (schools), 61,

INDEX

199
Springwood Avenue, Neptune, New Jersey, 60, 75, 78, 79
St. Paul, Minnesota, 297
stereo, 66, 110, 191
Steve Van Zandt, 72, 177
Stonewall Inn, 280
streetstyle, 5, 292
Studio 54, 281, 282
Style Wars, 236
subcultures, 293
suburbia, 36, 39, 47, 50, 52, 54, 57, 58, 63, 131, 132, 158, 186, 297, 299, 307–310, 312, 314
Summer of Love, 117, 137, 184
supermarkets, 59, 64, 65, 91, 307, 314
Surfers, 162
Suzy Creamcheese, 172

Tama Janowitz, 260
Ted Polhemus, 35, 60, 80, 97, 99, 114, 123, 125, 127, 137, 138, 140, 141, 149, 151, 166, 169, 175, 179, 185, 191, 192, 194, 213, 220, 237, 238, 240, 241, 254, 260, 266, 277, 295, 305
Teddy Boys, 164
teenagers, 17, 22, 160, 162, 164, 166, 183, 199, 225, 248, 250, 300, 301
television, 45, 85, 88, 94, 99, 131, 132, 157, 163, 170, 179–182, 242, 301
Temple University, 114, 125, 155, 206, 237
Texlahoma, 285
The Addams Family, 295
The Adventures of Ozzie and Harriet, 131
The Animals, 160, 230
The Bad Girl, 102, 113
The Beach Boys, 174
The Beatles, 97, 160, 172, 174, 212, 230
the DJ, 279
The Doors, 172
The Doors of Perception, 138

the draft, 110, 117, 206
The End of Suburbia, 312
The Face, 245
The Girl Next Door, 100, 101
The Grateful Dead, 172
The Great Masculine Renunciation, 232, 233, 235
The Marvelettes, 157
The Me Decade, 292
The Old Grey Whistle Test, 248
The Outsider, 192
The Phenomenology of Perception, 141
The Ramones, 275, 276
The Real Thing, 5
The Rocky Horror Show, 243, 295
The Rolling Stones, 160, 174, 230
The Roxy, 253
The Shirelles, 157
The Slits, 269
The Social Construction of Reality, 82, 143
The Sopranos, 49, 50, 71, 178
The Stone Pony, 70, 175, 177, 178
The Who, 230
The Wild One, 2, 162, 277
The Yardbirds, 230
Thelonious Monk, 6, 10
Tom Verlaine, 274
Tom Waits, 32, 177
Tom Wolfe, 137, 282, 292
Tower Bridge, London, 258
Toyah Willcox, 269
traditional styles (interior design), 93–95, 103
trickle down -v- bubble up, 15
turntable, 279
Twiggy, 18, 226, 230
unisex, 230
University College, London, 237, 254
vanilla cream pie, 85, 87
Variations for a Door and a Sigh, 148
Velvet Underground, 274
venereal disease, 98, 121
Vietnam, 107, 110, 112, 117, 138, 182, 183, 187, 195, 197, 206, 242,

295
Vivienne Westwood, 256–258, 271

War On Drugs, 153
Westerns (cinema), 41, 47
whatever, 3, 297
Wiffle ball, 55
William Blake, 143
Winchester, England, 218
Wolfman Jack, 178
Woodstock, 25, 172, 173, 205, 299
Woody Guthrie, 201, 202
World Wide Web, 291
Worlds End, London, 253
Wrong Side of the Tracks, 5

Yippies, 181
youth, 19, 26, 29, 224, 248, 249, 300, 302, 303
youth culture, 17, 21, 22, 29, 160–162, 164, 165, 225, 226, 247, 249, 250, 266, 299, 301–303
youthification, 18

Zandra Rhodes, 255, 258
Ziggy Stardust, 239, 240

www.tedpolhemus.com

Orbiting Neptune - a baby boomer memoir is a visual companion to **BOOM!** - for further information see **'What's Up?'** at

www.tedpolhemus.com